Physics Two

A Laboratory-Based Course

Third Printing 2003

Author and Publisher:

Gordon R. Gore
962 Sycamore Drive
Kamloops, B.C.
Canada V2B 6S2

Phone (250) 579-5722

Fax (250) 579-2302

Copyright © Gordon R. Gore (2001)

ISBN #0-9685526-8-4

Introduction

Physics Two is a companion book to **Physics One**, which provided an introduction to physics. Student *Investigations* emphasize thoughtful observation, measurement and graphical analysis, using real 'hands-on' materials. There are no computer simulations.

The author believes that genuine 'hands-on' laboratory work is absolutely essential to making the subject of physics 'real' to students. Physics should be much more than an exercise in applying algebra and trigonometry to 'formula' word problems.

Exercises and **Chapter Review Questions** vary in difficulty, but are selected to provide *manageable challenges* for students who are still relatively new to the subject. **Brain Busters** provide extra challenge where it is needed.

A *Self-Test* is provided for each chapter. Students may use these to test their own understanding in preparation for classroom tests provided by their instructor. Answers to the *Self-Tests* are at the back of the book.

Instructors will notice that some of the material on electricity is also in **Physics One**. This was done so that teachers have the option of doing some electricity in the first physics course, if they wish. Many students do not take a second physics course, and electricity is a very practical physics topic.

Acknowledgements

The author is grateful for positive and constructive responses of many, many students and teachers who, for fifteen years, used the British Columbia **Physics 12** book which preceded this book. Their suggestions for improvements have always been appreciated, and taken seriously. Computer illustrations in the book were created by **Moira Rockwell** of Mission, B.C. Cartoon drawings are by **Ehren Stillman**, of Deroche, B.C. All photographs are by the author.

Cover Photo

Jennifer Hoffbeck enjoys a hair-raising experience with a model Van de Graaff generator.

Physics Two

Contents

Chapter 1   Vectors and Static Equilibrium

1.1 Scalars and Vectors

If you add 5 L of water to another 5 L of water, you end up with 10 L of water. Similarly, if you add 5 kg of salt to 5 kg of salt, you will have 10 kg of salt. Volumes and masses are added by the rules of ordinary arithmetic. Volume and mass are **scalar quantities**. Scalar quantities have magnitude (size) only. Other scalar quantities with which you may be familiar are: length, energy, density and temperature.

If you add a 5 N force to another 5 N force, the two forces together *may* add up to 10 N, but they may also add up to 0 N or to any value between 0 N and 10 N! This is because forces have *direction* as well as magnitude. Quantities which have direction as well as magnitude are called **vector quantities.** Forces and other vector quantities must be added by the special rules of **vector addition,** which take into account direction as well as magnitude.

In addition to forces, other vector quantities you will encounter in this course include: velocity, displacement, acceleration, momentum, electrical field strength and magnetic field strength.

> *When you describe any velocity, displacement, acceleration, force, momentum or other vector quantity, you must specify both magnitude and direction!*

1.2 Adding Vectors

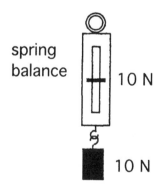

spring
balance

10 N

10 N

In **Figure 1.1**, an object is hanging from a spring balance. Two forces pull on the object. The earth exerts a 10 N force of gravity downward on it, and the spring balance exerts a 10 N force up on it. Both the earth and the spring balance exert the same *size* of force on the object. The **net force** on the object is not 10 N or 20 N as one might expect. It is, in fact, **0 N**!

To understand why the **net** or **resultant force** is zero in this situation, you must know (a) what a vector is and (b) how vectors are added.

Figure 1.1

To draw a vector you must construct a **line segment** whose length is proportional to the magnitude of the quantity being represented (in this case, a force). See **Figure 1.2.** You draw a segment in the direction the quantity is acting, and place an arrow tip on the line segment to show its proper direction. The line segment, drawn to an appropriate scale complete with arrow tip, is a **vector.**

(a)

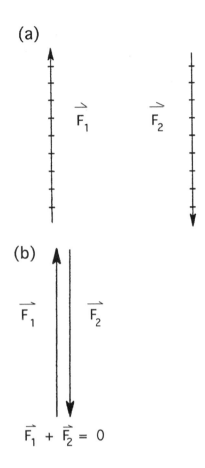

(b)

$$\vec{F_1} + \vec{F_2} = 0$$

Figure 1.2

Figure 1.2 shows how the two forces in **Figure 1.1** can be represented with vectors. **Figure 1.2 (a)** shows vectors representing the upward force F_1 exerted by the spring balance and the downward gravitational force F_2 individually, while **Figure 1.2(b)** shows the two forces added together by **vector addition**.

Note! There are two ways to indicate that a quantity is a vector quantity. In diagrams, or in hand-written notes, a small arrow may be drawn above the symbol for the quantity. For example, $\vec{F}$ indicates that a force vector is being discussed. In a textbook like this, the symbol for a vector quantity may be typed in **bold italics**, like this: **F**. This symbol also indicates that a force vector is being discussed. If only the *magnitude* of a vector is of importance, the symbol F (*italics*, but not bold) will be used.

To add vector F_1 to vector F_2, draw vector F_1 first, to scale and in the proper direction. Then draw vector F_2 so that its tail begins at the tip of vector F_1 and the line segment of F_2 points in the proper direction. Be sure to draw the tip of an arrow to show which way F_2 points. The **net** or **resultant force** is the vector going from the tail of F_1 to the tip of F_2.

In **Figure 1.2**, the resultant is clearly zero. When two or more forces acting on a body have a resultant of zero, the body is said to be in **equilibrium.** Sometimes a force like F_2, which balances one or more other forces and creates a condition where there is no net force, is called the **equilibrant.**

In **Figure 1.3**, a 10 N object is suspended by strings connected to two different spring balances. The strings form an angle of 120° where they are attached to the object. Notice that *both* scales read 10 N. Can the object possibly be in equilibrium if there are *two* 10 N forces pulling it up, and just *one* 10 N force pulling it down?

To find out what the **resultant** of the two upward forces is, the rule for adding vectors is used again. In **Figure 1.4**, vectors F_1, F_2 and F_3 have been drawn acting at a single point (where the three strings meet). The vectors are all drawn to a suitable scale and are aimed in the proper directions relative to one another.

Vector F_1 (dashed line) has been added to vector F_2. The tail of vector F_1 starts at the tip of vector F_2 and vector F_1 is aimed in the direction it acts, which is 60° left of the vertical.

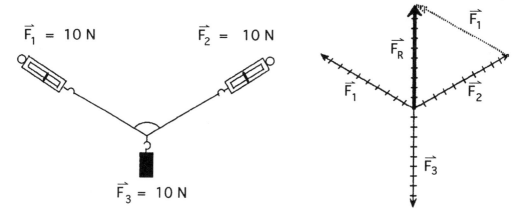

| Figure 1.3 | Figure 1.4 |

The resultant of F_1 and F_2 starts at the tail of F_2, and ends at the tip of F_1. The **resultant** is drawn with a **bold line** and is labelled F_R. Notice that F_R is equal in magnitude but *opposite in direction* to F_3. (You might call F_R the *equilibrant* of F_3.)

Exercises

1. What would the resultant be in **Figure 1.4** if you added F_2 to F_1 instead of F_1 to F_2?

2. What would the resultant be if you added F_R to F_3?

Adding Three Vectors

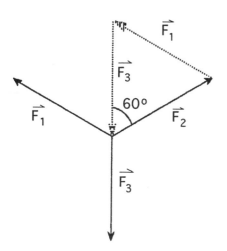

Figure 1.5

Figure 1.5 shows another way of looking at the vector situation in **Figure 1.3**. This time, all three forces have been added together by vector addition. The vector sum of the three forces is zero. The fact that the resultant force is zero should not surprise you. The point at which the three forces act was stationary, and you will recall from an earlier course that a body that is stationary will remain so if the net force on it is zero. (Recall **Isaac Newton's First Law of Motion**.)

Two ways of writing the result of the vector analysis in **Figure 1.5** are:

$$(1)\ \textbf{\textit{F}}_1 + \textbf{\textit{F}}_2 + \textbf{\textit{F}}_3 = 0\,,$$

and $$(2)\ \Sigma \textbf{\textit{F}} = 0\,.$$

The symbol Σ means 'the sum of'. In this situation, it is the **vector sum**.

Exercises

1. In how many ways might you add the vectors $\textbf{\textit{F}}_1$, $\textbf{\textit{F}}_2$, and $\textbf{\textit{F}}_3$?

2. Would it make any difference to the resultant you obtain if you added the three force vectors in a different order?

3. Displacement vectors are added in the same way as force vectors or any other vectors. If a golfer hits a drive 240 m toward the north, then hits a horrible second shot 100 m to the east, what is the resultant displacement of his golf ball? (Draw the two displacements to some suitable scale, then find their resultant.)

4. An inebriated (very drunk) man achieves the following successive displacements before being arrested for impaired walking: 3 steps north, 2 steps west, 5 steps east, and 7 steps south. What is his (a) resultant displacement? (b) total distance travelled?

1.3 'Subtracting' Vectors

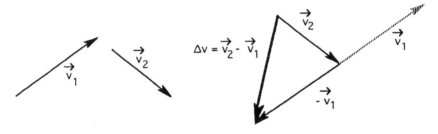

Figure 1.6(a)

On occasion you will have to find the difference between two vectors. For example, if the velocity of a body changes from v_1 to v_2, you may wish to calculate the **change in velocity,** Δv. A vector *difference* is defined as the vector *sum* of the second vector and the *negative* of the first vector.

$$\Delta \textbf{\textit{v}} = \textbf{\textit{v}}_2 + (-1)\textbf{\textit{v}}_1\,,$$

or,

$$\Delta \textbf{\textit{v}} = \textbf{\textit{v}}_2 - \textbf{\textit{v}}_1\,.$$

When 'subtracting' vectors, simply remember that the negative of any vector is a vector of the same magnitude (size) but pointing in the opposite direction. The difference of two vectors is the sum of the first vector and the *negative* of the second vector. See **Figure 1.6(a)**.

$$\Delta v = v_2 - v_1 = v_2 + (- v_1)$$

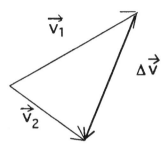

Figure 1.6(b)

Note! The difference between two vectors can also be found by drawing the vectors 'tail to tail' as in **Figure 1.6(b)**. The resultant, Δv, is the vector drawn from tip to tip.

From **Figure 1.6(b)**, $v_1 + \Delta v = v_2$,

$$\therefore \Delta v = v_2 - v_1.$$

Investigation 1-1   Experimenting with Force Vectors

Purpose: To analyze the force vectors in situations where three forces act at a single point, and where no motion results from the force.

Procedure

1. Set up the arrangement in **Figure 1.7**. Three forces act on the point where the three strings meet. The forces are 3.0 N, 4.0 N and 5.0 N. When all the masses are hanging stationary, place a sheet of polar graph paper or a protractor behind the point where the strings meet and measure angles A, B and C.

2. On a fresh piece of paper draw three lines meeting at a point, with the lines forming the same angles **A**, **B** and **C** as were formed by the three strings. See **Figure 1.8(a)**. On these lines draw force vectors representing the forces of gravity on the three hanging masses. Use a scale of 2.0 cm for each **newton** of force. See **Figure 1.8(b)**. Label the forces F_1, F_2, and F_3.

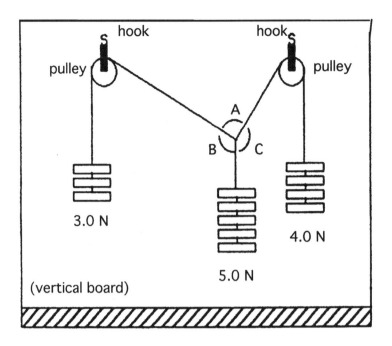

Figure 1.7

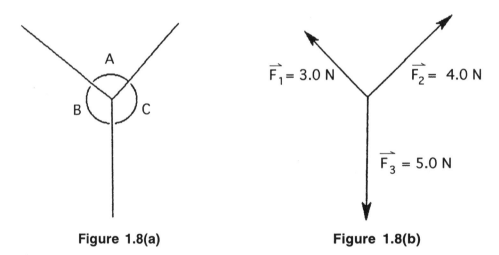

| **Figure 1.8(a)** | **Figure 1.8(b)** |

3. **Predict** what the resultant of these three force vectors will be. Now add them by the 'head-to-tail' system, as described in **Section 1.2**.

4. Use the same arrangement as in **Procedures 1** to **3**, but change the masses used so that the force of gravity on each mass is 4.0 N. Measure the new angles **A**, **B** and **C**. Draw and add by vector addition the three forces in this new situation.

Concluding Questions

1. Based upon your observations in **Procedures 1** to **4**, what is the resultant of the forces acting on a point if the point does not move?

2. In **Procedure 1**, explain why angle **A** is a right angle.

3. In **Procedure 4**, explain why angle **A** is 120°.

4. If the vector sum of all the forces acting on a point was not zero, what would you observe happening to the point (in this case, the junction of the three strings)?

5. Account for any small errors you may have encountered in this activity.

6. When a body is at rest even though there are numerous forces acting on it, we say it is in **static equilibrium**. According to your investigation, how would you describe the conditions needed for a point to be in static equilibrium?

Exercises

1. Two boys are pulling a girl along on a toboggan. Each boy pulls on a rope attached to the same point on the front of the toboggan with a force of 360 N. Using a scale diagram, determine the resultant of the two forces exerted by the boys if their ropes form each of these angles with each other:

   (a) 0°   (b) 60°   (c) 120°   (d) 180°.

2. A football player is pushed by one opponent with a force of 50.0 N toward the east. At the same time a second tackle pushes him with a force of 120.0 N toward the north. What is the magnitude and direction of the resultant force on the first player?

3. If the following three forces act simultaneously on the same point, what will their resultant be?

   100.0 N toward the north; 50.0 N toward the east; 220.0 N toward the south.

1.4 Vector Components

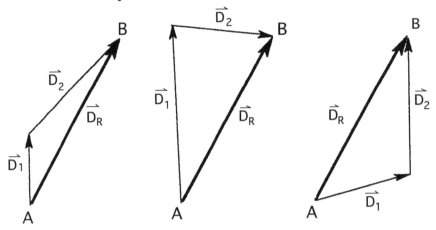

Figure 1.9

Figure 1.9 shows three ways one might travel from A to B. The vectors are **displacement** vectors. In each of the three 'trips', the resultant displacement is the same.

$$D_1 + D_2 = D_R$$

Any two or more vectors which have a resultant such as D_R are called **components** of the resultant vector. A vector such as D_R can be **resolved** into an endless number of component combinations. **Figure 1.9** shows just three possible combinations of components of D_R.

In many problems, the most useful way of resolving a vector into components is to choose components that are perpendicular to each other. **Figure 1.10** shows one situation where it is wise to use perpendicular components.

$$F_R = 60.0 \text{ N}$$

$37°$

(snowplow)

Figure 1.10

In **Figure 1.10**, a 60.0 N force is exerted down the handle of a snow shovel. The force that actually pushes the snow along the driveway is the **horizontal component**, F_x. The **vertical component**, F_y, is directed perpendicular to the road.

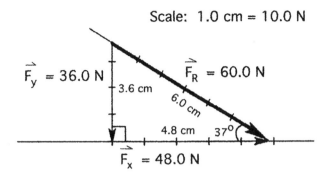

Scale: 1.0 cm = 10.0 N

$\vec{F}_y$ = 36.0 N

3.6 cm

$\vec{F}_R$ = 60.0 N

6.0 cm

4.8 cm   37°

$\vec{F}_x$ = 48.0 N

Figure 1.11

To find out what the horizontal component F_x is, a scale diagram like **Figure 1.11** can be drawn. First, you draw a horizontal reference line. Then you draw a line forming an angle of 37° with the horizontal reference line, because this is the angle formed by the snowplow handle with the road.

Using a scale of 1.0 cm for each 10.0 N, construct a force vector to represent F_R = 60.0 N. Next, drop a line down from the tail of F_R meeting the horizontal reference line at an angle of 90°. This gives you both the vertical and the horizontal component forces. Label these F_y and F_x, and place arrows on them to show their directions.

Since the horizontal component vector has a length of 4.8 cm, and each 1.0 cm represents 10.0 N, then F_x = 48.0 N. The vertical component vector is 3.6 cm long, therefore F_y = 36.0 N.

Sample Vector Questions

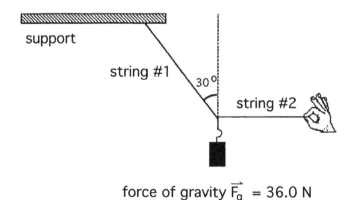

support

string #1

30°

string #2

force of gravity $\vec{F}_g$ = 36.0 N

Figure 1.12(a)

1. **Figure 1.12(a)** shows a typical force vector situation, where there are three forces acting, but no motion resulting. (**Static equilibrium** exists.) Two strings support a 36.0 N object. One string makes an angle of 30° with the vertical, and the other string is horizontal. The question is, "What is the **tension** in each string?" (The tension in a string is simply the force exerted along the string.)

Solution:

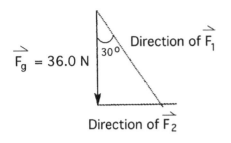

Figure 1.12(b) shows one way to look at this problem. The 36.0 N object is not moving, so the three forces acting on it must have a resultant of zero. That means *the vector sum of the three forces acting on the object is zero.*

The vector to draw first is the one about which you have the most complete information. You know that the force of gravity F_g has a magnitude of 36.0 N, and is directed *down.*

Figure 1.12(b)

You do *not* know the *magnitude* of the tension along **string #1** (F_1) but you know its *direction*, which is 30° to the vertical. You do *not* know the *magnitude* of the tension in **string #2** (F_2), but you know that it acts in a direction *perpendicular to* F_g. You also know that vectors F_1, F_2 and F_g form a **closed triangle** (since their resultant is zero).

In **Figure 1.12(b)**, dashed lines show the directions of F_1 and F_2. To complete the vector triangle of forces, arrows must be added to show that F_1 ends at the tail of F_g and F_2 starts at the tip of F_g. If F_g has been drawn to scale, then both F_1 and F_2 will have the same scale.

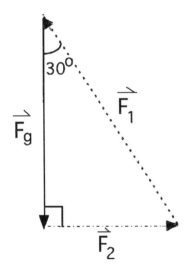

Figure 1.12(c) shows what the completed vector diagram looks like. To solve for tension forces F_1 and F_2, you must know to what scale F_g was drawn. In the next set of **Exercises**, you will be asked to complete the solution to this problem.

Figure 1.12(c)

(a)

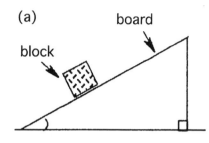

block

board

2. In **Figure 1.13(a)**, a block of wood rests on an inclined plane. Since the block is motionless, the forces acting on it must have a vector sum of zero. The block is in **static equilibrium.**

(a) What are the forces acting on the block?

(b)

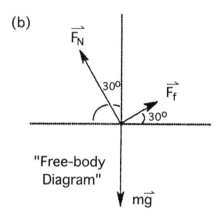

"Free-body Diagram"

Figure 1.13

Solution:

Let us represent the block by an imaginary 'particle', and draw all the forces that act *on* this 'particle'. A force diagram like **Figure 1.13(b)** is sometimes called a **free body diagram.**

There are **three** forces acting on the block. These forces are all shown on the **free body diagram.**

(1) The force of gravity exerted on the block, $F_g = mg.$

(2) The force exerted *outward* on the block by the inclined board. This force is **normal** perpendicular) to the board, so it is called the **normal force, F_N.**

(3) The force of **static friction, F_f,** which acts in a direction parallel to and toward the top of the inclined board.

(b) If the force of gravity on the block is 56 N, and the board is inclined at an angle of 30° to the horizontal, what is the magnitude of

(i) the **normal force** and

(ii) the **force of static friction?**

Solution

Since the three forces produce no acceleration, their **resultant** is zero.

$$\Sigma F = mg + F_N + F_f = 0.$$

The three force vectors form a vector triangle. See **Figure 1.14.**

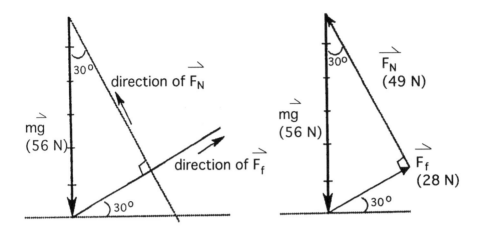

Figure 1.14

To solve this problem using a scale diagram, begin by drawing a vector to represent the force of gravity (*mg*), which is 56 N downward.

Use a scale of 1.0 cm = 10.0 N. The direction of the friction force, F_f, is 30° to the horizontal, so draw a line in that direction, beginning at the tip of the *mg* vector. The direction of the normal force vector F_N will be 30° to the vertical, and the F_N vector must end at the tail of the *mg* vector, because the three vectors form a closed triangle if their resultant is zero.

Since *mg* was drawn to scale, and the three angles in the vector triangle are correct, then the vector triangle just completed has all three forces to the same scale (1.0 cm = 10.0 N).

The vector triangle is completed by drawing tips on the vectors representing the normal force and the force of static friction.

Since the vector representing F_N on the scale diagram is 4.9 cm long, the normal force is 49 N. Similarly, the vector representing the force of static friction is 2.8 cm long, so that force is 28 N.

(c) What is the **coefficient of static friction, μ_s**, if the block is on the verge of sliding down the inclined board?

Solution:

$$\mu_s = \frac{F_f}{F_N} = \frac{28 \text{ N}}{49 \text{ N}} = 0.57.$$

The coefficient of static friction is 0.57.

Exercises

1. Complete the solution to **Sample Vector Question #1**.

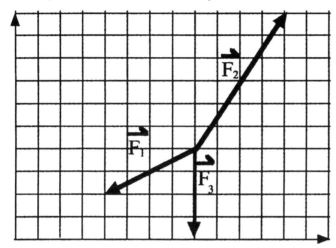

Figure 1.15

2. What is the **resultant** of

   (a) the three force vectors in **Figure 1.15**, added 'head-to-tail'?

   (b) the three **horizontal components**?

   (c) the three **vertical components**?

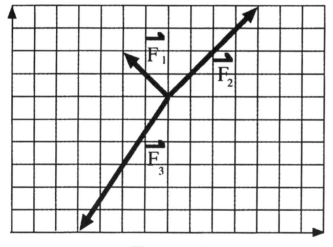

Figure 1.16

3. Copy **Figure 1.16** onto a sheet of graph paper with a similar grid. By any logical method, find the force F_4 that must be added to F_1, F_2, and F_3 to obtain a **resultant** of zero.

4. A dedicated physics student pulls his brand new shiny red wagon along a level road such that the handle makes an angle of 50° with the horizontal road. If he pulls on the handle with a force of 85 N, what is the horizontal component of the force he exerts along the handle? Draw a neat, labelled vector diagram. Use a scale of 1.0 cm for every 10.0 N. Why is the horizontal component more useful information than the force he exerts along the handle?

5. A skier stands on a sloped surface which forms an angle of 40° with the horizontal. If the force of gravity on her is 6.0×10^2 N, what component of this force is directed down the slope?

1.5 Trigonometric Ratios Used in Vector Problems

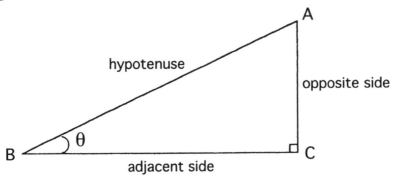

Figure 1.17

Three trigonometric ratios are particularly useful for solving vector problems. In the right-angled triangle ABC in **Figure 1.17**, consider the angle labelled with the Greek symbol, θ (*theta*). With reference to θ, AC is the **opposite side,** BC is the **adjacent side,** and AB is the **hypotenuse.** In any right-angled triangle, the hypotenuse is always the side opposite to the right angle. The three most commonly used trigonometric ratios are defined as follows:

$$\text{sine } \theta = \frac{\text{opposite side}}{\text{hypotenuse}} = \frac{o}{h}$$

$$\text{cosine } \theta = \frac{\text{adjacent side}}{\text{hypotenuse}} = \frac{a}{h}$$

$$\text{tangent } \theta = \frac{\text{opposite side}}{\text{adjacent side}} = \frac{o}{a}$$

Trigonometric ratios, available with the push of a button from your calculator, can help you solve vector problems quickly. Following is a sample vector question involving velocities. The rules for adding velocity vectors are the same as for displacement and force or any other vector quantities.

A Velocity Vector Problem

A motorboat operator is trying to travel across a fast-moving river. (See **Figure 1.18**.) Although he aims his boat directly across the stream, the water carries his boat to the right. If the boat's resultant velocity (as seen by an observer on the bank) is 15.0 m/s in the direction shown, how fast is the boat moving

(a) in a direction downstream?

(b) in a direction across the river?

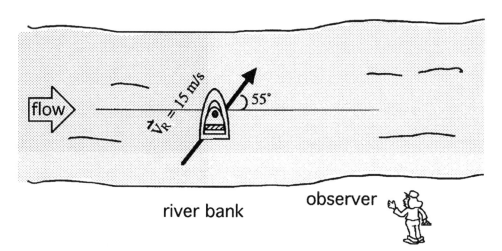

Figure 1.18

Solution

Consider the resultant velocity to have two **component velocities:** v_y, the boat's velocity relative to the water, and v_x, the water's velocity relative to the bank.

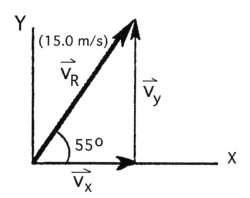

Figure 1.19

Component v_y is directed across the river, perpendicular to the bank, while component v_x is directed down the stream. For your vector diagram, only a neat sketch is needed, since you will be using **trigonometric ratios** rather than a scale diagram. See **Figure 1.19.**

To solve for v_y,

$$\sin 55° = \frac{v_y}{15.0 \text{ m/s}}.$$

$$\begin{aligned} v_y &= (15.0 \text{ m/s}) (\sin 55°) \\ &= (15.0 \text{ m/s}) (0.8192) \\ &= 12.3 \text{ m/s}. \end{aligned}$$

To solve for v_x, $\cos 55° = \dfrac{v_x}{15.0 \text{ m/s}}.$

$$\begin{aligned} v_x &= (15.0 \text{ m/s}) (\cos 55°) \\ &= (15.0 \text{ m/s}) (0.5736) \\ &= 8.60 \text{ m/s}. \end{aligned}$$

Exercises

1. It is 256 m across the river in **Figure 1.18**, measured directly from bank to bank.
   (a) If you wished to know how much time it would take to cross the river, which of the three velocity vectors would you use to obtain the answer most directly?
   (b) What is the magnitude of this vector?
   (c) How long would it take to cross the river?

2. You wish to calculate how far down the bank the boat in **Figure 1.18** will land when it reaches the other side.
   (a) Which velocity vector will give you the answer most directly?
   (b) What is the magnitude of this vector?
   (c) How far down the bank will the boat travel?

3. You absolutely *must* land your boat directly across from your starting point. This time, your resultant velocity will be 15.0 m/s, but in a direction straight across the river. In what direction will you have to aim the boat to end up straight across from your starting point?

Solving Vector Problems Using Trigonometry

Exercises

1. A girl is mowing her lawn. She pushes down on the handle of the mower with a force of 78 N. If the handle makes an angle of 40° with the horizontal, what is the **horizontal component** of the force she exerts down the handle?

2. A hunter walks 225 m toward the north, then 125 m toward the east. What is his resultant displacement?

3. An airborne seed falls to the ground with a steady terminal velocity of 0.48 m/s. A wind causes it to drift to the right at 0.10 m/s. What is the magnitude and direction of the resultant velocity?

4. A helium balloon is released and rises with a steady vertical velocity of 12 km/h. A wind from the east blows the balloon toward the west at 18 km/h.
   (a) What is the resultant velocity of the balloon?
   (b) How far west will the balloon drift in five minutes?

5. Any object in free fall in this locality will accelerate straight down at a rate $g = 9.80$ m/s^2. Imagine you are on skis on a very slippery slope (negligible friction), travelling downhill at an angle of 45° to the horizontal. What will your rate of **acceleration** down the slope be? (Find the component of g in a direction down the slope.)

6. (a) In **Figure 1.20,** what **horizontal force** must the boy exert to hold his friend on the swing still?
   (b) What is the **tension** in each of the two ropes of the motionless swing, if the two ropes share the load equally?

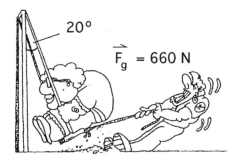

20°

$\vec{F_g}$ = 660 N

Figure 1.20

7. A 250 N crate rests on a smooth 24° inclined plane. What is the minimum value of the force of friction F_f keeping it from sliding down the ramp?

8. A hockey player is moving north at 15 km/h. A bodycheck changes his velocity to 12 km/h toward the west. Calculate the **change in velocity** of the hockey player.

For the moment, the downward force of gravity on these 'weights' is balanced by an upward force exerted by **Dean Corrigan**, and **static equilibrium** exists.

1.6 Statics: Forces in Equilibrium

You have already observed numerous situations where several forces acted on a body, yet the body did not move. If a body is at rest, and there are two or more forces acting on it, then the forces acting on the object must have a resultant of zero. Another way of saying this is that the *net force is zero*.

A trivial example of an object having two forces acting on it but a net force of zero is a pen sitting on a flat desk. The force of gravity pulls down on the pen, but it does not accelerate. The table exerts an equal force upward on the pen, so that the net force on the pen is zero.

If the net force on a body is zero, and it is not moving, the body is said to be in a state of **static equilibrium.** In physics, the subject of **statics** deals with the calculation of forces acting on bodies which are in **static equilibrium.**

Conditions for Equilibrium

First Condition for Static Equilibrium

For a body to be in static equilibrium, the vector sum of all the forces on it must be zero.

$$\Sigma F = 0$$

The sum of the components of F must also be zero. For forces acting in two dimensions,

$$\Sigma F_x = 0 \text{ and } \Sigma F_y = 0.$$

In this chapter, you have encountered situations where static equilibrium exists because the net force was zero. In situations encountered so far, all the forces acted through one point. *Investigation 1-1* dealt with this type of static equilibrium, as did many of the **Exercises** so far in this chapter.

What if the forces do NOT act through the same point?

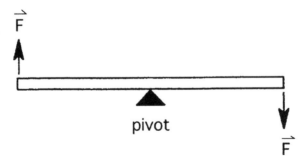

pivot

Figure 1.21

In **Figure 1.21** there are two forces, equal in magnitude, acting on a uniform bar. The forces act in opposite directions, and they act at *different* points on the bar. The net force is zero (because the forces are equal but opposite in direction), *but the bar is not in static equilibrium.* Obviously the bar would rotate about its mid-point. When forces on the same body do not act through the same point, there must be another condition required for static equilibrium. **Investigation 1-2** looks at this 'extra requirement'. First, some necessary definitions!

Torque

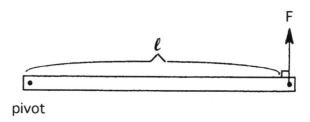

Figure 1.22

In **Figure 1.22**, a force F is exerted at a distance ℓ from the **pivot** or **fulcrum**. The product of a force F and its distance ℓ from the fulcrum, measured perpendicular to the direction of the force vector, is called the **torque** (τ) of that force about the pivot. The distance ℓ is called the **lever arm.**

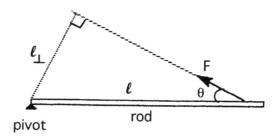

Figure 1.23

The force causing a torque is not always perpendicular to the line joining the pivot to the point where the force is applied. **See Figure 1.23**. Here, the line along which the force acts is at an angle θ to the rod. The force is applied at a distance ℓ from the pivot, but the distance you must use to calculate torque (τ) is the *perpendicular* distance from the pivot to the line of action of the force. This distance is labelled $\ell_\perp$ in the figure.

The **torque** due to force F is: $\tau = F \cdot \ell_\perp$, or $\tau = F \cdot \ell \cdot \sin\theta$.

Another way of looking at the same problem is to use the lever arm ℓ 'as is', but use the **component of F in a direction perpendicular to the rod.** See **Figure 1.24.** This component is labelled $F_\perp$.

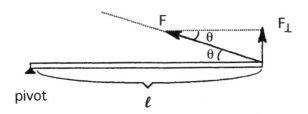

Figure 1.24

In **Figure 1.24**, the torque can be calculated as follows:

$$\tau = F_\perp \cdot \ell = [F \cdot \sin \theta] \cdot \ell = F \cdot \ell \cdot \sin \theta .$$

As you can see, this approach gives the same answer as the first method, used in **Figure 1.23**.

Exercise

The rod in **Figures 1.23** and **1.24** has a length of 2.5 m. A 60.0 N force is exerted at an angle of 30 ° to the rod, which tends to rotate in an *anticlockwise* direction. Calculate the **torque** produced by the force, using the method outlined in the text.

Centre of Gravity

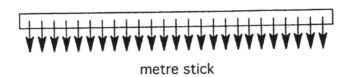

metre stick

Figure 1.25

Every molecule of wood in the metre stick in **Figure 1.25** has mass and therefore experiences a force due to gravity. The figure shows a few sample vectors which represent the force of gravity on individual molecules making up the wood. The resultant of all these force vectors would be the total force of gravity on the metre stick. Where would the resultant force appear to act?

You know from experience that there is a point within any rigid body where a single upward force can be used to balance the force of gravity on the body without causing any rotation of the body. For example, if you hold a metre stick with the tip of your finger at the mid-point of the uniform stick, the metre stick will remain in static equilibrium. (It will not move up, down or sideways, and it will have no tendency to rotate.)

There is a single point in a body where the force of gravity may be considered to act. This point is called the **centre of gravity** of the body. A body supported at its centre of gravity by a force equal to the force of gravity on the body (but in the opposite direction) will experience no translational or rotational motion as a result of the supporting force.

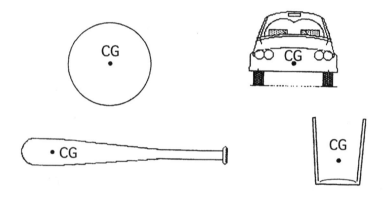

Figure 1.26

Figure 1.26 shows four objects with differing shapes. The probable location of the centre of gravity is indicated by the label **CG**. Notice that the **CG** may be *outside* the solid part of the object, as is the case with the drinking glass.

Centre of Mass

The **centre of mass** of an object is the point where the mass of the object might be considered to be concentrated (for the purpose of calculation). For most situations, the centre of mass is in the same place as the centre of gravity. An exception would be when the gravitational field over the object being considered is non-uniform. (This would have to be a very large object!) The centre of mass of a large spherical planet would be at the centre of the planet, if its mass is uniformly distributed. Where would you expect the centre of mass of the earth-moon system to be located?

Investigation 1-2   Rotational Equilibrium

Purpose: To investigate the conditions necessary to prevent the rotation of a loaded beam.

Procedure

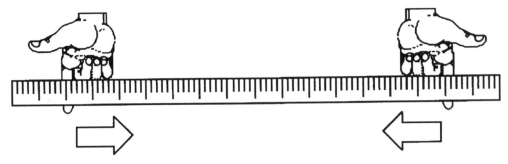

Figure 1.27

1. **Figure 1.27** shows you how you can find the **centre of gravity** of a metre stick very quickly. Hold the metre stick on your two index fingers, as in the figure. Slowly slide your fingers toward each other. When they meet, they will have the centre of gravity 'surrounded' . Try this several times.

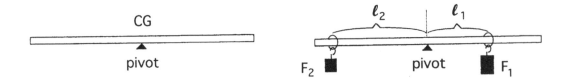

Figure 1.28   **Figure 1.29**

2. Mount your metre stick on a stand (**Figure 1.28**) with the pivot exactly at the centre of gravity. (Few metre sticks are perfectly uniform, so do not assume that the centre of gravity (CG) is at the 50.0 cm mark.) Adjust the pivot point precisely until the metre stick is in equilibrium. Record the position of the CG to the nearest millimetre.

3. Use a very thin, light piece of wire to attach a 1.00 kg mass at a distance of 20.0 cm from the pivot. The force of gravity on this mass will be 9.80 N. This force is labelled F_1 on the diagram. The distance from the pivot to the point where F_1 acts is called the **lever arm** and is labelled ℓ_1. The torque due to F_1 produces a clockwise turning effect, and is called a **clockwise torque**. It is labelled τ_1. $(\tau_1 = F_1 \ell_1)$ See **Figure 1.29**.

4. Suspend a 500 g mass by a light piece of wire on the other side of the metre stick. Adjust its lever arm until the metre stick is in a state of equilibrium. The force of gravity on the 500 g mass is 4.90 N. Call this force F_2 and its lever arm ℓ_2. The torque τ_2 is a **counterclockwise torque**. ($\tau_2 = F_2\,\ell_2$) Record the forces and lever arms in a table like **Table 1**. Calculate the torques and enter them in **Table 1** for Trial 1. (Torque is expressed in N·m.)

Table 1   Observations for *Investigation 1-2*

Trial	F_1 (N)	ℓ_1 (m)	τ_1 (N·m)	F_2 (N)	ℓ_2 (m)	τ_2 (N·m)	F_3 (N)	ℓ_3 (m)	τ_3 (N·m)	$\tau_2 + \tau_3$ (N·m)
1										
2										
3										
4										

5. Repeat the experiment, but place the 1.0 kg mass 25.0 cm from the pivot. Use *two* masses to produce **counterclockwise torques** and adjust their positions until the metre stick is at equilibrium. Measure and record all the forces and lever arms in **Table 1**. Calculate torques τ_1, τ_2 and τ_3 and record them in **Table 1**. (Trial 2.)

6. Try another combination of at least three forces of your own choosing. Record all the forces and lever arms and calculate all the torques needed to produce rotational equilibrium. (Trial 3.)

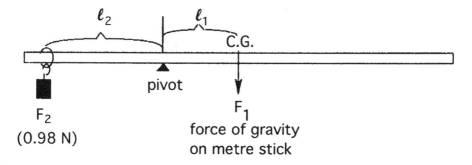

Figure 1.30

7. Finally, set up your metre stick as in **Figure 1.30** so that the force of gravity on the metre stick produces a clockwise torque. Place the CG 20.0 cm to the right of the pivot. Use a 100 g mass (force of gravity 0.980 N) to balance the metre stick. Move the mass to a position where the metre stick stays balanced. Record all your data in **Table 1** (Trial 4). Note that in this case F_1 is the unknown force of gravity on the metre stick.

8. Hang the metre stick from a spring balance and measure the force of gravity on the metre stick, according to the spring balance. Keep a record of this force.

Concluding Questions

1. Examine your calculated torques for each trial. When rotational equilibrium is achieved, what can you conclude regarding the **clockwise torque(s)** when compared with the **counterclockwise torque(s)**? State a general rule describing the condition(s) required for rotational equilibrium.

2. What are some likely sources of error which might cause discrepancies in your results? What is the maximum percent difference you observed when comparing the sum of the clockwise torques with the sum of the counterclockwise torques?

3. Use the general rule you described in (1) to calculate the force of gravity on your metre stick (**Procedure 7**), using only the torques involved. Calculate the percent difference between your calculated force of gravity and the force of gravity according to the spring balance. Explain any discrepancy you observe.

Challenges!

1. Explain why you can find the centre of gravity of a rod or metre stick using the method in **Procedure 1**. Why do you think your fingers always meet at (or surrounding) the centre of gravity?

2. An equal-arm balance will work only if there is a gravitational field, **g**. Explain why such a balance will 'read' the same mass whether it is used on the earth or on the moon, where **g** is only 1/6 what it is here.

3. A golfer wishes to know where the centre of gravity of his putter face is. He can find out quickly by holding the putter face horizontal and bouncing a golf ball on the face of the putter, which is held loosely in his other hand. How does he know when he is bouncing the ball off the CG?

Second Condition for Equilibrium

Earlier in this chapter it was shown that for a body to be in static equilibrium, the vector sum of all the forces on it must be zero. This means that the sum of all the forces acting up must equal the sum of all the forces acting down; the sum of all the forces acting to the left must equal the sum of all the forces acting to the right. No matter how you look at it, the first condition for static equilibrium is:

$$\Sigma F = 0.$$

Investigation 1-2 probably convinced you that for rotational equilibrium, a second requirement must be met. Not only must the vector sum of the forces on a body be zero, but also the sum of all the clockwise torques must equal the sum of all the counterclockwise torques.

Second Condition For Static Equilibrium

$$\Sigma \tau_{\text{clockwise}} = \Sigma \tau_{\text{counterclockwise}}$$

If a torque which tends to make an object rotate counterclockwise is assigned a positive (+) value, and a clockwise torque is assigned a negative (-) value, then the second condition for static equilibrium can be written this way:

$$\Sigma \tau = 0$$

Exercises

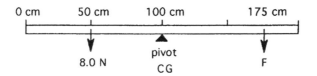

Figure 1.31

1. What force **F** is needed to balance the beam in **Figure 1.31**?

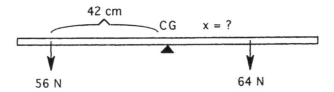

Figure 1.32

2. How far from the pivot must the 64 N object be placed to balance the beam in **Figure 1.32**?

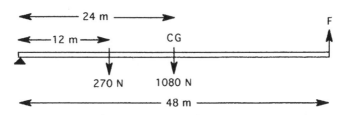

Figure 1.33

3. What upward force **F** is needed to achieve rotational equilibrium in **Figure 1.33**?

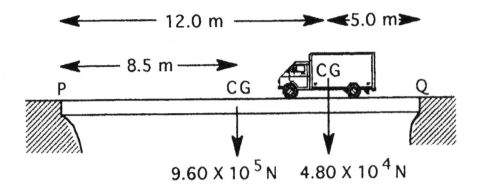

Figure 1.34

4. The force of gravity on the bridge in **Figure 1.34** is 9.60 x 10⁵ N. What upward
force must be exerted at end Q to support the bridge and the truck, if the force of
gravity on the truck is 4.80 x 10⁴ N? **Hint!** Treat the bridge as if it was a lever with an
imaginary pivot at P. What torques tend to rotate the 'lever' about pivot P?

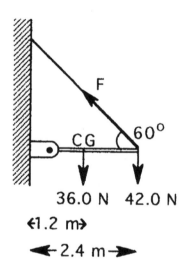

Figure 1.35

5. A small 42.0 N sign is suspended from the end of a hinged rod, which is 2.40 m long
and uniform in shape. **(Figure 1.35)** What tension force exists in the rope holding
up both the rod and the sign? The rope makes an angle of 60° with the 36.0 N rod.

Chapter Review Questions

1. What is the difference between a scalar quantity and a vector quantity?

2. A man walks 1.00×10^2 m south, then 2.4×10^2 m east. What is his resultant displacement?

3. Two forces act on point Q. One is 5.0 N toward the south and the other is 3.0 N toward the east. Find the magnitude and direction of the third force which will be needed to produce static equilibrium.

4. A girl pulls her friend across the ice on a sled with a force of 66.0 N. The rope on which she pulls makes an angle of 32° with the ice.

    (a) What is the horizontal component of the force she exerts along the rope?
    (b) If the friction force between the sled and the ice is 46.0 N, what is the unbalanced force in the horizontal direction?
    (c) Will her friend accelerate, decelerate or move with constant velocity?

5. A plane has a velocity of 951 km/h in a direction 35° west of north. What are its west and north components?

6. A jet aircraft is aimed south and travelling 851 km/h. A wind blows the plane toward the east at 36.0 km/h. What is its resultant velocity?

7. A man is lost in the woods. He wanders 3.0 km north, then 7.0 km east, then 7.0 km south, then 4.0 km west. What is the magnitude and direction of his resultant displacement?

8. A 6.0×10^3 kg vehicle is parked on a slight downslope making an angle of 6.7° with the horizontal.
    (a) What is the force of gravity on the vehicle?
    (b) What is the component of the force of gravity acting in a direction parallel with the slope?
    (c) What friction force is needed to keep the vehicle from accelerating down the slope?

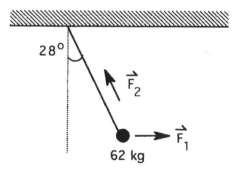

Figure 1.36

9. If the heavy pendulum in **Figure 1.36** is held motionless by the force on the horizontal rope, calculate:

(a) the tension in the horizontal rope and

(b) the tension in the rope supporting the pendulum at 28° to the vertical.

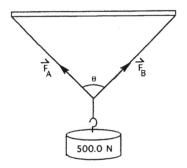

Figure 1.37

10. What is the tension in each supporting rope in **Figure 1.37** if the angle θ formed by the two sides of the 'V' made by the rope is:

(a) 0° ?   (b) 90° ?   (c) 120° ?   (d) 170°?   (e) 180°?

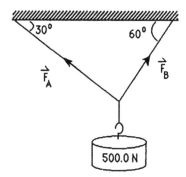

Figure 1.38

11. The two ropes in **Figure 1.38** support the 500.0 N load between them, but they act at different angles.

(a) What must the resultant of the two tension forces in the ropes be?

(b) What is the magnitude and direction of the tension in each of the two ropes?

12. A weather balloon rises upward at a rate of 6.4 m/s, but a wind blows it toward the east at 4.8 m/s.

   (a) What is its resultant velocity?

   (b) How long will it take to drift across a lake that is 12.0 km wide?

13. A 588 N mother sits on one side of a seesaw, 2.20 m from the pivot. One of her two children sits 2.00 m from the pivot on the other side of the seesaw. If the force of gravity on her is 256 N, where must the other child sit to balance the seesaw if the force of gravity on him is 412 N?

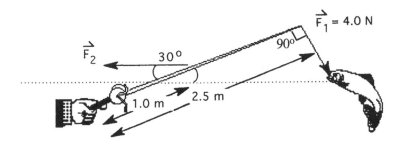

Figure 1.39

14. If the force exerted by the fish line on the tip of the rod is 4.0 N, what force must the fisherman exert in the direction and in the location shown in **Figure 1.39**? Ignore the rod's mass, and assume the rod is pivoted in the fisherman's other hand.

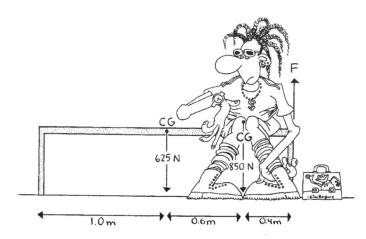

Figure 1.40

15. What upward force is exerted by the right support leg of the bench in **Figure 1.40**?

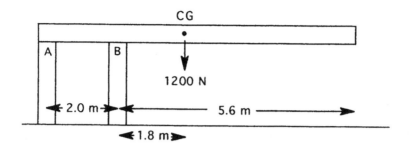

Figure 1.41

16. If the force of gravity on the beam in **Figure 1.41** is 1.2 x 10³ N, what forces must be exerted at A and B to maintain equilibrium? In what direction must each force act?

Brain Busters

17. A golfer hits his drive 225 m in a direction 15° east of north. His second shot is hit 175 m in a direction 20° west of north, and it ends up 3.0 m short of the hole on a direct line from the tee to the hole. How far is it from the tee to the hole?

18. A 9.0 kg box is sliding down a smooth flat ramp which makes an angle of 24° with the horizontal. If the coefficient of kinetic friction between the box and the ramp is 0.25, how long will it take the box to slide 2.0 m down the ramp from a standing start?

19. If the mass of the earth is 6.0 x 10²⁴ kg and the mass of the moon is 7.4 x 10²² kg, where is the centre of mass of the earth-moon system? The distance from the centre of the earth to the centre of the moon is 3.8 x 10⁵ km. Make a sketch showing approximately where the centre of mass of the earth-moon system would be located.

20. A uniform 15 kg ladder whose length is 5.0 m stands on the floor and leans against a vertical wall, making an angle of 25° with the vertical. Assuming that the friction between the ladder and the wall is negligible, what is the minimum amount of friction between the ladder and the floor which will keep the ladder from slipping?

21. If a ladder like the one in **Question 20** makes an angle θ with the wall, has a mass m and is uniform in design, show that the minimum force of friction which must exist between the ladder and floor to keep the ladder from slipping is given by

$$F_f = \frac{1}{2} mg \tan\theta .$$

Test Yourself!

Multiple Choice

1. Which list contains only **vector quantities**?

   A. mass, speed, force
   B. acceleration, distance, time
   C. momentum, speed, mass
   D. velocity, acceleration, force

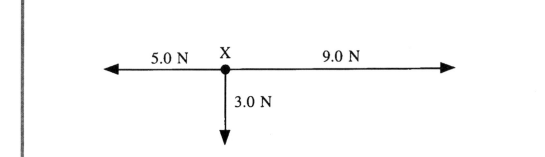

2. What is the *magnitude* of the **resultant** of the three forces acting at point X?

   A. 5.0 N
   B. 7.0 N
   C. 12.0 N
   D. 14.0 N
   E. 17.0 N

3. The current in a river is such that the water flows toward the north at 2.1 m/s. An alligator swims toward the west, at 2.4 m/s relative to the water. What is the resultant direction of travel of the alligator?

   A. 41° W of N
   B. 49° E of N
   C. 49° W of N
   D. 41° E of N

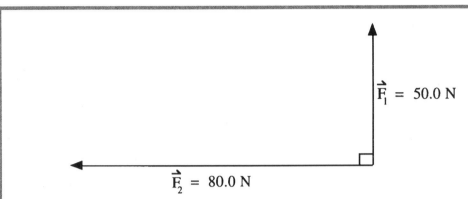

$\vec{F_1} = 50.0 \text{ N}$

$\vec{F_2} = 80.0 \text{ N}$

4. Two rugby players pull on a ball in the directions shown in the above diagram. What is the *magnitude* of the force that must be exerted by a third player, to achieve translational equilibrium of the ball?

    A. 130 N
    B. 94 N
    C. 65 N
    D. 30 N

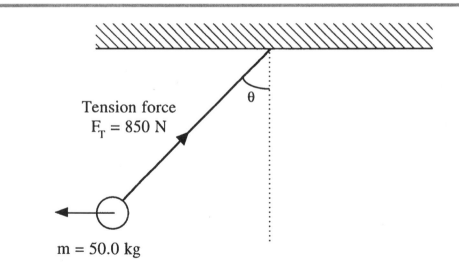

Tension force
$F_T = 850 \text{ N}$

θ

$m = 50.0 \text{ kg}$

5. A 50.0 kg mass is supported by a rope. When a horizontal force is used to hold the mass at an angle θ with the vertical, the tension in the rope is 850.0 N. What is angle θ?

    A. 30°
    B. 35°
    C. 55°
    D. 60°

Open-Ended Questions

6. An airplane heads due west with an airspeed of 84 m/s. Because of a wind blowing due north, the speed of the airplane relative to the ground is 98 m/s. What is the wind speed?

7. Golfer Arnold Hacker requires three putts from position A to put his ball in the hole. His first putt, from A to B, travels 8.0 m south. His second putt, from B to C, travels 1.2 m southwest. His third putt, from C to the hole at D, travels 0.50 m northwest. What would be the magnitude and direction of the single putt that would have put the ball into the hole, from A to D?

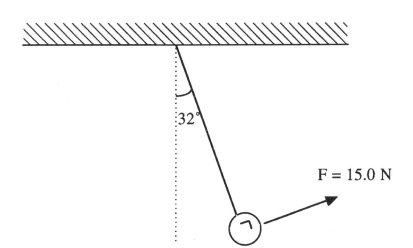

8. A 15.0 N force is used to hold a mass on a string at an angle of 32° from the vertical, as in the above diagram. What is the mass?

9. A 25 kg teeter-totter, of uniform density, is pivoted at its centre. A 35 kg girl is sitting on one side, 1.60 m from the centre. On the other side of the teeter totter, how far from the pivot must her 54 kg boyfriend sit in order to balance the teeter totter?

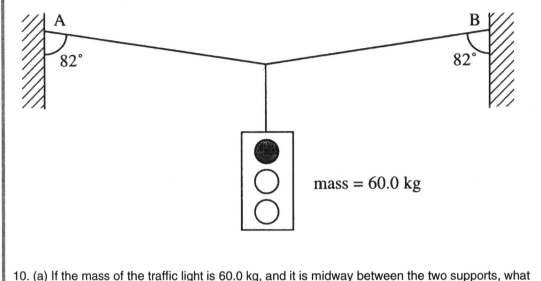

10. (a) If the mass of the traffic light is 60.0 kg, and it is midway between the two supports, what is the tension in the cord between A and B, supporting the light?

(b) Explain why it is not possible to have the cord absolutely straight between the two supports in this static equilibrium situation.

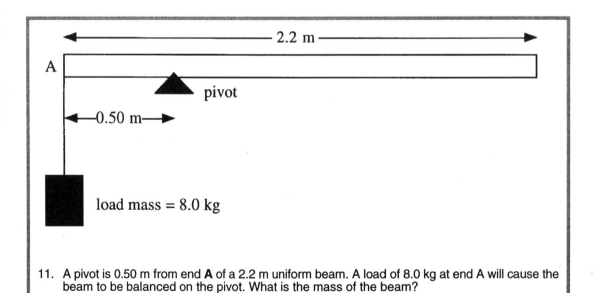

11. A pivot is 0.50 m from end **A** of a 2.2 m uniform beam. A load of 8.0 kg at end A will cause the beam to be balanced on the pivot. What is the mass of the beam?

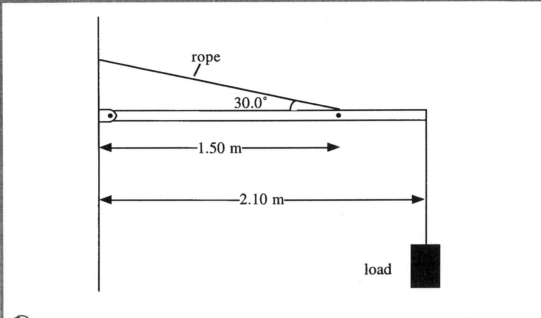

12. A horizontal beam 2.10 m long has negligible mass. If the rope exerts a 50.0 N *horizontal* force on the beam, what is the force of gravity on the load?

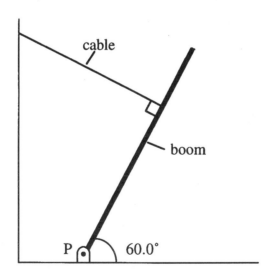

13. A cable supports a uniform boom, which is pivoted at point P. If the cable is attached two-thirds of the way along the boom from P, and the tension force in the cable is 840 N, what is the force of gravity on the boom?

Motocross trick rider **Mike Samson** of **Kamloops, BC**, demonstrates a move he calls the **'Helicopter Lookback'**. This is a spectacular example of motion in two dimensions.

Chapter 2 Motion in Two Dimensions

2.1 Review of Basic Definitions

Kinematics deals with the *description* of motion (without reference to the *causes* of the motion). A brief review of some of the definitions you studied earlier should be helpful to you.

Speed

The **average speed**, $\bar{v}$, of an object is defined as the **distance**, d, it travels divided by the **time**, t, it takes to travel that distance.

$$\textbf{Average speed} = \frac{\textbf{distance}}{\textbf{time}} \text{ , or } \bar{v} = \frac{d}{t}.$$

Speeds are expressed in a variety of units, such as **m/s, km/h**, or **km/s**.

A vehicle that travels 450 km in 5.5 h has an average speed of $\frac{450 \text{ km}}{5.5 \text{ h}}$, which equals 82 km/h. During the trip, the vehicle's speed would vary from minute to minute. Its speed *at a particular instant* (as shown on the speedometer) is called its **instantaneous speed**, v.

Velocity

Velocity is a **vector** quantity, whereas speed is a **scalar**. The velocity of an object is its speed *in a particular direction*. While speed is distance divided by time, velocity is **displacement, d**, divided by **time**. Displacement, of course, is also a vector quantity.

$$\textbf{Average velocity} = \frac{\textbf{displacement}}{\textbf{time}} \text{ , or } v = \frac{d}{t}.$$

If you travel 400.0 km south, then return 400.0 km north, and the whole trip takes you 10.0 h, your average **speed** for the trip is 800.0 km ÷ 10.0 h , or 80.0 km/h. Your average **velocity**, however, is *zero!* (This is because the vector sum of the south displacement vector and the north displacement vector is zero, which means that the average velocity for the trip is zero.)

Acceleration

A body **accelerates** when it changes speed or when it changes direction (or when it does both). Average acceleration is defined as the change in velocity divided by the time elapsed during the change in velocity.

$$\textbf{Average acceleration} = \frac{\textbf{change in velocity}}{\textbf{time interval}} \text{ , or } \bar{a} = \frac{\Delta v}{\Delta t} = \frac{v_f - v_o}{t_f - t_o}.$$

Generally speaking, the time interval, $t_f - t_o$, is simply called t. It must be remembered that **acceleration** and **velocity** are vector quantities, and in situations where changes in direction occur, the **vector difference** must be used. In many situations, we shall only be concerned with the *magnitudes* of velocities and/or accelerations. In these situations, the symbols v and a will be used.

Uniform Acceleration

You will often deal with situations where acceleration is uniform, or constant. A review of the laws governing uniform acceleration is provided here, because these laws are used often in this course. **Figure 2.1** is a graph showing how the velocity of a uniformly accelerated object varies with time. The object is moving with speed v_o at time t_o, and with speed v_f at the end of elapsed time t.

Graph of Speed vs Time for a Uniformly Accelerated Object

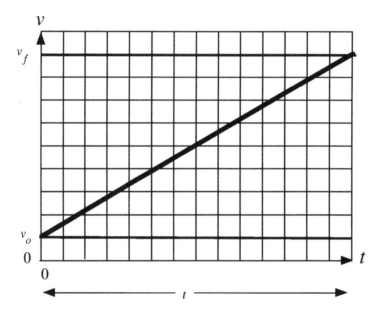

Figure 2.1

Consider the slope of the speed-time graph in **Figure 2.1**. Since we are interested in *speeds*, the symbol v is used. (Speed is the magnitude of a velocity, so it is a scalar quantity.)

$$\text{Slope} = \frac{\text{rise}}{\text{run}} = \frac{v_f - v_o}{t - 0}.$$

Obviously, the **slope** is equal to the **acceleration** of the body!

$$a = \frac{v_f - v_o}{t}.$$

The equation for the straight line graph in **Figure 2.1** can therefore be written:

$$v_f = v_o + at . \quad \textbf{I}$$

What distance, d, does the uniformly accelerating body travel during the time interval, t? You know that **distance = average speed x time,** or

$$d = \bar{v} \cdot t .$$

Now, for uniformly accelerated motion, the **average speed** occurs *halfway between* v_o and v_f, so we can write

$$d = \frac{v_o + v_f}{2} \cdot t . \quad \textbf{II}$$

From Equation I, we know that $v_f = v_o + at$, and we can substitute for v_f in Equation **II.**

$$d = \frac{v_o + v_o + at}{2} \cdot t , \text{ therefore}$$

$$d = v_o t + \tfrac{1}{2}at^2. \quad \textbf{III}$$

If time t is not known, but the other relevant variables are known, there is a fourth equation which often comes in handy in uniform acceleration problems. It can be derived by eliminating t from Equations **I** and **II.**

According to Equation I, $v_f = v_o + at$, therefore

$$t = \frac{v_f - v_o}{a} .$$

Substituting for t in Equation **II,** $d = \dfrac{v_o + v_f}{2} \cdot t$, therefore

$$d = \frac{v_f + v_o}{2} \cdot \frac{v_f - v_o}{a} , \text{ so}$$

$$d = \frac{v_f^2 - v_o^2}{2a} , \text{ and therefore}$$

$$v_f^2 = v_o^2 + 2ad . \quad \textbf{IV}$$

Thus, there are **four** equations one may use to solve problems involving uniform acceleration.

Acceleration of Falling Bodies

The most commonly used example of uniform acceleration is a body that is in **free fall**, where air resistance is either zero or negligible. On earth, a heavy body with a small surface area may approximate free fall. A falling sky diver is definitely **not** a good example of a body in free fall — especially when his or her parachute is deployed! On the moon, there is no atmosphere to contend with, and free fall would be achieved easily, but the rate of acceleration is about 1/6 of what it is here on earth.

The acceleration of a freely falling body is called the **acceleration due to gravity**, and is given the symbol **g**. The magnitude of **g** varies slightly from place to place on the earth's surface, but rarely varies much from **9.80 m/s²**. In this book we will assume that on earth, the magnitude of **g** is 9.80 m/s².

Acceleration is a vector quantity, of course, and in many situations where the acceleration is caused by the force of gravity. you will find it necessary to consider **down** as the **negative direction**. In gravitational acceleration problems, therefore, you use **a** $= -$ **9.80 m/s²**.

If a body is thrown into the air, it accelerates downward (**a** $= -$ **9.80 m/s²**) at all times during the trajectory, whether the velocity is upward (+), zero or downward (–).

Example

You throw a baseball straight up. It leaves your hand with an initial velocity of 10.0 m/s. **Figure 2.2** is a graph showing how the velocity of the ball varies with time, starting when you begin to throw the ball, and ending when you finish catching it. At **A**, the ball has just left your hand. At **C**, the ball has just reached the glove in which you will catch the ball. Notice that between **A** and **C**, the velocity is changing at a uniform rate. If you take the slope of this graph, you will obtain the acceleration of the ball due to gravity alone. See **Exercise 5**.

Exercises

1. A tourist averaged 82 km/h for a 6.5 h trip in her car. How far did she go?

2. Change these speeds so that they are expressed in m/s:
   (a) 1 km/h   (b) 50 km/h   (c) 80 km/h   (d) 100 km/h

3. A certain airplane has an acceleration of 15.0 m/s².
   (a) How fast will it be moving 2.5 s after it starts down the runway?
   (b) How far down the runway will it travel during the 2.5 s?
   (c) Minimum take-off speed is 60.0 m/s. How long must the runway be?

4. (a) You are driving along the road at 80 km/h (22 m/s) when you see a moose 50.0 m in front of your car. Your reaction time is 0.40 s, and when you finally hit the brakes, your car accelerates at a rate of $-$ 6.4 m/s². Will your car stop in time to avoid the moose?
   (b) If the road is wet, and your car accelerates at a rate of just $-$ 4.8 m/s², what will happen? Show your calculations.

Velocity vs Time
(for a Ball Thrown Straight Up)

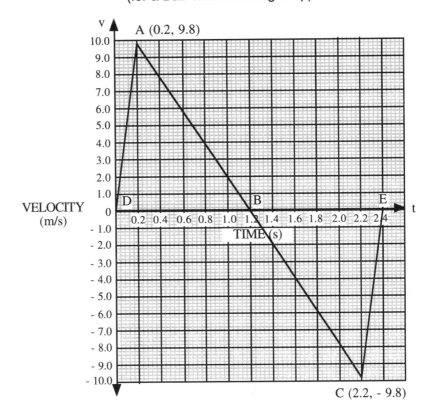

Figure 2.2

5. Refer to **Figure 2.2**, which is a graph of the velocity of a ball, as a function of time, when you throw a ball straight up in the air.
   (a) What was the acceleration of the ball
      (i) while it was being thrown?
      (ii) while it was in 'free flight'?
      (iii) while it was being caught?
   (b) What point on the graph corresponds with the instant when the ball reached the 'peak' of its flight? Explain how you know this.
   (c) What altitude did the ball reach? (**Hint**: The distance the ball travels equals the average speed multiplied by the time elapsed when it reaches its 'peak' altitude. What property of the graph would give you $d = \bar{v}t$?)

6. Equation **IV** for uniform acceleration, $v_f^2 = v_o^2 + 2ad$, can be used to show that a body thrown upward with a **speed** v will return to *the same level* with the same **speed** it had when it was thrown upward.
   (a) Show mathematically why the magnitude of v_f equals the magnitude of v_o.
   (b) Will the ball have the same **velocity** when it comes down as when it was thrown up in the air? Explain your answer.

7. A skateboarder accelerates uniformly down a hill, starting from rest. During the third one second interval from rest, the skateboarder travels 7.5 m. What is the acceleration of the skateboarder?

8. A frictionless air track is tilted at an angle of 2.5°.
   (a) At what rate will the glider accelerate down the sloped air track?
   (b) How long will the glider take to travel 1.5 m along the track, if its initial velocity was zero?

2.2 Projectile Motion

If you throw a baseball, your arm exerts a force on the ball until the ball leaves your hand. Once the ball is free of your hand, it continues moving because of its inertia, and will follow a curved path (unless you throw it straight up). A baseball thrown into the air is a good example of a **projectile**. If a marble rolls off the edge of a table, it follows a curved path to the floor. The marble, too, is a projectile.

Figure 2.3

Any object (a rock, a ball or a bullet) which is projected by some method, and then continues moving because of its inertia, is a **projectile**. **Figure 2.3** shows the path taken by a baseball thrown by highly skilled fielder. The dashed line shows the path the baseball would take if there was no force of gravity. The solid line shows the actual path taken by the baseball.

At first glance, it may appear to be a complicated matter to describe the motion of a projectile. After you have done **Investigation 2-1 (Projectiles)**, you will understand that the motion of a projectile can be described very simply if you look at the **vertical** motion and the **horizontal** motion separately.

Investigation 2-1   Projectiles

Purpose: To study the two-dimensional motion of a projectile.

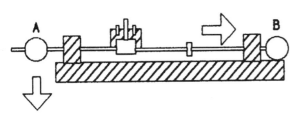

Figure 2.4

Procedure

1. Set up the projectile apparatus in **Figure 2.4**. When the horizontal bar is released by a spring mechanism, ball **A** falls straight down and ball **B** is projected horizontally. Once 'fired', both balls experience *one force only* (ignoring air resistance) — the **force of gravity**. Watch and *listen* as the two balls are projected simultaneously. Repeat the procedure several times.

2. **Figure 2.5** could be a tracing from a strobe photograph of two balls released simultaneously by a projectile apparatus similar to the one you just used. Make or obtain a copy of this tracing. Use a sharp, pencilled dot to mark the position of the centre of each image of the balls. **Figure 2.6** shows what to do.

3. Consider ball **A** first. (It is the one falling straight down.) Find out if its acceleration is *uniform* as follows: Call the time interval between images one **'time unit'** (tu). Measure the displacement of the ball during each successive **tu**. Since average velocity equals displacement divided by time, the **average velocity** during each successive time interval simply equals **displacement** divided by **1 tu.**

4. Make a graph of the average vertical velocity, $\bar{v}_y$, vs time, t. Find out if the acceleration of falling ball **A** is uniform. Remember that, since this is average velocity, you should plot velocities *midway* through each time interval.

5. Now consider ball **B**, which was projected horizontally. On your tracing, draw in the successive velocity vectors as in **Figure 2.6**. These vectors are cute to look at, but they do not help you understand what is happening to ball **B**! Therefore, construct both **horizontal** and **vertical components** of each of the velocity vectors. See **Figure 2.7**.

6. Compare successive **vertical components** of ball B's velocities with the corresponding vertical velocities of ball **A**. Plot a graph of $\bar{v}_y$ vs t for ball **B**.

7. Compare successive horizontal components (v_x) with each other. Plot $\bar{v}_x$ vs t.

8. (a) Plot **total vertical displacement from rest** (d_y) vs time (t) for the vertical motion of either ball.

   (b) Plot d_y vs t^2

9. Plot **total horizontal displacement from rest** (d_x) vs time (t) for ball **B**.

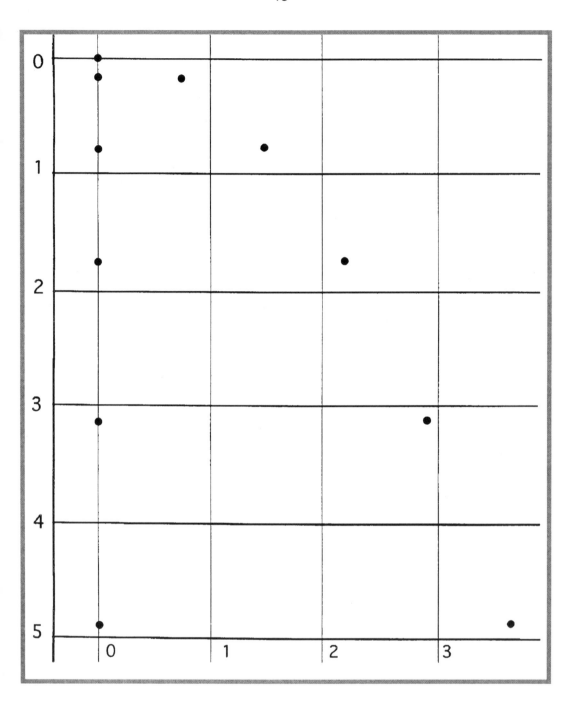

Figure 2.5

A tracing of a stroboscopic photograph made of a *projected* ball, falling simultaneously with a ball falling straight down, might look like this.

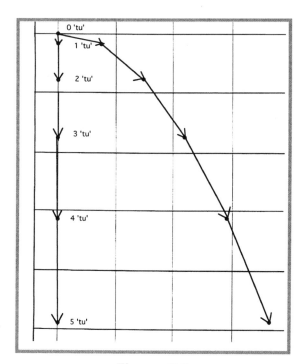

Figure 2.6

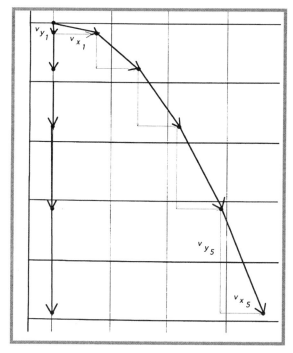

Figure 2.7

Concluding Questions

1. A rifle fires a bullet horizontally on level ground. Just as the bullet leaves the rifle, the rifle falls to the ground. Which will hit the ground first, the bullet or the rifle? Explain your answer.

2. When a ball is projected horizontally, what conclusions do you arrive at regarding

   (a) its **horizontal velocity components**?

   (b) its **vertical velocity components**?

3. Write a simple mathematical relationship (such as $d_x = kt$, where k is the constant of proportionality) connecting the following variables in a projectile situation:

   (a) v_y vs t,

   (b) v_x vs t, and

   (c) d_y vs t.

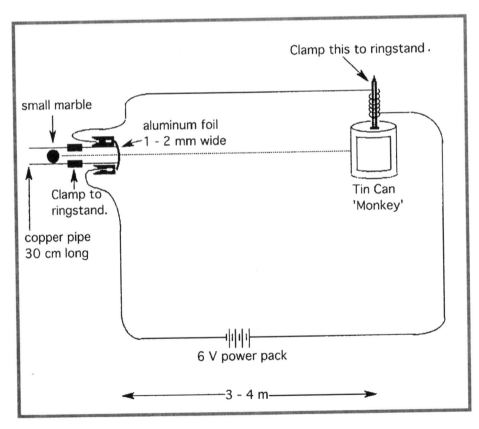

Figure 2.8

Challenges

1. Build a 'monkey gun' apparatus. See **Figure 2.8**. The projectile is a small marble which is propelled by a 'blow gun' made of a copper pipe, the diameter of which is just slightly larger than the marble. When the marble leaves the gun, it breaks a thin piece of aluminum foil, which opens an electric circuit. An electromagnet holding up a tin can target (the 'monkey' in a tree?) is deactivated. Just as the marble leaves the gun, the 'monkey' starts to fall to the ground. Will the marble hit the monkey or miss it? Explain your answer. Now test your prediction!

2. Imagine that the 'blow gun' is aimed upward at some angle greater than zero relative to the horizontal. It is aimed at the 'monkey' to begin with. Will it still hit the monkey if the monkey falls at the instant the marble leaves the gun? Explain your answer!

2.3 Vectors and Projectile Problems

You will use the four laws of uniform acceleration frequently when solving problems involving projectile motion. For your convenience these laws are summarized here:

$$v_f = v_o + at \qquad \text{I}$$

$$d = \frac{v_o + v_f}{2} \cdot t \qquad \text{II}$$

$$d = v_o t + \tfrac{1}{2} at^2 \qquad \text{III}$$

$$v_f^2 = v_o^2 + 2ad \qquad \text{IV}$$

When solving projectile problems, you must remember that velocities, displacements and accelerations are **vector quantities**. Upward motion is generally considered positive (+) and downward motion is negative (-). On or near the earth's surface, the magnitude of the acceleration due to gravity is $g = 9.80$ m/s², and since it is always acting downward, you should use

$$a = -9.80 \text{ m/s}^2 .$$

When analyzing the motion of a projectile, the velocity is almost always resolved into its **horizontal** and **vertical** components. The laws of uniform acceleration may be applied to the vertical motion of the object. The horizontal motion is simple to deal with, since horizontal velocity is **constant** (ignoring air resistance).

The Parabolic Nature of Projectile Motion

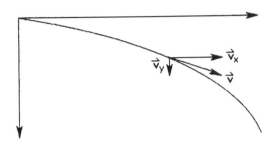

Figure 2.9

When a projectile is fired, its path is **parabolic** if air resistance is negligible. That this is so can be shown quite simply for the situation where an object is thrown out horizontally.

Let the magnitude of the horizontal displacement of an object thrown out horizontally be x. Horizontal velocity, which has magnitude v_x, is constant.

$$v_x = \frac{x}{t}, \quad \text{so } t = \frac{x}{v_x}.$$

Let the magnitude of the vertical displacement be y. Assuming the object starts from rest, so that v_o = zero, then

$$y = \tfrac{1}{2}at^2, \text{ or } \quad y = \tfrac{1}{2}a[\frac{x}{v_x}]^2.$$

Now, '$\tfrac{1}{2}$', 'a' and 'v_x' are all constant, therefore we can say that $y = kx^2$.

This is the simplest possible equation for a **parabola**. A ball thrown out by a pitcher, or a stream of water issuing from a hose, will follow a parabolic path. If air resistance is negligible, any object given a horizontal motion in a gravitational field will move with a parabolic path.

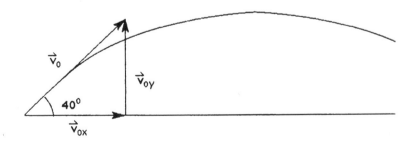

Figure 2.10

Sample Problem: Projectile Motion

A golf ball was struck from the first tee at Lunar Golf and Country Club, a private golf course for astronauts stranded on the moon. It was given a velocity of 48 m/s at an angle of 40° to the horizontal. On the moon, the magnitude of $g = 1.6$ m/s².

(a) What is the vertical component of the golf ball's initial velocity?

Solution: Since the velocity of the ball is initially 48 m/s, then $v_o = 48$m/s.

$$v_{oy} = v_o \sin 40° = (48 \text{ m/s})(0.6428) = 30.9 \text{ m/s*}.$$

(*Keep one extra significant figure for now.)

(b) For what interval of time is the ball 'in flight'?

Solution: The most direct way of solving for time is to use Equation III for uniform acceleration.

$$d = v_o t + \tfrac{1}{2} at^2$$

Since the ball will eventually return to ground level, its displacement for the entire trip, in a vertical direction, is zero! $(d = y = 0.)$

Therefore, $0 = (30.9 \text{ m/s})t + \tfrac{1}{2}(-1.6 \text{ m/s}^2) t^2$
or, $(0.80 \text{ m/s}^2)t^2 = (30.9 \text{ m/s})t$

$$t = \frac{30.9 \text{ m/s}}{0.80 \text{ m/s}^2} = 38.6 \text{ s*}$$

(*Keep one extra significant figure for now.)

(c) How far will the ball travel horizontally?

Solution: Horizontal displacement $x = v_{ox} t$. Horizontal velocity remains constant. It can be calculated as follows:

$$v_{ox} = v_o \cos 40°.$$

Therefore, $x = (v_o \cos 40°) \cdot t = (48 \text{ m/s})(0.7660)(38.6 \text{ s}) = 1.42 \times 10^3 \text{ m}.$

The final answers, rounded off to two significant figures, are:
(a) 31 m/s,
(b) 39 s, and
(c) 1.4×10^3 m or 1.4 km.

Just think! The golf ball would travel 1.4 km on the moon!

Exercises   Use $g = -9.80$ m/s^2 .

1. A girl throws a rock horizontally from the top of a cliff 98 m high, with a horizontal velocity of 27 m/s.

   (a) How many seconds was the rock in the air?
   (b) How far out from the base of the cliff does the rock land?

2. A golfer gives a golf ball a velocity of 48 m/s at an angle of 45° with the horizontal.

   (a) What is the **vertical component** of the ball's initial velocity?
   (b) How long is the ball in the air?
   (c) What is the **horizontal distance** covered by the ball while in flight? Compare your result with that for the same question on the moon . (See the **Sample Problem** preceding these exercises.)

3. A rescue pilot wishes to drop a package of emergency supplies so that it lands as close as possible to a downed aircraft. If the plane travels with a velocity of 81 m/s and is flying 125 m above the downed craft, how far away (horizontally) from the downed craft must the rescue pilot drop his package? (Assume negligible air resistance.)

4. An archer standing on the back of a pickup truck moving at 28 m/s fires an arrow straight up at a duck flying directly overhead. He misses the duck. If the arrow was fired with an initial vertical velocity of 49 m/s relative to the truck,

   (a) For how many seconds will the arrow be in the air?
   (b) How far will the truck travel while the arrow is in the air?
   (c) Where, in relation to the archer, will the arrow come down? (Ignore air friction.) Will the archer have to 'duck'? Explain.

5. A bullet is fired with a horizontal velocity of 330 m/s from a height of 1.6 m above the ground. Assuming the ground is level, how far from the gun, measured horizontally, will the bullet hit the ground?

6. A ball is thrown with a velocity of 24 m/s at an angle of 30° to the horizontal. Assume air friction is small enough to be ignored.

   (a) What is the horizontal component of the initial velocity?
   (b) What is the vertical component of the initial velocity?
   (c) How long will the ball be in the air?
   (d) What horizontal distance (range) will the ball carry?
   (e) To what maximum height will the ball rise?

7. Solve **Exercise 6** for angles of (a) 45° and (b) 60°. Which of the three angles results in the greatest range? (It can be shown that, for a given initial velocity, this angle is the best of **all** angles for obtaining the maximum range in the ideal, 'no air resistance' situation.)

8. A student measured the horizontal and vertical components of the velocity of a projectile in a laboratory situation. Here is the data. Times and velocities are 'true' (not scaled).

Vertical velocity	v_y	m/s	3.58	4.56	5.54	6.52	7.50
Horizontal velocity	v_x	m/s	2.12	2.12	2.13	2.11	2.12
Time	t	s	0.10	0.20	0.30	0.40	0.50

(a) Plot vertical velocity vs. time.
(b) Find the slope and Y-intercept of your graph.
(c) Write an equation **specifically** describing your graph.
(d) On the same graph sheet, plot horizontal velocity vs time.
(e) Write an equation **specifically** describing your second graph.

Ehren Stillman Cartoon

Chapter Review Questions   Use $g = -9.80$ m/s^2.

1. Define the meaning of (a) speed, (b) velocity, and (c) acceleration.

2. Assuming no air resistance, how far must a small steel ball fall from rest before it reaches a speed of 100.0 km/h?

3. How far does a freely falling body travel during the **fourth** second of its fall?

4. A youngster hits a baseball giving it a velocity of 22 m/s at an angle of 62° with the horizontal. Ignoring air friction, how far will the ball travel before it is caught by a fielder? Would this hit be a likely home run? Explain.

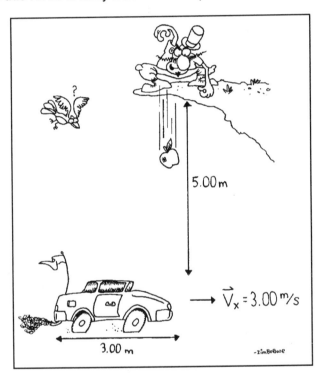

Figure 2.11

5. A disgruntled physics student sees the front end of his teacher's car directly below him at the base of a cliff. See **Figure 2.11**. If the student is 5.00 m above the car, which is 3.00 m long and travelling only 3.00 m/s to the right, will the apple the student drops hit the teacher's car? (Will Physics be a core subject?) Show all details of your argument.

6. A pebble is fired from a slingshot with a velocity of 30.0 m/s. If it is fired at an angle of 30° to the vertical, what height will it reach? If its fall is interrupted by a vertical wall 12 m away, where will it hit the wall in relation to the starting position of the pebble in the slingshot?

Brain Busters

7. A fireman is standing on top of a building 20.0 m high. He finds that if he holds the hose so that water issues from it horizontally at 12.0 m/s, the water will hit a burning wall of an adjacent building, at a height of 15.0 m above the ground. What is the horizontal distance from the fireman to the burning wall?

8. The fireman in **Brain Buster 7** wants the water from the same hose to reach the burning wall at the *same level* above the ground as he is standing. At what angle must he aim the hose relative to the horizontal?

9. A penny is dropped down a very deep well. One hears the sound of the penny hitting the water 2.5 s later. If sound travels 330 m/s, how deep is the well?

10. A stone is thrown straight up with a speed of 15.0 m/s. How fast will it be moving when its altitude is 8.0 m above the point from which it was thrown? How much time elapses while the stone is reaching that height? (Is there one answer or are there two answers? Why?)

11. A small, free-falling pebble takes 0.25 s to pass by a window 1.8 m high. From what height above the window was the pebble dropped?

Physics is everywhere! This basketball thrown by **Cindie Edamura** follows a parabolic path.

Test Yourself!

Multiple Choice

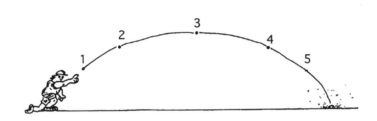

(1-3) A ball is thrown into the air, following the path shown in the diagram. At **1**, the ball has just left the thrower's hand. At **5**, the ball is at its original height above the ground. Assume negligible air friction when answering these questions:

1. The **acceleration** of the ball while it is in flight has magnitude *'g'* when the ball is at

   A. 1, 2, 3, 4 and 5.
   B. 1 only.
   C. 1 and 5 only.
   D. 1, 2, 4 and 5 only.

2. The **horizontal velocity** of the ball is at a maximum at

   A. 1, 2, 3, 4 and 5.
   B. 1 only.
   C. 3 only.
   D. 5 only.
   E. 1 and 5 only.

3. The magnitude of the **vertical velocity** of the ball is at a maximum at

   A. 1 only.
   B. 5 only.
   C. 1 and 5 only.
   D. 3.
   E. 1, 2, 3, 4, and 5.

4. A ball is tossed in a direction 72° above the horizontal, with a velocity of 12 m/s. What is the maximum height the ball will reach?

   A. 0.70 m
   B. 6.6 m
   C. 7.3 m
   D. 70 m

5. A projectile is launched with a velocity of 16.3 m/s, at an angle of 37° with the horizontal. How much time will elapse before the vertical component of the velocity is zero?

    A. 1.66 s
    B. 1.33 s
    C. 1.25 s
    D. 1.00 s

6. An observer records time (t), displacement (d) and velocity (v) of a skier sliding from rest down a ski slope, with uniform acceleration. He plots graphs using different variables. In which case will the observer **not** obtain a straight line?

    A. d vs t.
    B. d vs t^2.
    C. v vs t.
    D. v^2 vs d.

Open-Ended Questions

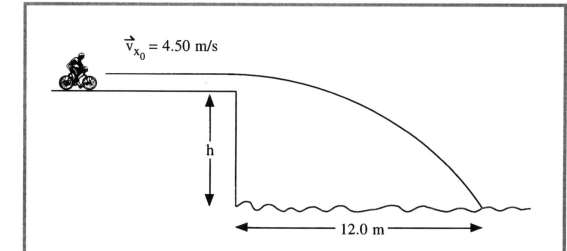

7. A daredevil BMX rider runs his bike off a cliff with a horizontal velocity of 4.5 m/s, and lands in the water 12 m from the base of the cliff.

    (a) How long does it take the rider to hit the water?

    (b) How high is the cliff?

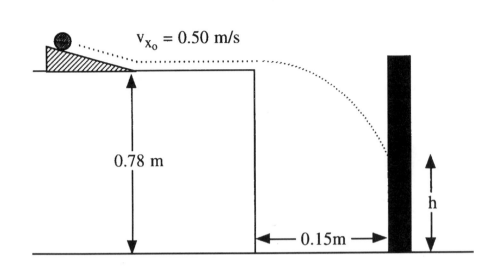

$v_{x_o} = 0.50$ m/s

0.78 m

0.15m

h

8. A marble is accelerated to a horizontal velocity of 0.50 m/s by rolling it down a small ramp. The marble rolls off the table, which is 0.78 m high. As it falls, it hits a barrier on the way down. If the barrier is 0.15 m from the edge of the table, at what height from the ground, h, will the marble hit the barrier?

9. As part of a NASA experiment, golfer Tiger Woods drives a golf ball on the moon, where $g = 1.60$ m/s². He 'launches' a golf ball with a speed of 285 km/h, at an angle of 42° with the horizontal. What horizontal distance will his drive travel before landing back on the surface of the moon. Ignore the curvature of the moon.

10. A projectile is launched with a speed of 128 m/s, at an angle of 60° with the horizontal.

(a) After 2.0 s, what is the vertical component of the projectile's velocity?

(b) After 2.0 s, what is the speed of the projectile?

Chapter 3 Momentum and Energy

3.1 Dynamics

While **Galileo** was chiefly responsible for establishing the science of **kinematics** (which is concerned with describing motion, without reference to its cause), it was **Isaac Newton (1642-1727)** who laid the foundations for the science of **dynamics.** Newton was the first to clearly explain the relationship between motion and forces, which is the basis for dynamics.

Review of Newton's Laws of Motion

Newton's First Law of Motion

If there is no net force acting on a body, it will continue to move with constant velocity. This means that a body at rest will stay at rest; a body moving at a certain speed will continue to move at that speed and in the same direction unless and until an unbalanced (net) force acts on it. This property, possessed by all bodies having mass, is called **inertia**.

Your own experience tells you that if you want to push a book across your desk at constant velocity, you must exert a force on the book. Does this contradict the First Law? No! To move the book along at steady velocity, your force just has to balance the friction force opposing its motion. When the force you apply equals the friction force, the *net* force is zero, because the vector sum of your applied force and the friction force is zero.

Newton's Second Law of Motion

In an earlier course, you performed experiments to find out what happens when there is a net force acting on a body. These experiments showed you two facts about motion:

(1) A **net force** on a given body causes it to **accelerate** in the direction of the net force. If the net force is doubled, the acceleration will double. If the net force is tripled, the acceleration will also triple. Experiments show that the acceleration is directly proportional to the net force on the object.

$$\text{acceleration} \quad \propto \quad \text{net Force}$$

In symbols, $a \propto F.$

(2) For a given net force, the **acceleration** of a body is *inversely proportional* to the **mass** of a body. For example, if a 10 N force will accelerate a 5 kg mass at a rate of 2 m/s^2, the same force will accelerate a 10 kg mass at a rate of one-half the original acceleration, which is 1 m/s^2.

$$\text{acceleration} \quad \propto \quad \frac{1}{\text{mass}}$$

In symbols, $a \propto \frac{1}{m}.$

Newton's Second Law can be summarized as follows:

The acceleration of a body is directly proportional to the net force acting on it, and inversely proportional to its mass. Acceleration is in the same direction as the net force.

In symbols, $\quad a \propto \dfrac{F}{m}$, $\quad$ or $\quad a = k \cdot \dfrac{F}{m}$.

If units for force and mass are chosen so that k = 1, then $a = \dfrac{F}{m}$.

Rearranging terms, the familiar form of Newton's Second Law is obtained:

$$F = ma.$$

Newton's Third Law of Motion

When you do 'push-ups', which way do you exert your force? If you think about it, you will realize that you cannot push yourself up! You exert a force *downward* on the floor. What raises your body is the force exerted on you by the floor. When you climb stairs, you push down. The stairs push you up. When you swim forward, you push backward; the water pushes you forward.

Isaac Newton realized that when a force is applied to a body, it has to be applied by *another body!* Imagine an axe striking a block of wood. That the axe exerts a force on the wood is obvious. The force exerted by the wood on the axe might be less apparent, but if you think about it, the axe is decelerated very quickly when the wood 'hits back' at it!

Newton's Third Law may be stated as follows:

When one body exerts a force on a second body, the second body exerts an equal force on the first body, but in the opposite direction. The forces are exerted during the same interval of time.

In popular literature, the Third Law is sometimes called the **Law of Action and Reaction**. The first force is the 'action' force and the second is the 'reaction' force. The action force equals the reaction force, but is opposite in direction. *The two forces act on different bodies.* If we call the first body **A** and the second body **B**, then Newton's Third Law can be written symbolically as:

$$F_{A \text{ on } B} = -F_{B \text{ on } A}.$$

Examples Illustrating Newton's Laws

1. A 110 kg motorbike carrying a 50 kg rider coasts to a stop in a distance of 51 m. It was originally travelling 15 m/s. What was the stopping force exerted by the road on the motorbike and rider?

Solution

The stopping force is friction, which opposes the motion of the bike. Newton's Second Law will permit you to solve for **F,** if first you calculate acceleration using the appropriate uniform acceleration equation, namely:

$$v_f{}^2 = v_o{}^2 + 2ad.$$

$$a = \frac{v_f{}^2 - v_o{}^2}{2d}$$

$$a = \frac{0 - (15 \text{ m/s})^2}{2(51 \text{ m})} = -2.2 \text{ m/s}^2.$$

The acceleration is negative because its direction is opposite to the direction of the motion of the motorbike. (It is decelerating.) Newton's Second Law can now be used to solve for the **net force** (which is the stopping force due to friction):

$$F = ma = (160 \text{ kg})(-2.2 \text{ m/s}^2) = -3.5 \times 10^2 \text{ N}$$

The negative sign simply means that the stopping force is in a negative direction relative to the motion of the motorbike.

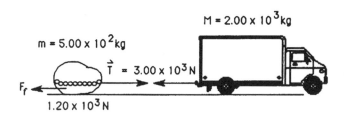

$M = 2.00 \times 10^3 \text{kg}$

$m = 5.00 \times 10^2 \text{kg}$

$\vec{T} = 3.00 \times 10^3 \text{N}$

F_f

$1.20 \times 10^3 \text{N}$

Figure 3.1(a)

2. A truck of mass 2.00×10^3 kg is towing a large boulder of mass 5.00×10^2 kg using a chain (of negligible mass). The tension in the chain is 3.00×10^3 N, and the force of friction on the boulder is 1.20×10^3 N. See **Figure 3.1(a)**.

(a) At what rate will the boulder accelerate?

(b) How far will the boulder move in 3.0 s, starting from rest?

Solution

First, draw a **free body diagram**, showing the forces acting on the body in question, which is the boulder. See **Figure 3.1(b)**.

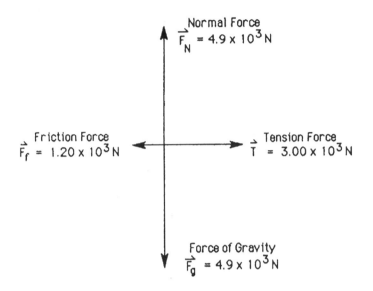

Figure 3.1(b)

To solve for the acceleration of the boulder, one must know the **net force** or **resultant force** acting on the boulder. There are four forces exerted on the boulder: (1) the **force of gravity** (mg), (2) the **normal force** (F_N) exerted upward by the road (equal in magnitude but opposite in direction to mg), (3) the **tension force** (T) exerted by way of the rope, and (4) the **friction force** (F_f) between the road and the boulder. **Figure 3.1(b)** illustrates these four forces. Their resultant is clearly 1.80×10^3 N in the direction the truck is moving. The two Y-components, mg and F_N, add up to zero. The X-components, F_f and T, have a resultant of 3.00×10^3 N - 1.20×10^3 N = 1.80×10^3 N.

Applying Newton's Second Law to the **boulder,** one can solve for its acceleration:

$$a = \frac{F}{m} = \frac{1.80 \times 10^3 \text{ N}}{5.00 \times 10^2 \text{ kg}} = 3.60 \text{ m/s}^2 .$$

To determine how far the boulder will move in 3.0 s, use the appropriate uniform acceleration equation, which is:

$$d = v_o t + \frac{1}{2}at^2 = 0 + \frac{1}{2}(3.6 \text{ m/s}^2)(3.0 \text{ s})^2 = 16 \text{ m} .$$

The boulder will move 16 m during the 3.0 s it is being pulled by the truck.

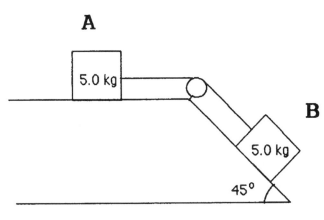

A

5.0 kg

B

45°

Figure 3.2

3. In **Figure 3.2**, a 5.0 kg block is connected to another 5.0 kg block by a string of negligible mass. The inclined plane down which the second block slides makes an angle of 45° with the horizontal. Friction is negligible.

(a) At what rate will the masses accelerate?

(b) What is the tension in the string joining the two masses?

Solution

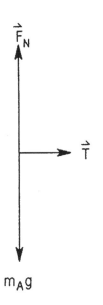

Figure 3.3(a)

Consider block **A** by itself. **Figure 3.3(a)** is a **free body diagram** showing the forces acting on block **A**. Forces F_N and m_Ag are the **Y-component forces** acting on mass **A**. Clearly, they are equal and opposite in direction, so their vector sum is zero.

$$(\Sigma F_y = 0.)$$

The resultant force on **A** will just equal the tension force **T** exerted on the rock by the rope. There is no friction force to oppose **T**.

For body **A**, then, $T = m_A a.$

Therefore, $T = $ (5.0 kg) $a.$ (1)

Consider block **B** by itself. **Figure 3.3(b)** is a **free body diagram** showing the forces acting on **B**. The direction *along the plane* is taken as the **X-component** direction. Again, the vector sum of the Y-component forces, F_N and F_y, is zero.

$$(\Sigma F_y = 0.)$$

The **resultant force** causing acceleration is $\Sigma F_x = F_p - T$, where F_p is the X-component of the force of gravity, m_Bg, on mass **B**.

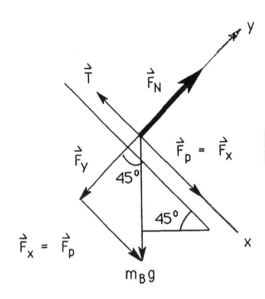

Figure 3.3(b)

Since $F_p = m_Bg \sin 45°$, the net force causing acceleration is:

$$m_Bg \sin 45° - T = m_Ba.$$

$$(5.0 \text{ kg})(9.8 \text{ N/kg})(0.707) - T = (5.0 \text{ kg}) \, a$$

$$34.6 \text{ N} - T = (5.0 \text{ kg}) \, a \qquad \text{(2)}$$

To solve for **acceleration, a,** add Equations (1) and (2):

Then, 34.6 N = (10.0 kg) **a.**

Therefore, **a** = 3.46 m/s².

To solve for **T,** use Equation (1).

$$T = (5.0 \text{ kg})(3.46 \text{ m/s}^2) = 17.3 \text{ N.}$$

Therefore, **acceleration** of the blocks is **3.5 m/s²**, and the **tension force is 17 N.**

Exercises

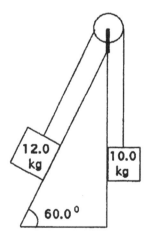

Figure 3.4

1. At what rate and in which direction will the 10.0 kg mass accelerate when the masses in **Figure 3.4** are released? Assume friction in all parts of the system may be ignored.

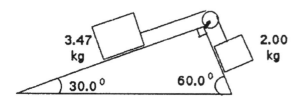

3.47 kg

2.00 kg

30.0°   60.0°

Figure 3.5

2. The two masses in **Figure 3.5** are connected by a rope of negligible mass. Friction is negligible. In what direction and at what rate will the 2.00 kg mass accelerate?

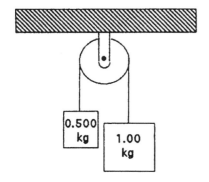

0.500 kg

1.00 kg

Figure 3.6

3. In **Figure 3.6**, a cord of negligible mass connects a 0.500 kg mass to a 1.00 kg mass. There is negligible friction in the system.
   (a) At what rate will the masses accelerate?
   (b) What is the tension in the cord while the masses are accelerating?

4. A criminal wants to escape from the third storey window of a jail, by going down a rope to the road below. Having taken high school physics, he thinks he can escape down the rope even though his mass is 75 kg and the rope can only support 65 kg without breaking. Explain how he can get down safely without breaking the rope.

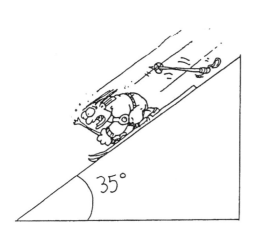

35°

Figure 3.7

5. The skier in **Figure 3.7** is descending a 35° slope on a surface where the coefficient of kinetic friction between his skis and the icy surface is 0.12.
   (a) If his mass (including his skis) is 72 kg, at what rate will he accelerate?
   (b) How fast is he moving after 8.0 s?

6. A 60.0 kg skydiver experiences air resistance during his jump. At one instant, the resistance is 320 N. At that instant, what is his acceleration? Describe his motion when the air resistance increases to the point where it equals the force of gravity on him.

3.2 Momentum and Impulse

One of the most important concepts in physics is the idea of **momentum.** Newton first used the concept when he phrased his Second Law of Motion. He called the product of mass and velocity **'quantity of motion'**, but this product has come to be known as momentum.

What makes momentum so important is the fact that it is a **conserved** quantity. *In an isolated system (a system in which no external forces interfere) the total momentum of the objects in the system will remain constant.* This is the **Law of Conservation of Momentum.**

Any moving object has momentum. Momentum (**p**) is calculated by multiplying the **mass** of the body by its **velocity**.

---

momentum = mass x velocity

$$p = mv$$

Momentum is a vector quantity, and the direction of the momentum vector is the same as the direction of the velocity vector. When you add momenta, you must use **vector addition**.

Newton's Second Law in Terms of Momentum

Newton's Second Law can be re-written in terms of momentum.

$$F = ma = m\frac{\Delta v}{\Delta t} = m\frac{[v_f - v_o]}{\Delta t} = \frac{[mv_f - mv_o]}{\Delta t} = \frac{\Delta[mv]}{\Delta t} = \frac{\Delta p}{\Delta t}.$$

Newton's Second Law can be stated in words, in terms of momentum, as follows:

An unbalanced (net) force acting on a body changes its motion so that the rate of change of momentum is equal to the unbalanced force.

Impulse

If the equation for net force just derived is re-arranged by multiplying both sides of the equation by Δt, then

$$F\Delta t = \Delta (mv).$$

The product of the **net force** and the **time interval** during which it acts is called the **impulse** of the force. *The impulse of the force equals the change in momentum it causes.* A given change in momentum can be produced by a large force acting for a short time *or* by a small force acting for a long time!

Units for Momentum and Impulse

Momentum has measuring units which have the dimensions of [mass] x [velocity], which are **kg·m/s**. **Impulse** has units with the dimensions of [force] x [time], which are **N·s**. However,

$$1 \text{ N·s} = 1 \text{ kg·}\frac{m}{s^2}\text{·s} .$$

Therefore, $$1 \text{ N·s} = 1 \text{ kg·}\frac{m}{s} .$$

Therefore the **N·s** is equivalent to the **kg·m/s**. Momentum can be expressed in either units, and so can impulse.

Conservation of Momentum

Consider an isolated system consisting of two laboratory carts with a compressed spring between them. Before the spring is released by a suitable triggering mechanism, the carts are stationary, and the carts have masses m_a and m_b respectively. The total momentum is zero, since neither cart is moving.

The spring is now released. Cart A pushes on cart B and, according to Newton's Third Law, cart B exerts the same force on cart A, but in the opposite direction.

$$\boldsymbol{F}_{a \text{ on } b} = - \boldsymbol{F}_{b \text{ on } a}$$

$$\frac{\Delta[m_b \boldsymbol{v_b}]}{\Delta t} = - \frac{\Delta[m_a \boldsymbol{v_a}]}{\Delta t} .$$

Since the time intervals are the same for both forces, Δt can be eliminated.

Therefore $$\Delta[\, m_b \boldsymbol{v_b}\,] = -\Delta[\, m_a \boldsymbol{v_a}\,],$$

$$\text{or } \Delta \boldsymbol{p_b} = - \Delta \boldsymbol{p_a} .$$

This means that $$\Delta \boldsymbol{p_a} + \Delta \boldsymbol{p_b} = 0.$$

The total change of momentum of the isolated system is zero. Since the momentum of the two-cart system was zero to begin with, it must be still zero. Both carts are moving after the spring pushes them apart, and both have momentum, but the directions are opposite. *The vector sum of the momenta is still zero.*

Similar arguments can be used for interacting bodies which have momentum to begin with; the *change* in momentum will still be zero, and the *total* momentum will remain constant.

> **The Law of Conservation of Momentum** applies to any isolated system.
>
> *The total momentum of an isolated system of objects will remain constant.*

Sample Problem

A rifle bullet of mass 0.060 kg leaves the muzzle with a velocity 6.0×10^2 m/s. If the 3.0 kg rifle is held very loosely, with what velocity will it recoil when the bullet is fired?

Solution

Momentum is conserved. Since before the rifle is fired the momentum of the isolated rifle-bullet system is zero, the total momentum after the bullet is fired is still zero!

$$p_r + p_b = 0$$

The subscript 'r' denotes 'rifle', and 'b' denotes bullet.

$$m_r v_r + m_b v_b = 0$$

$$(3.0 \text{ kg})(v_r) + (0.060 \text{ kg})(6.00 \times 10^2 \text{ m/s}) = 0$$

$$v_r = \frac{-(0.060 \text{ kg})(6.00 \times 10^2 \text{ m/s})}{3.0 \text{ kg}} = -12 \text{ m/s}.$$

The rifle will recoil with a velocity of 12 m/s in the opposite direction to the velocity of the bullet.

Exercises

1. What is the momentum of a 0.25 g bug flying with a speed of 12 m/s?

2. (a) What is the momentum of a 112 kg football player running at 4.8 m/s?
   (b) What impulse must a tackler impart to the football player in (a) to stop him?
   (c) If the tackle is completed in 1.2 s, what average force must the tackler have exerted on the other player?

3. You are doing a 'space walk' outside the Space Shuttle, with no cable between you and the shuttle. Your small maneuvering rocket pack suddenly quits on you, and you are stranded in space with nothing but a $10,000 camera in your hands. What will you do to get back to the shuttle?

4. A rocket expels 1.2×10^3 kg of gas each second, and the gas leaves the rocket with a speed of 5.0×10^4 m/s. Will the thrust produced by the rocket be sufficient to lift it if the force of gravity on the rocket is 5.8×10^7 N?

5. A 3.2 kg cart travelling 1.2 m/s collides with a stationary 1.8 kg cart, and the two carts stick together. What is their common velocity after the collision?

6. A 6.0 x 10^3 kg railway car is coasting along the track at 7.0 m/s. Suddenly a 2.0 x 10^3 kg load of coal is dumped into the car. What is its new velocity?

7. A 1.2 x 10^3 kg car travelling 33 m/s collides head-on with a 1.8 x 10^3 kg car travelling 22 m/s in the opposite direction. If the cars stick together, what is the velocity of the wreckage immediately after impact?

8. A 0.060 kg rifle bullet leaves the muzzle with a velocity of 6.0 x 10^2 m/s. The 3.0 kg rifle is held firmly by a 60.0 kg man. With what initial velocity will the man and rifle recoil? Compare your answer with the answer to the **Sample Problem** preceding these **Exercises**.

9. A bullet of mass *m* is fired into a steel wall with velocity **v**, then rebounds with velocity − 1/2**v**. A second bullet of the same mass *m* is fired into a wall covered with Plasticine™, and it does not rebound. Which bullet exerts a greater force on the wall: the one that rebounds or the one that does not? Show your reasoning.

10. (a) What impulse must be imparted to a 145 g baseball to change its velocity from 40.0 m/s south to 50.0 m/s north?
    (b) If the collision between the baseball and the bat lasted 1.00 ms (milliseconds), what force did the bat exert on the baseball?

11. To measure the speed of a bullet, a physicist fired a 45.0 g bullet into a large block of Plasticine™, which rested on a metal disk floating on a large air table. The combined mass of the Plasticine™ and disk was 18.0 kg. By using strobe photography, the speed of the disk was measured to be 0.900 m/s immediately after the impact of the bullet. What was the speed of the bullet?

12. A 2.0 x 10^3 kg car travelling 15 m/s 'rear-ends' another car of mass 1.0 x 10^3 kg. The second car was initially moving 6.0 m/s in the **same** direction. What is their common velocity after the collision if the cars lock together during the impact?

13. What impulse is needed to change the speed of a 10.0 kg body from 20.0 m/s to 12.0 m/s in a time of 5.0 s? What force is needed to do this?

Momentum in Two-Dimensional Situations

All the examples and exercises with momentum have, so far, dealt with motion in a straight line. The principles involved all apply, however, to two- or three- dimensional situations as well.

In *Investigation 3-1*, you will review conservation of momentum in one dimension, and then investigate a collision in two dimensions. (Parts 1, 2, and 3 might be treated as demonstrations if time is short.)

Investigation 3-1
Momentum in Explosions and Collisions

Purpose: To measure and compare momentum before and after
(a) 'explosions' and (b) 'collisions'.

Part 1 An 'Explosion' of Two Carts (Demonstration)

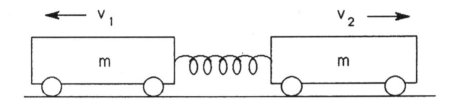

Figure 3.8

1. Two laboratory carts of equal mass are equipped with spring bumpers. See
   Figure 3.8. **Predict** how the speeds of the carts will compare when the springs
   are compressed, and the two carts are allowed to 'explode' apart. Design a way to
   compare speeds using only a metre stick. Test your prediction!

2. Place an extra laboratory cart on top of one of the other identical carts, so that you
   double the mass of the bottom cart. Again, **predict** how the speeds will compare
   after the carts 'explode' apart, and test your prediction.

Question: On what basis did you make your predictions? Were they correct?
If not, explain why they were not.

Part 2 Straight-Line Collisions of Carts of Equal Mass (Demonstration)

1. (a) **Predict** what will happen if a spring-bumpered cart moving with a speed v is
   made to collide 'head-on' with a second cart of equal mass, which is
   initially at rest. Test your prediction.

   (b) Repeat the procedure in (a), but this time attach a strip of Velcro™ to two
   identical carts so that when they collide they will stick together upon collision.
   Predict what the speed of the combined carts will be after the collision, if the
   incoming cart has speed v.

2. (a) **Predict** what will happen if two identical spring-loaded carts, travelling toward
   each other at speed v, collide 'head-on'. Test your prediction.

   (b) **Predict** what will happen if two identical carts, equipped with Velcro™
   bumpers, approach each other, both at speed v, and stick together following
   the collision. Test your prediction.

Question: On what basis did you make your predictions in **Procedures 1** and **2**? Were they correct? If not, explain why they did not work out.

Part 3 Oblique Collisions of Pucks on an Air Table (Demonstration)

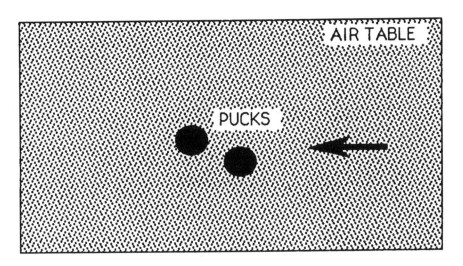

Figure 3.9

1. Place two pucks of identical mass on an air table. Observe what happens when a moving puck collides with a stationary puck (a) 'head-on' and (b) at an oblique angle. Pay particular attention to the angle between the *incident* puck and the *struck* puck.

If you have the equipment, take a strobe photograph of these two types of collision and measure the angles from the photograph. You may substitute Part 3 for Part 4 if you use this method for Part 3.

---

2. Try varying the masses of the pucks. Observe whether the angle between the incident puck and the struck puck is the same as it was when the pucks had identical mass.

Questions

1. What do you conclude regarding the angle between the incident puck and the struck puck after they have collided (a) 'head-on' and (b) obliquely, when their masses are identical?

2. Does this conclusion hold true when the masses are different?

Part 4 Collisions of Steel Balls of Equal Mass (Student Experiment)

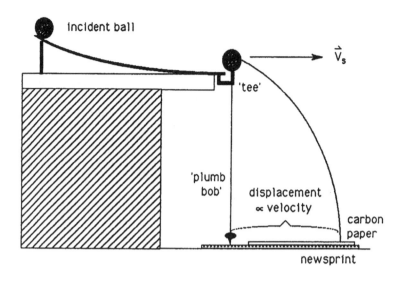

Figure 3.10

Introduction

If one sphere of mass m collides with a second sphere of equal mass *m*, we expect momentum should be conserved, and therefore

$$mv_{io} + mv_{so} = mv_{if} + mv_{sf}$$

where v_{io} is the velocity of the incident ball **before the collision;**
v_{so} is the velocity of the struck ball **before the collision;**
v_{if} is the velocity of the incident ball **after the collision;** and
v_{sf} is the velocity of the struck ball **after the collision.**

*Keep in mind that velocity and momentum are **vector** quantities.*

Figure 3.10 shows the arrangement for this experiment. From your study of projectile motion, you know that no matter what the horizontal velocity of a ball coming off the ramp is, it will take the same time to fall to the floor. This means that you can use the **horizontal displacement** of the ball from its position during the collision as a measure of its **velocity**. Since the time of fall for either ball will always be the same, let that time be one arbitrary time unit (**tu**). If, for example, the horizontal displacement of the struck ball was 32 cm, then its velocity is v_{sf} = **32 cm/tu**.

Also, since the incident ball and the struck ball are of equal mass *m*, mass 'cancels out' of the momentum equation, and you can compare momenta simply by comparing velocities (or, in this case, displacements). This only works when the colliding balls are of equal mass!

Procedure

1. Set up the apparatus in **Figure 3.10**. Place several sheets of carbon paper with the carbon side *down* on top of a large sheet of newsprint paper, so that when a ball lands on the floor it will leave a black mark showing where it landed.

2. The 'plumb bob' shows the exact location of the centre of the struck ball. Make a pencil mark at this location. Also make a pencil mark where the centre of the incident ball will be at the moment of collision. (It should be one ball diameter in front of the struck ball's centre.)

3. To measure the velocity (displacement) of the incident ball, let it run down from the very top of the ramp at least five times. Measure the *average displacement* using the close cluster of ball marks. Record this average as the value of v_{io}.

4. Set the 'target' ball on its 'tee', making sure that the collision will be truly 'head-on'. Allow the incident ball to run down the ramp from the very top again, but let it collide with the target ball, which should be identical with the incident ball. Repeat this four more times and measure the *average displacement* of the target (struck) ball from the cluster of ball marks. Record this average as the value of v_{sf}. Why can the displacement of the incident ball after the collision be disregarded in this particular type of collision? (Remember Parts 2 and 3.)

5. Draw vector diagrams (scaled down if necessary) showing the following:

   (a) the **momentum** of the incident ball before the head-on collision;
   (b) the **momentum** of the incident ball after the collision;
   (c) the **momentum** of the struck ball after the collision.
   Label these vectors p_{io}, p_{if} and p_{sf}.

6. Arrange the target ball so that the collision will be **oblique** (i.e. the incident ball will strike the target ball at an angle other than 'head-on'). Let the incident ball run down from the very top of the ramp and collide with the target ball. **Mark the landing positions of both balls.** Repeat four more times and average the displacement of each ball after the collision. **Be sure to record the angles between the two balls after the collision.** Also record the angle between their displacement vectors and the displacement vector the incident ball would have had if it had not collided with the struck ball. (You need to know the direction of the initial momentum vector.)

7. Draw a vector diagram (scaled down if necessary) showing the following:

   (a) the **momentum** of the incident ball before the oblique collision;
   (b) the **momentum** of the incident ball after the collision;
   (c) the **momentum** of the struck ball after the collision;
   (d) the **vector sum of the momenta** of the incident ball after collision and the struck ball after the collision.

   Label these vectors respectively: p_{io}, p_{if}, p_{sf}, and p_R.

Concluding Questions

1. Compare the total momentum before with the total momentum after a 'head-on' collision of two steel balls of equal mass. Calculate the percent difference between the two, and discuss sources of error.

2. Compare the resultant momentum of the incident and struck balls after an oblique collision, with the momentum of the incident ball before the collision.
*If there is a difference, remember you must use the **vector difference.***
What percent is the magnitude of the *vector difference* between p_R and p_{io} of the initial momentum, p_{io}, of the incident ball? Discuss **sources or error**.

Challenges

1. Repeat **Procedures 1** to **7**, using a steel ball colliding with a less massive glass ball. Note that you can no longer use just displacement vectors to compare momenta. Each displacement (velocity) must be multiplied by the appropriate mass.

2. If two identical steel balls collide obliquely, and **no kinetic energy is lost** in the collision, then

$$\frac{1}{2} mv_{io}^2 = \frac{1}{2} mv_{if}^2 + \frac{1}{2} mv_{sf}^2 \ .$$

This type of collision is called a **perfectly elastic collision**. Show that, if $v_{if} > 0$, the incident and struck balls must leave the collision at 90° to each other.

3. Find out if the collisions in your experiment were perfectly elastic.

3.3 Two-Dimensional Momentum Problems

Three sample questions involving momentum in two dimensions will help show how useful the **Law of Conservation of Momentum** can be in solving problems.

Example 1

A 60.0 kg hockey player travelling 2.0 m/s toward the north collides with a 50.0 kg player travelling 1.0 m/s toward the west. The two become tangled together. With what velocity will they move after the collision?

Solution:

Momentum is a **vector quantity**, and the rules for vector addition must be followed!

Before the collision, the momentum of the first player was
$$p_1 = (60.0 \text{ kg})(2.0 \text{ m/s}) = 120 \text{ kg·m/s (north)}.$$

Before the collision, the momentum of the second player was
$$p_2 = (50.0\text{kg})(1.0 \text{ m/s}) = 50. \text{ kg·m/s (west)}.$$

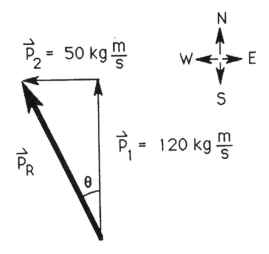

Figure 3.11

After the collision, the tangled players have a momentum equal to the vector sum of p_1 and p_2. **Figure 3.11** shows how to find the vector sum. Since the vector triangle has a right angle, **Pythagoras' Theorem** can be used to solve for p_R.

$$p_R{}^2 = p_1{}^2 + p_2{}^2$$

$$p_R{}^2 = (120 \text{ kg·m/s})^2 + (50 \text{ kg·m/s})^2$$

$$p_R = 130 \text{ kg·m/s}.$$

Since $p_R = (m_1 + m_2) v_R$, the velocity of the tangled players will have magnitude

$$v_R = \frac{p_R}{m_1 + m_2} = \frac{1.3 \times 10^2 \text{ kg·m/s}}{1.1 \times 10^2 \text{ kg}} = 1.2 \text{ m/s}.$$

The answer is not yet complete, since velocities have specific directions! From the momentum vector diagram,

$$\tan \theta = \frac{50 \text{ kg·m/s}}{120 \text{ kg·m/s}} = 0.4167.$$

$$\theta = 22.6° \text{ to the west of north}.$$

The **resultant velocity** of the hockey players is **1.2 m/s**, directed **23° W of N**.

Example 2

A 0.050 kg air puck moving with a velocity of 2.0 m/s makes an *elastic* collision with an identical but stationary air puck. The direction of the incident puck is changed by 60° from its original path, and the angle between the two pucks after the collision is 90°. What are the speeds of the two pucks after they collide?

Solution:

Momentum is conserved, so the resultant momentum after the collision must equal the momentum of the incident puck. The directions of the momenta of the two pucks are known. The resultant momentum must equal p_{io}.

$$p_{io} = (0.050 \text{ kg})(2.0 \text{ m/s}) = 0.10 \text{ kg·m/s}.$$

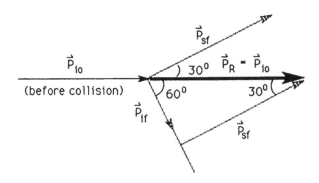

Figure 3.12

In **Figure 3.12** the resultant momentum ($p_R = p_{io}$)was drawn first. Then the *directions* of p_{if} and p_{sf} were constructed. As you can see, it is then a simple task to complete the momentum vector triangle.

After the collision, $p_R = p_{io} = 0.10$ kg·m/s in the direction shown. Trigonometry can be used to solve for the magnitudes of p_{if} and p_{sf}.

$$p_{if} = p_R \cos 60° = (0.10 \text{ kg·m/s})(0.500) = 0.050 \text{ kg·m/s}$$

$$V_{if} = \frac{p_{if}}{m_i} = \frac{0.050 \text{ kg·m/s}}{0.050 \text{ kg}} = 1.0 \text{ m/s}.$$

Similarly, $p_{sf} = p_R \sin 60° = (0.10 \text{ kg·m/s})(0.866) = 0.087 \text{ kg·m/s}$

$$V_{sf} = \frac{p_{sf}}{m_s} = \frac{0.087 \text{ kg·m/s}}{0.0500 \text{ kg}} = 1.7 \text{ m/s}$$

Challenge! Can you see a shorter way to solve this particular problem?

Example 3

A metal disk explodes into three pieces, which fly off in the same geometric plane. The first piece has a mass of 2.4 kg, and it flies off north at 10.0 m/s. The second piece has a mass of 2.0 kg and it flies east at 12.5 m /s. What is the speed and direction of the third piece, which has a mass of 1.4 kg?

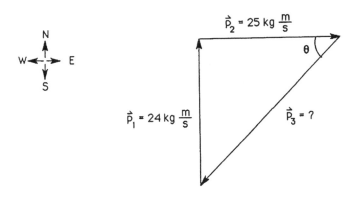

Figure 3.13

Solution

Before the explosion, total momentum was zero. After the explosion, the vector sum of the three momenta must be zero, as well, since momentum is conserved. Begin by drawing momentum vectors for the two fragments for which you have full information. The momentum of the third fragment must be such that the three momenta have a vector sum of zero. (They must form a closed triangle.) See **Figure 3.13.**

The momentum of the first fragment, p_1 = (2.4 kg)(10.0 m/s) = 24 kg·m/s (north)

The momentum of the second fragment, p_2 = (2.0 kg)(12.5 m/s) = 25 kg·m/s (east)
Since these momentum vectors form a right-angled triangle, use Pythagoras' Theorem to solve for the magnitude of p_3.

$$p_3 = \sqrt{(24 \text{ kg·m/s})^2 + (25 \text{ kg·m/s})^2} = 35 \text{ kg·m/s.}$$

$$v_3 = \frac{p_3}{m_3} = \frac{35 \text{ kg·m/s}}{1.4 \text{ kg}} = 25 \text{ m/s.}$$

Since $\tan \theta = \frac{24 \text{ kg·m/s}}{25 \text{ kg·m/s}} = 0.9600$, the angle is 44°.

Therefore, the **velocity** of the third fragment is 25 m/s in a direction 44° south of west.

Special Note

In each of the three examples, the angle between vectors has been a right angle. If there is no right angle, the problem may be solved using a scale diagram or by using sine law or cosine law. Another method is to use X- and Y- components of velocities or momenta.

Exercises

1. A hockey player of mass 82 kg is travelling north with a velocity of 4.1 m/s. He collides with a 76 kg player travelling east at 3.4 m/s. If the two players 'lock together' momentarily, in what direction will they be going immediately after the collision? How fast will they be moving?

2. A 2.5 x 10³ kg car travelling west at 6.0 m/s is hit by a 6.0 x 10³ kg truck going south at 4.0 m/s. The two vehicles lock together on impact. What is the speed and direction of the wreckage immediately after impact?

3. In **Exercise 2**, calculate the **kinetic energy** $(E_K = \frac{1}{2}mv^2)$ of each of the vehicles before the collision. Also, calculate the kinetic energy of the *combined* wreckage immediately after the collision. How much energy is not accounted for after the collision? To what forms do you think it was transformed?

4. A frustrated physics student blew up her Physics textbook, using a small amount of an explosive. It broke into three pieces, which miraculously flew off in directions that were all in the same geometric plane. A 0.200 kg piece flew off at 20.0 m/s, and a 0.100 kg piece went off at 90° to the first piece, at 30.0 m/s.

   (a) What was the momentum of the third piece?

   (b) If the mass of the third piece was 0.150 kg, what was its velocity right after the explosion?

5. A proton of mass **m** collides obliquely with another proton. The first proton is moving with a speed of 6.0 x 10⁶ m/s before it hits the second, stationary proton. Assuming the collision is perfectly elastic (no kinetic energy is lost), and using the fact that the first proton is moved 30° from its initial path after the collision, figure out the speed and direction of each proton after the collision.

6. A 0.40 kg model airplane is travelling 20 km/h toward the south. A 0.50 kg model airplane, travelling 25 km/h in a direction 20° east of south, collides with the first model airplane. The two planes stick together on impact. What is the direction and magnitude of the velocity of the combined wreckage immediately after the collision?

7. What impulse is needed to change the velocity of a 90.0 kg football player from 3.6 m/s toward the north and make it 1.2 m/s toward the northeast? In what direction must the force be exerted?

3.4 Work

Imagine you have just spent the past hour finishing a physics experiment, writing a quiz, then solving five difficult problems from your physics textbook. After all this, your physics teacher says "You people have done very little work this period!" Your reaction to this statement would be very predictable. You would be very annoyed with your teacher — unless you know what a physics teacher really means by **work!** In physics, **work** has a very special meaning.

Work is done on a body when a force or a component of that force acts on the body, causing it to be displaced. Work is calculated from the product of the force component in the direction of motion and the distance moved.

Work = Force component in direction of motion x distance

$$W = F_d \cdot d$$

The measuring unit for work is the **newton·metre**, which is called a **joule.**

---

1 J = 1 N·m.

Examples

F=150 N

d=1.2m

Figure 3.14

1. How much work does the man in **Figure 3.14** do to lift the 150 N of firewood from the ground up to a height of 1.2 m?

   Solution:

   Lifting the wood at a steady speed, he will exert a force equal to the force of gravity on the wood. The direction of the force is straight up, so

   $$W = Fd = (150\ N)(1.2\ m) = 180\ J.$$

   The man does 1.8×10^2 J of work on the wood.

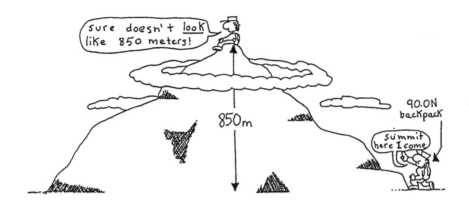

Figure 3.15

2. How much work does the hiker in **Figure 3.15** do on the 90.0 N backpack he carries to the top of the 850 m high hill?
Solution:

When the hiker reaches the top of the hill, his vertical displacement will be 850 m. The force component in the vertical direction is equal to the force of gravity on the backpack (but in the opposite direction), assuming the vertical velocity component is constant.

$$W = Fd = (90.0 \text{ N}) (850 \text{ m}) = 7.7 \times 10^4 \text{ J.}$$

The work done on the backpack is 77 kJ.

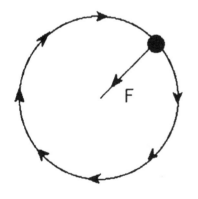

**Figure 3.16
(top view)**

3. A ball on the end of a rope is following a circular path because of a constant force exerted on the ball by the rope in a direction toward the centre of the circle. How much work is done on the ball by this force?

Solution

Since the ball is moving in a direction perpendicular to the force acting on it, **no work** is done. There is no force component in the direction of motion, therefore no work is done.

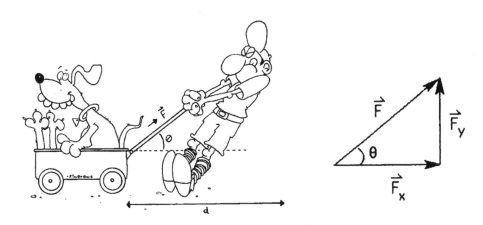

Figure 3.17

4. A child is pulling a wagon along the driveway, exerting a force **F** along the handle of the wagon. How would you calculate the work done by the child on the wagon?

Solution:

The *component* of the force exerted by the child in the direction of motion is F_x , the horizontal component.

$$F_x = F \cdot \cos \theta .$$

The work done is therefore $W = F \cdot \cos \theta \cdot d$.

Exercises

1. (a) How much work must be done to lift a 110 kg motorbike directly up 1.1 m to the back of a truck?

   (b) If a 2.6 m ramp is used to push the bike up to the back of the truck, the force needed is 550 N. Does this ramp 'save you work'? Why is it used?

2. In **Figure 3.17**, if the force exerted on the handle of the wagon is 45 N, and the angle θ is 28° , how much work will be done pulling the wagon 17 m along the driveway?

3.5 Work Done by a Changing Force

Frequently the force acting on an object is not constant over the distance it is exerted. Three examples of situations involving *changing* forces will be used to illustrate how the work done could be calculated.

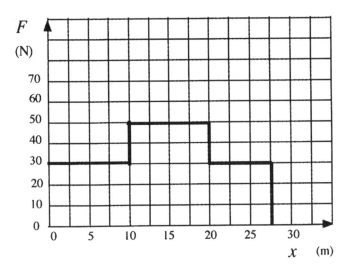

Figure 3.18

Example 1

A young girl is pushing a laboratory supply cart down the hallway of a school. She pushes in a direction parallel with the floor. On a linoleum floor, she exerts a force of 30.0 N over a distance of 10.0 m. She then has to push the cart over a carpeted floor for a distance of 10.0 m, and this requires a force of 50.0 N. Finally, she must push it another 7.5 m on another stretch of linoleum floor, again with a force of 30.0 N. How much work does she do on the cart during the whole trip?

Solution

The **total work** done will be the sum of the work done on each stretch of floor:

Total work W = (30.0 N)(10.0 m)+(50.0 N)(10.0 m) + (30.0 N)(7.5 m)
= 300. J + 500. J + 225 J = **1025 J**.

The total work done is 1.025×10^3 J. If you examine **Figure 3.18**, you will see that this work is equal to **the *area* under the force vs distance graph.** As a general rule, where the force is parallel with the displacement of the object, the area under the force vs distance graph is equal to the amount of work done.

Example 2

A coiled spring is stretched by hanging known weights from its end, and the stretch is measured in metres. **Figure 3.19** is a graph showing how the force on the spring varies with the amount of stretch. How much work must be done to stretch the spring 0.50 m?

Solution

Since the force is changing all the time the spring is being stretched, the **average force** must be used. From the graph, the average force is 3.0 N, so the work done while stretching the spring is

$$W = \bar{F} \cdot x = (3.0 \text{ N})(0.50 \text{ m}) = \textbf{1.5 J}.$$

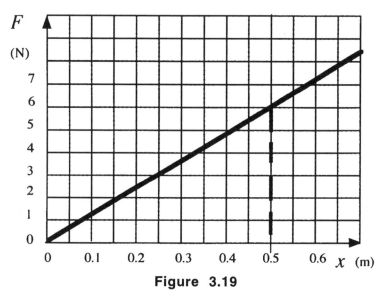

Figure 3.19

The work done to stretch the spring is 1.5 J. Notice that this is the **area under the force vs distance graph.** The area of the triangle underneath the line on the graph is [1/2·height·base], which is $1/2 \cdot F \cdot x$. This is the same as $\overline{F} \cdot x$.

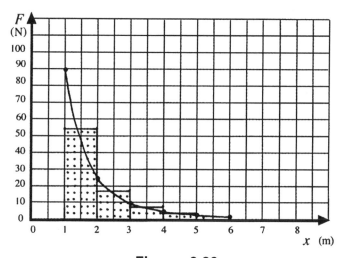

Figure 3.20

Example 3

Figure 3.20 shows a common situation in physics. The force in this case changes radically with distance. In fact, if you study the graph carefully you will notice that as the distance doubles, the force is reduced to one quarter of what it was. If the distance triples, the force is reduced to one ninth of its original value. You will encounter at least two situations where this happens. The gravitational attraction between any two masses is one example of a force which varies as the **inverse of the square** of the distance between the two bodies. Electrostatic forces are in the same class. You will learn about these situations later.

How much work would be done moving an object from a distance of 1.0 m (**Figure 3.20**) to a distance of 5.0 m? If you knew the average force between these two distances, you could use it to calculate the work done. Obviously that is not a simple thing to determine. You could draw a series of rectangles which average the force over a sequence of short distances, and then total their areas. Or, you can wait until you learn the calculus method of finding the area under such a curve. This area is what will give you the amount of work done.

Exercises

1. In **Figure 3.19**, how much work is done to stretch the spring from a starting stretch of 0.20 m to a new stretch of 0.40 m?

2. If 1.0 J of work is done to stretch the spring in **Figure 3.19** from its relaxed position, by how much will the spring be extended?

3.6 Kinetic Energy

A moving object can do work. A falling axe does work to split a log. A moving baseball bat does work to stop a baseball, momentarily compress it out of its normal shape, then reverse its direction and send it off at high speed. Since a moving object has the ability to do work, it must have **energy**. We call the energy of a moving object its **kinetic energy**.

A body which is at rest can gain kinetic energy if work is done on it by an external force. To get such a body moving at speed v, a **net force** must be exerted on it to accelerate it from rest up to speed v. The amount of work, W, which must be done can be calculated as follows:

$$W = F{\cdot}d = (ma)d = m(ad).$$

Remember that for an object accelerating from rest at a uniform rate,

$$v_f^2 = 2ad.$$

Therefore,

$$(ad) = \frac{v_f^2}{2}, \text{ and}$$

$$W = m(ad) = m\frac{v_f^2}{2} = \frac{1}{2}mv^2.$$

The work done on the object to accelerate it up to a speed v results in an amount of energy being transferred to the object, which is equal in magnitude to $\frac{1}{2}mv^2$. The energy an object has because of its motion is called **kinetic energy**, E_k.

$$E_k = \frac{1}{2}mv^2$$

Once an object has kinetic energy, the object itself can do work on other objects.

Exercises

1. A golfer wishes to improve his driving distance. Which would have more effect, (a) *doubling the mass* of his golf club or (b) *doubling the speed* with which the clubhead strikes the ball? Explain your answer.

2. How much work must be done to accelerate a 110 kg motorbike and its 60.0 kg rider from 0 to 80 km/h?

3. How much work is needed to slow down a 1200 kg vehicle from 80 km/h to 50 km/h? What does this work?

4. How much work is needed to accelerate a 1.0 g insect from rest up to 12 m/s?

5. If the speed of a proton is tripled by a particle accelerator, by how much will its kinetic energy increase? (Ignore relativistic effects.)

3.7 Potential Energy

Potential energy is sometimes referred to as 'stored' energy. A skier has *potential energy* at the top of a hill, because work has been done (by the skier or by a ski tow) to raise the skier from the bottom of the hill to the top. If the skier has been lifted a height h from the bottom of the hill, and the force of gravity on the skier is mg, then the amount of **work** done on the skier is $W = mgh$.

The energy transferred to the skier because of this amount of work done on the skier is now 'potentially available' to do work. In this situation, it can be said that the skier has **gravitational potential energy**.

Gravitational E_p = mgh.

A stretched spring or a compressed spring has potential energy. Work must be done to stretch or compress a spring. In the example of **Figure 3.19** the work done to stretch the spring a distance x is $\frac{1}{2}F{\cdot}x$. For this particular spring, force is directly proportional to extension (stretch), so $F = kx$.

The work done to stretch the spring is therefore

$$W = \tfrac{1}{2}(kx)x = \tfrac{1}{2}kx^2 \, .$$

The amount of energy transferred to the spring because of the work done on it is 'potentially available' to do work. In this case, the stored energy is called **elastic potential energy**.

Elastic $E_p = \frac{1}{2}kx^2$.

An object has kinetic energy because of its motion; it will have potential energy because of its position (in the case of gravitational potential energy) or its shape (elastic potential energy).

Exercises

1. How much gravitational energy is gained by a 45 kg girl if she climbs a flight of stairs 6.0 m high?

2. (a) A spring in a toy gun requires an average force of 1.2 N to compress it a distance of 3.0 cm. How much elastic potential energy is stored in the spring when it is fully compressed?
   (b) If all the elastic potential energy is transferred to a 10.0 g 'bullet' (a plastic rod with a suction cup on the end), how fast will the 'bullet' move as it leaves the gun?

3. Discuss the forms of energy involved when a basketball is dropped from your hand, bounces on the floor and back up into your hand.

Ehren Stillman Cartoon

Investigation 3-2   Energy Changes of a Swinging Pendulum

Purpose: To predict the maximum speed reached by a pendulum swinging from a known height above its rest position, and to check the prediction by measurement.

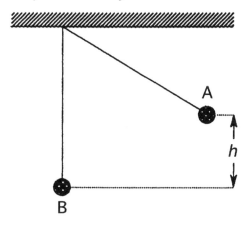

Figure 3.21

Procedure

1. Attach a massive pendulum bob (1 kg) by a sturdy cable to a support on the roof of your classroom.

2. Design a system so that you can raise the bob to the same height h repeatedly. Measure h from the lowest position the bob reaches during each swing.

3. Choose the value of h you are going to use, then calculate how much gravitational potential energy, E_p , the bob will have at height h.

4. Let the bob swing once, and record the height h' reached by the bob on its *return swing*. Repeat this measurement four more times and average your five measurements of h'. Calculate the **loss** of E_p during one full swing ($mgh - mgh'$).

5. The loss of energy during one complete swing can be accounted for by assuming that work is done by the bob and string to overcome the force of friction due to the air. As the bob moves from its starting position **A** to the bottom of its swing at **B**, it will lose an amount of energy equal to 1/4 of the loss for one full swing, which you calculated in **Procedure 4**. What happens to the rest of the **potential energy** the bob has when it is at **A**?

Let us assume that all the remaining potential energy is changed into **kinetic energy**. At the bottom of the swing, all the bob's energy is kinetic energy, $E_k = \frac{1}{2}mv^2$. This energy was initially the potential energy of the bob at **A**. If there was no air friction (or other forms of friction), we could predict that

$$E_k \text{ (bottom of swing)} = E_p \text{ (top of swing)} .$$

Since there **is** a loss of potential energy due to friction, this loss must be taken into account. The loss of energy during the swing from **A** to **B** is $\frac{1}{4}(mgh - mgh')$.

To predict the speed of the bob at **B**, calculate v using the following:

$$\frac{1}{2}mv^2 = mgh - \frac{1}{4}(mgh - mgh') .$$

6. Attach a short length of ticker tape (no longer than needed) to the 1 kg mass, and use a recording timer to measure the **maximum speed** reached by the swinging mass. (If your timer vibrates with a frequency of 60 Hz, the time between dots is 1/60 s.) When several groups have duplicated the same measurement using the same starting height, average the values of v.

Concluding Questions

1. What is the percent difference between your predicted speed and your measured speed?

2. What are some **sources of error** in this experiment?

3. If you had used a bob with a different mass, how would that affect the predicted speed? Explain your answer.

4. Do your results suggest that the **total energy** of the bob (potential and kinetic) remains constant during a full swing? Discuss your answer.

Challenge

Predict what these graphs would look like, for one-half swing of the pendulum:

(a) v vs x;

(b) E_p vs x;

(c) E_k vs x;

(d) Total E vs x.

Design and carry out an experiment to test your predictions.

3.8 The Law of Conservation of Mechanical Energy

Consider a frictionless pendulum as it makes a swing from one side to the other. If we decide to assign the bob **zero potential energy** at the bottom of its swing, as we did in *Investigation 3-2,* then it gains **potential energy** equal to *mgh* when it reaches the highest point in its swing. When it swings through the lowest part of its swing, its potential energy returns to zero, but it still has the same **total energy**. At the bottom of the swing, all the potential energy the bob had at the top of its swing has been transformed into **kinetic energy**. Ignoring energy lost because of friction in the system,

$$E_k \text{ (bottom of swing)} = E_p \text{ (top of swing)}$$

At *any* point in the swing, ignoring energy losses because of work done overcoming friction, the **total mechanical energy** *($E_k + E_p$)* is constant.

Total Mechanical Energy $= E_K + E_P = $ **constant**

If the subscripts '1' and '2' are used to represent any two positions of the pendulum, the **Law of Conservation of Mechanical Energy** for this situation can be written:

$$\tfrac{1}{2}mv_1{}^2 + mgh_1 = \tfrac{1}{2}mv_2{}^2 + mgh_2$$

This description would also apply to a body falling under the influence of the force of gravity, from an initial height *h.*

Although we have looked at only a single example of a mechanical situation (the pendulum), the Law of Conservation of Energy applies in a very general way to all similar energy transformations. Taking *all* forms of energy into account, a broader statement can be made about energy in general:

Energy can be transformed from one form to another, but it is never created and it is never destroyed. Total energy remains constant.

Exercises

1. A 45.93 g golf ball is struck by a golf club and leaves the clubface with a speed of 75 m/s.
   (a) How much kinetic energy does the golf ball have as it leaves the face of the club?
   (b) If air friction is ignored, from what height would the same golf ball have to be dropped to gain this much kinetic energy?

2. A 1.00 kg pendulum bob is released from a height of 0.200 m. Its speed at the bottom of its swing is 1.95 m/s on the first pass. How much energy is lost due to friction during one complete swing of the pendulum?

3. A rope is hanging from the roof of the gymnasium. You are going to run at the rope, grab it, and see how high you are carried off the floor by the swinging rope. How fast must you run if you want to swing to a height of 1.5 m off the floor? Does your mass matter? Does the length of the rope matter? Discuss your answers.

4. A skier slides down a frictionless 25° slope from a height of 12 m. How fast is she moving at the bottom of the hill? Does the slope of the hill matter? Explain.

5. A 45 kg youngster slides down a homemade 'snowslide', which is 3.0 m high. At the bottom of the slide he is moving 7.0 m/s. How much energy was lost during the trip down the slide? What would account for this loss?

3.9 Applying the Conservation Laws

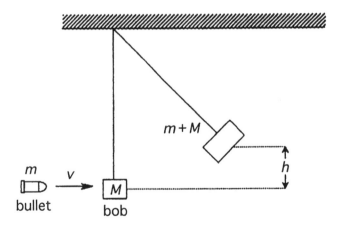

Figure 3.22

A **ballistic pendulum**, used to measure the speed of a bullet indirectly, is a good illustration of the use of both the Law of Conservation of Momentum and the Law of Conservation of Mechanical energy.

A bullet of mass m is fired at an unknown speed v into a sand-filled pendulum bob of mass M, causing the bob to swing to the right and rise to a height h. How can the speed v be calculated? (See **Figure 3.22.**)

The bullet entering the bob transfers its momentum to the bob, and the combined masses continue merrily on at initial speed v'. Since momentum is conserved,

$$mv = (m + M)v' \quad \text{(I)}$$

The bob and bullet together now have kinetic energy due to their motion.

$$E_k = \tfrac{1}{2}(m + M)v'^2 \quad \text{(II)}$$

The bob and bullet rise and momentarily come to rest at height h, where all the mechanical energy is in the form of gravitational potential energy.

$$E_p = (m + M)gh \quad \text{(III)}$$

If we assume that mechanical energy is conserved (energy loss due to friction is negligible), then

$$\tfrac{1}{2}(m + M)v'^2 = (m + M)gh.$$

Therefore,
$$v'^2 = 2gh.$$

According to equation I,
$$v' = \frac{m}{m + M} \cdot v.$$

However,
$$v' = \sqrt{2gh},$$

therefore,
$$\frac{m}{m + M} \cdot v = \sqrt{2gh},$$

and
$$v = \frac{m + M}{m} \cdot \sqrt{2gh}.$$

Exercises

1. A 5.0 g bullet is fired into the ballistic pendulum described in **Figure 3.22**. If the bob has a mass of 2.0 kg and the bob rises a vertical distance of 8.0 cm, how fast was the bullet moving? (Use $g = 9.80$ m/s^2 .)

2. In designing a ballistic pendulum, you want a bullet of mass 6.0 g and speed 6.0×10^2 m/s to make the pendulum bob rise 3.0 cm. What mass must the bob have?

3. A 56 kg boy jumps down from a 2.0 m high ladder. Using only the Law of Conservation of Mechanical Energy, determine his kinetic energy and his speed when he is half way down.

3.10 Power

The word **power** is used in a variety of ways in everyday language, but in physics it has a specific meaning. *Power is the rate at which work is done, or the rate at which energy is transformed from one form to another.*

$$\textbf{Power} \; = \; \frac{\textbf{Work done}}{\textbf{time}} \; = \; \frac{\textbf{Energy Transformed}}{\textbf{time}}$$

Power is measured in **watts (W)**, where $\textbf{1 W} \; = \; 1\frac{\textbf{J}}{\textbf{s}}$.

A typical household lightbulb transforms energy at the rate of 60 W. Most of the electrical energy, unfortunately, is transformed into heat instead of light! Approximately 57 W of heat and 3 W of light are produced by the lamp. (An incandescent light bulb is only about 5% efficient.) A kettle might transform electrical energy into heat at the rate of 1500 W. The power rating of an electrical appliance is usually printed somewhere on the appliance.

A commonly used unit for power is the **horsepower (hp)**. In the metric system, the hp is defined as 750 W. (The electrical kettle just described is 2 hp.) The hp was originally defined by **James Watt**, who was looking for a way to describe the power of his newly invented steam engines, in terms that people accustomed to using horses to do their work could understand.

Exercises

1. How much work can a 5.00 hp motor do in 10.0 min?

2. A 60.0 kg girl runs up a flight of stairs 3.32 m high in 2.60 s.
   What is her power output in (a) watts? (b) in hp?

3. How long would it take a 5.0 hp motor to lift a 500.0 kg safe up to a window 30.0 m above the ground?

4. A man slides a 100.0 kg box along the floor for a distance of 4.0 m. If the coefficient of kinetic friction is 0.250, and the man does the job in 3.6 s, what is his power output (a) in watts? and (b) in hp?

5. A certain automobile engine is rated at 350 hp. What is its power
   (a) in watts? (b) in kilowatts (1 kW = 1 000 W)?

Chapter Review Questions

1. Two monkeys are connected by a rope of negligible mass which passes over a pulley. Friction in the pulley is negligible. One monkey has a mass of 20.0 kg while the other has a mass of 22.0 kg. At what rate will the monkeys accelerate? What will be the tension in the rope connecting the monkeys?

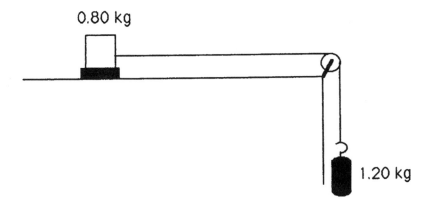

0.80 kg

1.20 kg

Figure 3.23

2. (a) At what rate will the system in **Figure 3.23** accelerate, assuming no friction? (b) What is the tension in the string while the system accelerates?

3. How much momentum does a 0.500 kg rock have when thrown at 25.0 m/s?

4. What impulse must be imparted to a 100.0 g ball to get it moving at 40.0 m/s?

5. A 2.4 kg cart moving 0.64 m/s collides with a stationary 1.8 kg cart. The carts lock together. What is their combined velocity after the collision?

6. A 1.5×10^3 kg car collides 'head-on' with a 1.2×10^3 kg car. Both cars were travelling at the same speed, 20.0 m/s, but in opposite directions. What will the velocity of the combined wreckage be immediately after the collision?

7. A 52 kg girl is coasting along the floor on a large 2.0 kg skateboard. If she is moving 1.8 m/s when a 46 kg boy jumps on to the same skateboard, what is the speed of the skateboard immediately after the boy jumps on it?

8. A 0.050 kg bullet leaves the muzzle of a 2.0 kg rifle with a velocity of 6.0×10^2 m/s. With what velocity will the rifle start to recoil if the rifle is (a) held loosely? (b) held firmly against the shoulder of a 98.0 kg man?

9. A 30.0 kg hockey player travelling 1.0 m/s toward the south collides with a 25.0 kg hockey player moving 0.50 m/s toward the west. They get tangled and move off together. With what speed and in what direction will the two players move right after the collision?

10. A 5.00 x 10^{-3} kg steel ball moving 1.20 m/s collides elastically (i.e. with no loss of kinetic energy) with an identical, stationary steel ball. The incident ball is deflected 30° from its original path.

(a) Draw a vector diagram showing the paths of both balls after the perfectly elastic collision.
(b) What is the velocity of the incident ball after the collision?

(c) What is the velocity of the struck ball after the collision?

(d) How much of the incident ball's kinetic energy was transferred to the struck ball?

11. If an amateur astronomer carries a 5.0 kg telescope to the top of a 250 m hill, how much work will he do on the telescope?

12. A child pulls a toy wagon along the road for a distance of 250 m. The force she exerts along the handle is 32 N. The handle makes an angle of 30° with the horizontal road. How much work does the child do on the wagon? Express your answer in kJ.

13. A girl pushes a 3.0 x 10^2 N box along the floor for a distance of 4.0 m. The coefficient of kinetic friction is 0.33. She then lifts the box straight up 1.2 m. What is the total amount of work she has done?

14. A spring with a force constant, k, of 12 N/m is compressed horizontally by a distance of 0.30 m. A 0.100 kg mass is then placed at the end of the compressed spring. When the spring is released, with what speed will the mass be thrown out by the spring?

15. How much kinetic energy does a 1.0 x 10^3 kg car travelling 90 km/h have?

16. How much gravitational potential energy does a 75 kg skier have when at the top of a hill 2.0 x 10^3 m high?

17. A large ball of Plasticine™ is dropped from a height of 2 m to the floor. The ball does not bounce back up in the air. Explain in terms of the conservation laws discussed in this chapter.

18. The pendulum bob in **Figure 3.24** has a mass of 0.500 kg. The pendulum is 1.20 m long. The bob is raised up a vertical distance of 0.150 m relative to its starting height. If friction is ignored, how fast will the bob be moving as it swings through A?

19. A girl lifts a 30. kg box from the ground up to a table 1.0 m high in a time of 1.5 s. A weightlifter friend carries a 100. kg load across the gym in 5.0 s, without dropping it or lifting it higher. Who has the greater power output? Explain.

20. A conveyor belt lifts 15 large 75 kg boxes from the road up to a window 4.2 m high, in a time of 8.2 s. What is the power rating of the conveyor in this situation?

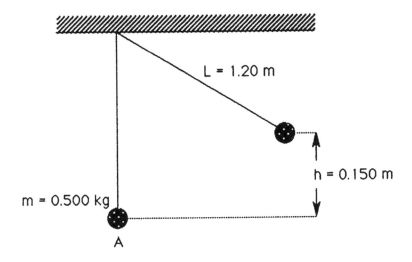

Figure 3.24

21. How much work can a 6.0 hp motor do in an 8.0 h working day? Express your answer in megajoules. (**1 MJ = 10^6 J.**)

Brain Busters

22. An 80 kg rider on a 120 kg motorbike, travelling 25 m/s in a direction 12° west of north, enters a highway without properly checking that the road is clear. He collides with a 1200 kg car travelling north at 20 m/s. The two vehicles and rider become entangled. In what direction and at what speed will the wreckage move immediately after the collision? (Assume the car's mass includes its occupants.)

23. A 9.6 kg box slides down a ramp inclined at 32° to the horizontal. At what rate will it accelerate if the coefficient of kinetic friction is 0.28?

24. Joe Physics is travelling on a jet airliner. As it accelerates down the runway, he holds a pendulum (consisting of a small washer on the end of a thread) in front of him and observes that the pendulum is displaced 10.0° from its usual vertical alignment. Help him by calculating the acceleration of the aircraft.

25. A block slides down a smooth inclined plane at steady speed when one end of the plane is raised to form an angle θ with the horizontal. Show that the coefficient of kinetic friction, μ, can be calculated as follows:

$$\mu = \tan \theta.$$

26. A 5.00 g bullet is fired into a 6.00 kg block, which is suspended from a string 1.00 m long. The string deflects through an angle of 12.0°. How fast was the bullet moving?

27. A large superball and a small superball are dropped from the same initial height *H*. Both balls bounce back up to a height *h* , which is just a bit less than *H*. If, however, the small superball is placed immediately above the large superball and both are dropped to the ground simultaneously from height *H,* the small superball rebounds to a height *h′ >>> H!* Explain this in terms of the Conservation Laws discussed in this chapter.

Ehren Stillman Cartoon

Test Yourself!

Multiple Choice

1. Change in momentum can be calculated from:

    A. $F\Delta d$.
    B. $F\Delta t$.
    C. $F\Delta v$.
    D. $v\Delta t$.

2. Both momentum and impulse can be measured in these units:

    A. N·m
    B. N·m/s
    C. N·s
    D. kg·m/s^2

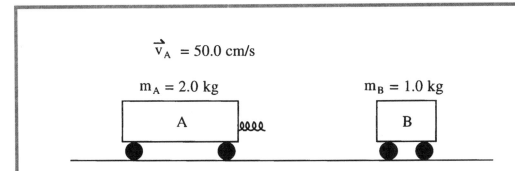

3. Spring-loaded cart A is moving with a speed of 50.0 cm/s when it collides with stationary cart B. After the collision, cart A is moving 30.0 cm/s. How fast is cart B moving after the collision?

A. 40.0 cm/s
B. 50.0 cm/s
C. 100 cm/s
D. 160 cm/s

4. Which best describes an **elastic collision** between two objects?

	total energy	total momentum	kinetic energy
A	conserved	conserved	conserved
B	conserved	conserved	not conserved
C	conserved	not conserved	not conserved
D	not conserved	not conserved	not conserved

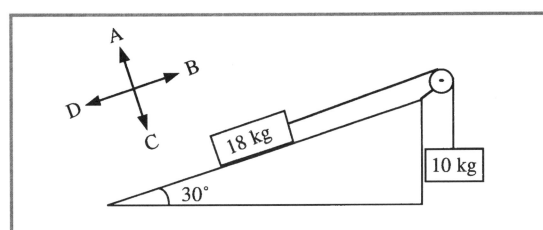

5. Two blocks are connected by a string over a frictionless pulley, as in the above diagram. If the system remains motionless, in which direction does the force of friction act on the 18 kg block?

A   B   C   D

Open-Ended Questions

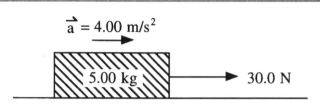

6. A 5.00 kg block is accelerated along a level surface at 4.00 m/s². The applied force is 30.0 N.
   (a) What is the net force?
   (b) What is the friction force?
   (c) What is the coefficient of friction, μ, between the block and the surface?

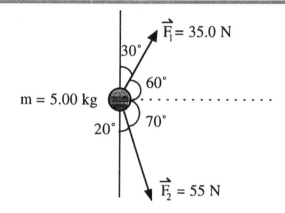

7. If the two forces F_1 and F_2 act simultaneously on the 5.00 kg mass in the above diagram, what will the magnitude of the acceleration be?

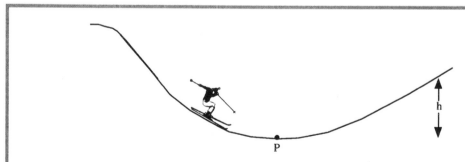

8. Skier Bob slides down the ice-covered hill on the left, passing **P**, and coasts up the hill on the right to a vertical height, *h*, of 12 m. How fast was Bob moving when he passed point **P**? Assume that frictional effects are negligible.

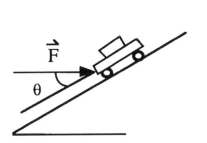
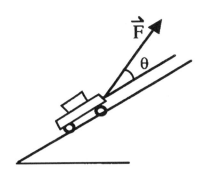

9. Is it easier to push a lawnmower up a slope as in the diagram on the left, or to pull it up the same slope as in the diagram on the right? Explain your answer using sketched vector diagrams.

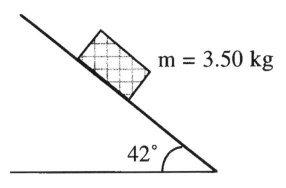

m = 3.50 kg

42°

10. The 3.50 kg block in the above diagram starts to slide at steady speed down the ramp when the ramp is raised to an angle of 42° with the horizontal. What is

(a) the normal force?
(b) the force of friction?
(c) the coefficient of kinetic friction, μ?

11. A gun fires 10 bullets per second, each of mass 0.020 kg, travelling 400 m/s. What is the average recoil force exerted on the gun?

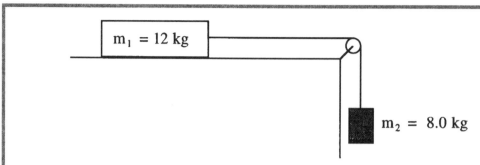

$m_1 = 12$ kg

$m_2 = 8.0$ kg

12. Two objects are connected by a light string, as in the above diagram. The horizontal surfaces and the pulley are frictionless.

(a) At what rate will the 12 kg mass accelerate?

(b) What is the tension in the connecting string?

13. A 10.0 kg pumpkin explodes into three fragments. The first fragment has a mass of 4.00 kg, and it travels north at 2.0 m/s. The second fragment has a mass of 1.5 kg, and it travels east at 4.0 m/s. In what direction and at what speed will the third fragment travel?

I used to have a lot more *energy*. Now all I have is a lot of *inertia*.

Chapter 4   Circular Motion and Gravity

4.1 Motion in a Circle

In a previous course, you may have solved problems involving the force of gravity and the acceleration due to gravity. You assumed **g** remains constant as a body falls from a height, and you considered many situations, most of which happened on or near the surface of the earth. Here are some questions you should be able to answer after you study this chapter:

> ➡ Is **g** the same for a satellite orbiting the earth several hundred kilometres above its surface?
> ➡ Does the earth exert a force of gravity on the moon?
> ➡ Why does the moon not 'fall down' to earth?

The force that keeps you firmly attached to this planet is of the same nature as the force that keeps earth in orbit around the sun. The force of **gravity** exists between any two masses in the universe.

All the planets orbit the sun in elliptical orbits. Satellites (both artificial and our moon) orbit the earth in elliptical paths. The ellipses are usually very close to being circular, however, so we begin our study of gravity by learning about objects moving in circular paths.

Uniform Circular Motion

Imagine you are driving a car around a circular track, maintaining the same speed all the way around the track. Any object that moves in a circle at steady speed is said to be in **uniform circular motion.** Is such an object *accelerating?* It may seem to have zero acceleration, but in fact an object moving in a circle has a constant acceleration — not because of a change in speed, but because of its *change in direction.* Remember, *acceleration is defined as change in velocity divided by change in time, and velocity is a vector quantity.*

$$a = \frac{\Delta v}{\Delta t}$$

Centripetal Acceleration

If a body is moving in a circular path, in what direction does it accelerate? **Figure 4.1** shows two consecutive positions of a body moving in a circle. Velocity vectors are labelled v_o and v_1. To find out the direction of the acceleration, we need the direction of Δv. Since Δv is the **vector difference** between v_1 and v_o, we use the rules for **vector 'subtraction'**.

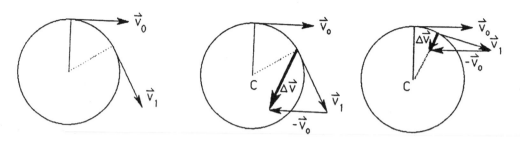

| Figure 4.1 | Figure 4.2 | Figure 4.3 |

Figure 4.2 shows how to find the vector difference, Δv, between v_1 and v_0 .

$$\Delta v = v_1 - v_0$$

$$\Delta v = v_1 + (-v_0).$$

Vector Δv is the **resultant** of v_1 and $(-v_0)$.

In **Figure 4.2**, the velocity vectors chosen represent the velocity of the body at two different times. The time interval between the occurrence of the velocities is relatively long. If this time interval (Δt) is shortened, the direction of Δv becomes closer and closer to being **toward the centre of the circle.** See **Figure 4.3**.

In fact, as $\Delta t \rightarrow 0$, the direction of Δv and therefore the direction of the acceleration, **a,** for all practical purposes, is **toward the centre of the circle**.

Since the direction of the acceleration of a body moving at uniform speed in a circle is toward the centre of the circle, the acceleration is called **centripetal acceleration. Centripetal** means *directed toward a centre.*

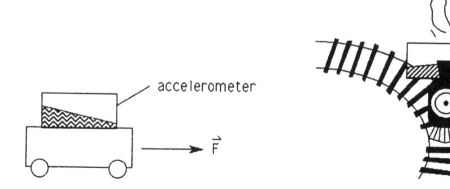

accelerometer

$\vec{F}$

| Figure 4.4 | Figure 4.5 |

A device called an **accelerometer** (**Figure 4.4**) can be used to show that a body moving in a circle accelerates toward the centre of the circle. If the accelerometer is attached to a cart accelerating in a straight line, the coloured water inside it forms a 'wedge' pointing in the direction of the acceleration. If the same accelerometer is attached to a toy train on a circular track (as in **Figure 4.5**), the accelerometer shows no acceleration in the direction of travel, but a definite acceleration **perpendicular to the direction of travel.** In other words, the train on the circular track accelerates **toward the centre** of the track.

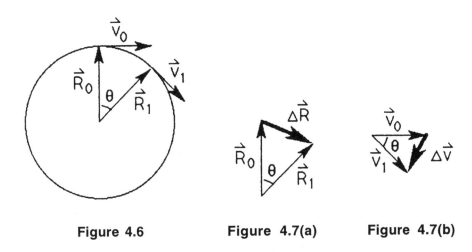

| Figure 4.6 | Figure 4.7(a) | Figure 4.7(b) |

In **Figure 4.6**, a body is moving in a circle of radius R_o. The radius is a **displacement vector**. The velocity of the body is v_o. Following a very short time interval Δt, the body has moved through a small angle θ, and the body has a new velocity, v_1, the **same magnitude as** v_o, **but in a new direction.**

In **Figure 4.7(a)**, ΔR is the vector difference between R_1 and R_o ;

$$R_1 + (-R_o) = \Delta R$$

or $R_o + \Delta R = R_1$, as in **Figure 4.7(a).**

Figure 4.7 (b) shows vector subtraction of the **velocity** vectors.

Vector Δv is the vector difference between v_1 and v_o.

$$v_1 + (-v_o) = \Delta v$$

or $v_o + \Delta v = v_1$ as in **Figure 4.7 (b).**

Now, consider the triangles formed by the **radius vectors** in **Figure 4.7(a)** and the **velocity vectors** in **Figure 4.7(b)**. Both are isosceles triangles with a common angle θ, so they are **similar triangles.** Corresponding sides of similar triangles are proportional; therefore,

$$\frac{\Delta v}{\Delta R} = \frac{v}{R} .$$

(The subscripts have been dropped because the *magnitudes* of the speeds and the radii do not change.)

$$\Delta v = \frac{v}{R} \cdot \Delta R$$

During a time interval Δt, the **average acceleration** is $\frac{\Delta v}{\Delta t}$, so

$$\bar{a} = \frac{\Delta v}{\Delta t} = \frac{v}{R} \cdot \frac{\Delta R}{\Delta t} .$$

Consider what happens during one complete circle during the motion of the body in **Figures 4.6** and **4.7**.

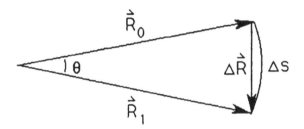

Figure 4.8

If the time interval Δt is chosen to be very small ($\Delta t \to 0$), **Figure 4.8** shows that each ΔR becomes closer to being equal to the section of corresponding arc Δs on the circumference of the circle. If Δs is the arc in question, then $\Delta R \to \Delta s$ as $\Delta t \to 0$.

The speed v of the body as it moves around the circle is $v = \frac{\Delta s}{\Delta t}$, and if $\Delta t \to 0$,

$$v = \frac{\Delta R}{\Delta t} .$$

It can therefore be said that the average acceleration during time Δt is

$$\bar{a} = \frac{\Delta v}{\Delta t} = \frac{v}{R} \cdot \frac{\Delta R}{\Delta t} = \frac{v}{R} \cdot v = \frac{v^2}{R} .$$

If $\Delta t \to 0$, the magnitude of the average acceleration approaches the **instantaneous centripetal acceleration, a_c**. The magnitude of the **centripetal acceleration** is therefore

$$a_c = \frac{v^2}{R} .$$

To summarize, when a body moves in a circle with uniform speed, it accelerates toward the centre of the circle, and the acceleration has a magnitude of $\dfrac{v^2}{R}$.

Newton's Second Law suggests that since the acceleration is toward the centre of the circle, the net force causing it should also be a **centripetal force.** If the centripetal force causing the centripetal acceleration is 'turned off' , the body will travel off in a direction which is along a tangent to the circle.

Another useful equation for calculating centripetal acceleration can be derived from $a_c = \dfrac{v^2}{R}$. If **one full revolution** of the body is considered, its **speed** will equal the **circumference** of the circle divided by the **period** of the revolution. That is, $v = \dfrac{2\pi R}{T}$, where R is the **radius** of the circle, and T is the period of one revolution.

Since $a_c = \dfrac{v^2}{R}$, then $a_c = (\dfrac{2\pi R}{T})^2 \cdot \dfrac{1}{R}$; therefore

$$a_c = \frac{4\pi^2 R}{T^2} \ .$$

Both equations for centripetal acceleration find much use. You will use them when studying the motion of planets around the sun, satellites around the earth, electrons in a magnetic field, and any kind of circular motion.

Examples

1. What is the centripetal acceleration of the moon toward earth?
Given: $R = 3.84 \times 10^8$ m and $T = 2.36 \times 10^6$ s

Solution

$$a_c = \frac{4\pi^2 R}{T^2} = \frac{4\pi^2 [3.84 \times 10^8 \ m]}{[2.36 \times 10^6 \ s]^2} = 2.72 \times 10^{-3} \ m/s^2 \ .$$

2. A skater travels at 2.0 m/s in a circle of radius 4.0 m. What is her centripetal acceleration?

Solution

$$a_c = \frac{v^2}{R} = \frac{[2.0 \ m/s]^2}{4.0 \ m} = 1.0 \ m/s^2 \ .$$

Centripetal Force

The net force that causes centripetal acceleration is called **centripetal force.** *Acceleration and net force are related by Newton's Second Law,* which says that $F = ma.$

$$\text{Centripetal force } F_C = ma_c .$$

Therefore, $\qquad F_c = m\dfrac{v^2}{R}$ or $F_c = m\dfrac{4\pi^2 R}{T^2} .$

Exercises   Use $g = 9.80$ m/s^2.

1. A 1.00 kg rock is swung in a horizontal circle of radius 1.50 m, at the end of a rope. If one complete revolution takes 0.80 s,
   (a) What is the speed of the rock?
   (b) What is the centripetal acceleration of the rock?
   (c) What is the centripetal force exerted on the rock?
   (d) What exerts the centripetal force?
   (e) The circle traced out by the rock was described as being horizontal.
      Would the rope, as it swings, be horizontal too? Explain.

2. A spider who could not find his web site (because his computer crashed?) is on the outside edge of an old phonograph record. He holds on for dear life, as the record rotates at 78 rpm. The radius of the record is 15 cm.
   (a) What is the linear speed, v, of the record at its outside edge?
   (b) What is the centripetal acceleration of the spider?
   (c) How much frictional force must there be to keep the spider from flying off the spinning record, if his mass is 1.0 g?

3. A satellite is orbiting the earth at a distance of 6.70 x 10^6 m from the centre of the earth. If its period of revolution around the earth is 5.45 x 10^3 s, what is the value of g at this distance?

4. A 1.2 x 10^3 kg car rounds a curve of radius 50.0 m at a speed of 80.0 km/h (22 m/s).
   (a) What is the centripetal acceleration of the car?
   (b) How much centripetal force is needed to cause this acceleration?
   (c) If the coefficient of kinetic friction, μ, is 0.25 on a slippery road, will the force of friction between the road and the wheels of the car be enough to keep the car from skidding?

5. A pendulum 1.00 m long and with a 1.20 kg bob is swinging with a maximum speed of 2.50 m/s. Calculate the **total force** exerted by the string on the swinging mass when the mass is at the bottom of its swing.

6. A 61 kg skater cuts a circle of radius 4.0 m on the ice. If her speed is 4.00 m/s, what is the centripetal force? What exerts this force?

7. What centripetal force is needed to keep a 12 kg object revolving with a frequency of 5.0 Hz in an orbit of radius 6.0 m?

8. A motocross rider at the peak of his 'jump' has a speed such that his centripetal acceleration is equal to *g.* As a result he does not feel any supporting force from the seat of his bike, which is also accelerating at rate *g.* Therefore he feels as if there is no force of gravity on him, a condition described as *apparent weightlessness.* If the radius of the approximately circular jump is 75.0 m, what was the speed of the bike?

9. Planet earth has a period of rotation of 24 h and a radius of 6.4×10^6 m.

   (a) What is the centripetal acceleration toward the centre of the earth of a person standing on the equator?
   (b) With what frequency *f,* in hertz, would the earth have to spin to make the centripetal acceleration a_c equal in magnitude to *g*? Compare this with the earth's normal frequency of rotation. (1 rotation in 24 h = 1.16×10^{-5} Hz.)
   (c) If the earth could be made to spin so fast that $a_c = g$, how would this affect the apparent force of gravity on you? Explain.

10. A 25 kg child is on a swing, which has a radius of 2.00 m. If the child is moving 4.0 m/s at the bottom of one swing, what is the centripetal force exerted by the ropes of the swing on the child? What is the **total force** exerted by the ropes when the swing is at its lowest point?

11. At the bottom of a power dive, a plane is travelling in a circle of radius 1.00 km at a speed of 2.50×10^2 m/s. What is the **total force** exerted upward on the 90.0 kg pilot by his seat?

12. Tarzan is swinging on a vine that will break if the force exceeds 2.0×10^3 N. If the length of the vine is 5.0 m and Tarzan's mass is 1.00×10^2 kg, what is the highest speed he can safely travel while swinging on the vine? (Hint: At what point in the swing will the tension in the vine be greatest?)

13. Earth orbits the sun at a distance of 1.5×10^{11} m. What is its centripetal acceleration toward the sun? If the mass of the earth is 6.0×10^{24} kg, what is the centripetal force exerted by the sun on the earth? What provides this force?

14. A roller coaster loop has a radius of 12 m. If the passengers in a car are not to fall out at the top of the loop, what is the minimum speed the car must have at the top?

15. A highway curve is designed to handle vehicles travelling 50 km/h safely. Assuming the coefficient of kinetic friction between the rubber tires and the road is 0.60, what is the minimum radius of curvature allowable for the section of road? For added safety, the road might be built with a 'banking'. In what direction should the road be 'banked'? Why does this help?

Investigation 4-1   Circular Orbits

Purpose: To investigate factors involved in the uniform circular motion of a mass revolving at the end of a string.

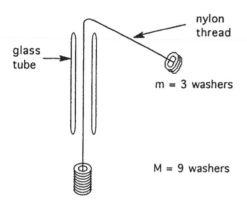

Figure 4.9

Introduction

Some aspects of circular motion can be studied using the simple equipment shown in **Figure 4.9**. A small mass m (a bundle of 3 washers) 'orbits' on the end of a string. A large mass M experiences a force of gravity Mg. In this **Investigation**, M is chosen to be a bundle of 9 identical washers, so that $M = 3m$.

The glass tube is smoothly polished at the top, and strong, smooth nylon thread joins the two masses. In effect, the edge of the tube acts like a pulley, changing the direction of the tension force in the string without changing its magnitude.

When the small mass m is made to 'orbit' around the top end of the glass tube, mass M remains static, so the tension in the string along its length L is equal to the downward force of gravity on M, which is Mg.

The radius of the orbit is not L, however, but R (the horizontal distance from m to the vertical glass tube). See **Figure 4.10**.

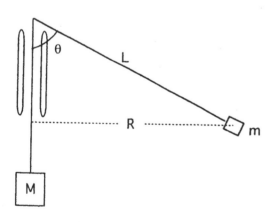

Figure 4.10

When the small mass m is made to 'orbit' the top of the glass tube, we will assume the upward force on the stationary mass M has a magnitude of Mg. The reaction force exerted on m through the string has the same magnitude (Mg) but is exerted in the opposite direction. In **Figure 4.11**, this tension force is labelled $T = Mg$. Consider the two *components* of **T**. The vertical component F_y, balances the downward force of gravity on m, so $F_y = mg$. The horizontal component of **T** is the **centripetal force**, so $F_x = F_c$.

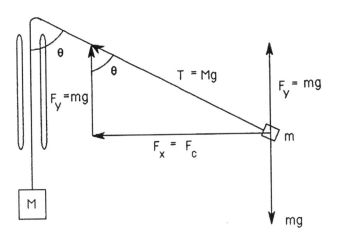

Figure 4.11

Procedure

1. Prepare the apparatus, using 3 identical washers for the orbiting mass and 9 washers for the large mass. **Predict** what the angle θ between the thread and the vertical glass tube will be, using the fact that

$$\text{cosine } \theta \;=\; \frac{F_y}{T} \;=\; \frac{mg}{Mg} \;=\; \frac{m}{M}.$$

2. In this investigation, you will vary L and measure the period of revolution T for each length L. Measure from the centre of gravity of the mass m along the string, and mark off distances of 20 cm, 40 cm, 60 cm, 80 cm and 100 cm with chalk or a small dab of correction fluid.

3. Hold the glass tube vertically in your hand, and swing mass m until it achieves a stable orbit such that length L is 20.0 cm. While you keep the orbiting mass revolving, have your partner make the following measurements (as best he can, for it will be difficult!):

   (a) the radius of the orbit, R. Your partner will have to hold a metre stick as near to the orbiting mass as he dares (to avoid decapitation) and estimate R as closely as possible;

   (b) the period of revolution, T. Your partner will time how long the mass takes to make ten revolutions, then divide the total time by 10.

4. Repeat **Procedure 3** for lengths of 40.0 cm, 60.0 cm, 80.0 cm and 100.0 cm. Record all your measurements in a table like **Table 1**.

5. Calculate the ratio of R/L . From **Figure 4.10** you can see that this ratio equals sine θ. Calculate θ knowing sine θ.

Table 1   Data for *Investigation 6*

Length of String, L [cm]	Radius of Orbit, R [cm]	Period of Revolution, T, [s]	sin θ $= \dfrac{R}{L}$	θ [°]	cos θ $= \dfrac{m}{M}$	θ [°]
20.0	18 cm	0.54s				
40.0	30 a	0.725s				
60.0	36.5 cm	0.872s				
80.0						
100.0						

6. Plot a graph with *T* on the Y-axis (since it is the *dependent variable*) and *L* on the X-axis (since it is the *independent variable*).

7. Examine the shape of your graph of *T* vs *L* , and make an educated guess at what the power law might be. For example, if you think the power law is most likely $T^n = k \cdot L$, then plot a graph of T^n vs *L*. If you choose the correct value of n, your graph should be a straight line passing through (0,0).

8. Determine the slope of your final, straight-line graph, and express it in appropriate units. Then write an **equation** for your straight line, incorporating the **slope**.

---

9. You can use the results of your experiment to do a check on the formula for centripetal force.

$$\text{Since } \ F_c = \frac{m4\pi^2 R}{T^2} \ , \quad \text{therefore,} \quad T^2 = \frac{m4\pi^2 R}{F_c}.$$

Figure 4.10 shows you that $R = L\sin\theta$, and **Figure 4.11** makes it clear that $F_c = F_x = Mg \sin\theta$. Therefore, we can write

$$T^2 = \frac{m4\pi^2 L\sin\theta}{Mg\sin\theta} = \frac{m4\pi^2}{Mg} L.$$

Thus, the **theoretical** slope of a graph of T^2 vs *L* should be $\dfrac{m4\pi^2}{Mg}$.

Concluding Questions

1. Compare the average value of angle θ calculated from sin θ $= R/L$ with the value of θ predicted using cosine θ $= m/M$. What is the **percent difference** between the two results?
2. According to your results, how does the period, *T*, of the orbiting mass vary with the length, *L*? Write a **specific equation** for your graphical result.

3. What is the **theoretical value** of your slope for the graph in **Concluding Question 2**? What is the **percent difference** between your graph's actual slope and the theoretical slope?
4. Discuss **sources of error** in this experiment and how you might be able to reduce their effects.

Ehren Stillman Cartoon

Challenges

1. Discuss how the results of your experiment would be affected if the ratio of the masses used was 1:2 instead of 1:3. How would this affect (a) the angle θ made by the string with the vertical glass tube? (b) the relationship between the period of revolution and the length of the string?

2. Design a way of testing out the centripetal force formula using an air puck on an air table. See if you can design a way of showing that Newton's Second Law really does apply to centripetal acceleration.

4.2 Gravity and 'Free Fall'

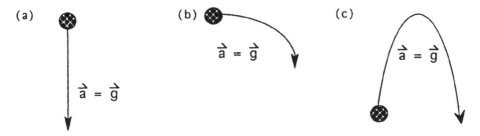

Figure 4.12

If gravity is the only force acting on a body, the body is in **free fall**. If there is no friction, each of the bodies in **Figure 4.12** is in free fall. Each is *accelerating downward at rate g,* which is independent of the mass of the body and has a magnitude of 9.80 m/s² near the surface of the earth.

"What goes up must come down!" This simple 'truth' has been known for centuries. Any unsupported object will fall to the ground. According to legend, **Isaac Newton (1642-1727)** was sitting under an apple tree when he saw an apple fall to the ground. He looked up at the moon and wondered, "Why should the moon not fall down, as well?"

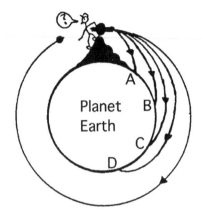

Figure 4.13

Might the moon be in 'free fall'? If it is, then why does it not fall to the earth like other unsupported bodies? Newton created a diagram like the one in **Figure 4.13** to explain why the moon circles the earth without 'falling down' in the usual sense.

Imagine you are at the top of a mountain that is high enough so that there is essentially no air to offer resistance to the motion of a body projected horizontally from the top of the mountain. If a cannon is loaded with a small amount of gunpowder, a cannonball will be projected horizontally at low speed and follow a curved path until it strikes the ground at A. If more gunpowder is used, a greater initial speed will produce a curved path ending at B. With more and more initial speed, paths ending at C and D will be achieved. If the initial speed is just high enough, the path will have a curvature *parallel with the earth's curvature,* and the cannonball will circle the earth for an indefinite period. The cannonball will, like the moon, be *in orbit around the earth.*

Isaac Newton actually anticipated artificial earth satellites. Of course, the technology for sending a satellite into orbit was not available 300 years ago. (Incidentally, to place an artificial satellite in orbit 500 km above the earth's surface requires a horizontal speed of approximately 7.6 km/s. It will take such a satellite approximately 90 minutes to complete one orbit.)

The moon was our first satellite, of course. No one knows how or why it attained its orbit, but it is in a nearly circular path around this planet. The moon is, indeed, in 'free fall'. It does 'fall toward the earth'. Its horizontal speed is great enough that it completes its orbit with no danger of colliding with the earth's surface — just like the cannonball in **Figure 4.13** but at a much greater altitude. The moon's mean distance from earth is 3.84×10^5 km. The orbit is actually slightly elliptical; hence 'mean' (average) distance.

Could the centripetal force needed to keep the moon in a near-circular orbit around the earth be the same force that makes an apple fall from a tree? What would exert this force of gravity on the moon?

Since every known thing on earth experiences the pull of gravity, Newton was certain that it was the earth itself which exerted a gravitational force on objects near its surface. At the earth's surface, gravity makes objects accelerate at a rate of 9.8 m/s^2. What would the acceleration due to gravity be at a distance as far away as the moon?

Treating the moon as a body in circular orbit, the acceleration due to gravity is just the centripetal acceleration of the moon. Therefore,

$$a_c = \frac{4\pi^2 R}{T^2} = \frac{4\pi^2(3.84\times10^8 \text{ m})}{[(27.3 \text{ d})(24 \text{ h/d})(3600 \text{ s/h})]^2} = 2.7 \times 10^{-3} \text{ m/s}^2.$$

If this value of a_c was really the magnitude of g at the moon's distance from the earth, it is much smaller than the value of g at earth's surface. Newton was convinced that, since $F = ma$, the **force of gravity** causing this acceleration must decrease rapidly with distance from the earth.

In **Investigation 4-2,** you will be provided with data about most of the planets in the solar system. Given their **orbital radii** and their **periods of revolution**, you will calculate their **centripetal accelerations** toward the sun. You will then use graphical analysis to determine the nature of the relationship between a_c (caused by the force of gravity of the sun on the planet) and distance R from the sun.

Investigation 4-2
Centripetal Acceleration of Planets

Purpose: **Using planetary data, to determine how the centripetal acceleration of planets varies with their distances from the sun.**

Introductory Notes: The orbits of the planets are actually **elliptical**, but they are close to being **circular**. The radii given in **Table 2** are **mean orbital radii**.

Procedure

1. Prepare a table similar to **Table 2**. Calculate values of a_c for each of the planets listed, using $a_c = \dfrac{4\pi^2 R}{T^2}$.

2. Plot a graph of a_c (on the Y-axis) vs R (on the X-axis). Label your graph using appropriate units.

3. Make an educated guess at the power law involved. Plot a_c vs R^n, where n is your reasoned best choice. Repeat this procedure if necessary until you obtain a straight line.

Table 2   Planetary Data: Mean Orbital Radii and Periods

Planet	Mean Orbital Radius, R [m]	Period of Revolution, T [s]	Centripetal Acceleration, a_c [m/s²]	
Mercury	0.58×10^{11}	7.60×10^6		
Venus	1.08×10^{11}	1.94×10^7		
Earth	1.49×10^{11}	3.16×10^7		
Mars	2.28×10^{11}	5.94×10^7		
Jupiter	7.78×10^{11}	3.74×10^8		
Saturn	14.3×10^{11}	9.30×10^8		
Uranus	28.7×10^{11}	2.66×10^9		

Concluding Question

Write an equation for your final, straight-line graph, complete with a numerical value for the slope, in appropriate units. Describe the nature of the relationship between centripetal acceleration and distance, in words.

4.3 Johannes Kepler (1571 - 1630)

Johannes Kepler was a German mathematician, who had worked in the astronomical laboratory of Danish astronomer **Tycho Brahe (1546-1601).** Brahe is famous for his precise observations of the positions of almost 800 stars, and his accurate records of the positions of planets over a period of two decades. Tycho did all his work *without a telescope!* The telescope had not yet been invented.

Kepler was fascinated with planetary motions, and devoted his life to a search for mathematical patterns in their motions. To find these patterns he relied completely on the observations of Tycho Brahe. Kepler formulated three laws describing the orbits of the planets around the sun.

Kepler's Three Laws of Planetary Motion

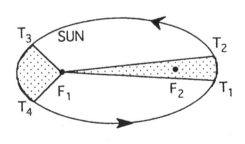

Figure 4.14

1. **Each planet orbits the sun in an elliptical path, with the sun at one of the two foci of the ellipse.**

2. **A line joining the centre of the sun and the centre of any planet will trace out equal areas in equal intervals of time. See Figure 4.14.**

If *time intervals* $T_2 - T_1$ and $T_4 - T_3$ are equal, the *areas* traced out by the orbital radius of a planet during these intervals will be equal. (The diagram is not to scale.)

3. **For any planet in the solar system, the cube of its mean orbital radius divided by the square of its period of revolution is a constant.**

$$\frac{\overline{R}^3}{T^2} = K$$

The three laws of Kepler can be neatly summarized in half a page of this text, but remember that to arrive at these laws required many years of work by this dedicated mathematician, not to mention the twenty years spent by Tycho Brahe making his painstaking observations of the heavenly wanderers, the planets.

In **Investigation 4-3**, you will calculate Kepler's constant, K for the solar system.

Investigation 4-3
Determining Kepler's Constant for the Solar System

Purpose: Using astronomical data for the planets in the solar system, to calculate the value of K, Kepler's constant.

Procedure

1. **Table 2** in **Investigation 4-2** lists the **mean orbital radii** and **periods** for seven planets. Prepare a Table of Data and calculate **K** = R^3/T^2 for each planet. Express **K** in appropriate units.

2. In **Investigation 4-2,** you obtained a straight line graph when you plotted a_c vs $(1/R^2)$. Therefore, $a_c = k \cdot \dfrac{1}{R^2}$, where k is the slope of your graph.

As you know, $a_c = \dfrac{4\pi^2 R}{T^2}$.   The slope of your graph was

$$k = \frac{\Delta a_c}{\Delta \dfrac{1}{R^2}} = \frac{a_c - 0}{\dfrac{1}{R^2} - 0} = a_c R^2 = \frac{4\pi^2 R}{T^2} \cdot R^2 = 4\pi^2 \cdot \frac{R^3}{T^2} = 4\pi^2 \cdot K,$$

where **K** is **Kepler's constant.**

Slope k = $4\pi^2$ **K**, where **K** is Kepler's constant for the solar system. Calculate **K** using the slope k your graph from **Investigation 4-2.** (**K** = $\dfrac{k}{4\pi^2}$.)

Concluding Questions

1. What is the mean value of **K**, according to **Procedure 1? Procedure 2?**

2. Planet Neptune has a mean orbital radius of 4.50×10^{12} m. What is its period of revolution according to Kepler's Third Law? How many 'earth-years' is this?

3. Pluto has a period of revolution of 7.82×10^9 s. What is its mean orbital radius?

4. For satellites of the **earth**, Kepler's Law applies, but a different constant K must be used. Calculate what K would be for the earth's satellites, using only the fact that the **moon** has a mean orbital radius of 3.84×10^8 m and a period of revolution of 2.36×10^6 s.

5. Using K for the earth's satellites, calculate the mean orbital radius of an earth satellite which is in **geosynchronous orbit** (a communications satellite which orbits the earth in the plane of the equator in a period of 24 h, and therefore stays above one point on earth's surface as the earth completes its daily rotation).

Example

Planet Xerox (a close copy of planet Earth) was discovered by Superman on one of his excursions to the far extremes of the solar system. Its distance from the sun is 1.50×10^{13} m. How long will this planet take to orbit the sun?

Solution

Earth's orbital radius, R_e = 1.5×10^{11} m.
Earth's period of revolution, T_e = 1.0 a.
Xerox's orbital radius, R_x = 1.50×10^{13} m.

The problem *could* be solved using Kepler's constant derived in **Investigation 4-3.** You would use Kepler's Third Law and simply solve for T_x. Another way to solve the problem is to use data for the earth (above) and the fact that

$$\frac{R_x^3}{T_x^2} = \frac{R_e^3}{T_e^2} = K_{sun}$$

$$T_x^2 = \frac{R_x^3}{R_e^3} \cdot T_e^2 = \frac{[1.5 \times 10^{13} m]^3}{[1.5 \times 10^{11} m]^3} \cdot [1.0\ a]^2 = 1.0 \times 10^6\ a^2$$

$$T_x = 1.0 \times 10^3\ a.$$

The planet Xerox has a period of revolution around the sun of 1.0×10^3 a.

Exercises

1. A certain asteroid has a mean orbital radius of 5.0×10^{11} m. What is its period of revolution around the sun?

2. A satellite is placed in orbit around the earth with an orbital radius of 2.0×10^7 m. What is its period of revolution? Use the facts that the moon's period of revolution is 2.36×10^6 s and its orbital radius is 3.84×10^8 m.

3. A satellite has period T and orbital radius R. If you wish the period to be increased to $8T$, what must the new orbital radius be?

4.4 Newton's Law of Universal Gravitation

Kepler's three laws *describe* the orbits of the planets around the sun. Newton used Kepler's Laws to derive a law outlining the nature of the gravitational forces that *cause* the planets to move in these orbits.

Newton believed that the force that keeps planets in orbit is the same force that makes an apple fall to the ground. He believed that there is a gravitational force between *any* two bodies in the universe. Like all other forces, gravity is a *mutual* force. That is, the force with which the earth pulls on a falling apple is equal to the force with which the apple pulls on the earth, but in the opposite direction. The earth pulls on your own body with a force of gravity which is commonly referred to as your 'weight'. Simultaneously, your body exerts a force on planet earth of the same magnitude but in the opposite direction. (Relative to each other, the earth 'weighs' the same as your body!)

Newton was able to use Kepler's Laws as a starting point for showing that the force of gravity between the sun and the planets varied as the inverse of the square of the distance between the sun and the planets. He was convinced that the inverse square relation would apply to everyday objects near the surface of the earth, as well. He produced arguments suggesting that the force should depend on the product of the masses of the two bodies being attracted to one another. The mathematical details of how Newton arrived at his famous **Law of Universal Gravitation** can be found in many references, but are too lengthy to reproduce here.

Newton's Law of Universal Gravitation can be summarized as follows:

Every body in the universe attracts every other body with a force which is (a) directly proportional to the product of the masses of the two bodies and (b) inversely proportional to the square of the distance between the centres of mass of the two bodies.

The equation for Newton's Law of Universal Gravitation is:

$$F = G\frac{Mm}{R^2}.$$

The constant of proportionality, G, is called the **universal gravitation constant.** Isaac Newton was unable to measure G, but it was measured later in experiments by **Henry Cavendish (1731-1810).**

The modern value for **G** is **6.67 x 10⁻¹¹ Nm²/kg².**

4.5 Cavendish's Experiment to Measure 'G'

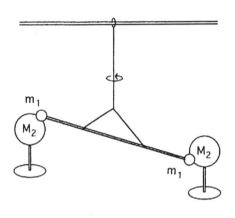

You can imagine how difficult it is to measure the gravitational force between two ordinary objects. In 1797, **Henry Cavendish** performed a very sensitive experiment which was the first 'earth-bound' confirmation of the Universal Law of Gravitation. Cavendish used two lead spheres mounted at the ends of a rod 2.0 m long. The rod was suspended horizontally from a wire which would *twist* an amount proportional to the gravitational force between the suspended masses and two larger fixed spherical masses placed near each of the suspended spheres. (See **Figure 4.15.**)

Figure 4.15

The forces involved in this experiment were extremely small (of the order 10^{-6} N), so great care had to be taken to eliminate errors due to air currents and static electricity. Cavendish did manage to provide confirmation of the Universal Law of Gravitation, and he also arrived at the first measured value of 'G'.

4.6 Gravitational Field Strength of the Earth

If you wish to calculate the force of gravity on a mass m, you simply multiply the mass by the gravitational field strength, g. ($F = mg$.) You could also use the Law of Universal Gravitation,

$$F = G\frac{Mm}{R^2},$$ where M is the mass of the earth.

This means that $mg = G\dfrac{Mm}{R^2}$, and therefore,

$$g = G\frac{M}{R^2}.$$

Thus, the **gravitational field strength of the earth** depends only on the **mass of the earth** and the distance, R, from the centre of the earth to the centre of mass of the object which has mass m.

Exercises

$$G = 6.67 \times 10^{-11} \text{ Nm}^2/\text{kg}^2 \qquad g = 9.80 \text{ N/kg}$$
$$\text{Earth's mass} = 5.98 \times 10^{24} \text{ kg} \qquad \text{Earth's radius} = 6.38 \times 10^6 \text{ m}$$

1. What is the force of gravity on a 70.0 kg man standing on the earth's surface, according to the Universal Law of Gravitation? Check your answer using $F = mg$.
2. What is the force of gravitational attraction between a 75 kg boy and a 60.0 kg girl (a) when they are 2.0 m apart? (b) when they are only 1.0 m apart?
3. What is the force of gravity exerted on you if you are standing on the moon, if your mass is 70.0 kg and the moon's mass is 7.34×10^{22} kg? The moon's radius is 1.74×10^6 m.
4. What is the force of gravity exerted on you by Mars, if your mass is 70.0 kg and the mass of Mars is 6.37×10^{23} kg? The radius of Mars is 3.43×10^6 m, and you are standing on its surface, searching for Mars bars.
5. What is the force of gravity exerted on a 70.0 kg person on Jupiter (assuming the person could find a place to 'stand')? Jupiter has a mass of 1.90×10^{27} kg and a radius of 7.18×10^7 m.
6. What is the gravitational field strength of the earth at a distance equal to the moon's orbital radius, 3.84×10^8 m? Compare this with the centripetal acceleration of the moon, calculated earlier in the chapter.
7. Calculate the orbital speed of the moon around the earth, using the moon's orbital radius (**Exercise 6**) and the value of the earth's gravitational field strength at that distance.
8. Both G and g are 'constants'. Why is G a **universal** constant and not g? Under what conditions is g a constant?

9. Calculate the value of g at each of these locations:

	mass	radius
(a) on the moon	7.34×10^{22} kg	1.74×10^6 m
(b) on planet Mercury	3.28×10^{23} kg	2.57×10^6 m
(c) on Ganymede*	1.54×10^{23} kg	2.64×10^6 m
(d) on the surface of the sun	1.98×10^{30} kg	6.95×10^8 m

Express each answer as a multiple or a decimal fraction of Earth's g. Would the force of gravity on you be greatest on the moon, on Ganymede (*one of Jupiter's moons), or on Mercury?

10. Use Newton's Law of Universal Gravitation *and* the formula for centripetal force to show that you can calculate the mass of the earth knowing only the orbital radius and the period of an earth satellite. Then calculate Earth's mass using the moon's period (2.36×10^6 s) and orbital radius (3.84×10^8 m).

11. Calculate the gravitational force between the sun and Pluto. The mass of the sun is 2×10^{30} kg, and the mass of Pluto is 6×10^{23} kg. Pluto is 6×10^{12} m away from the sun.

4.7 Weightlessness

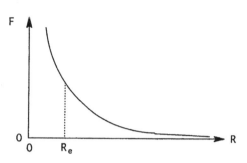

Figure 4.16

According to Newton's Law of Universal Gravitation, the force of gravity between any two bodies varies inversely as the square of the distance between the centres of mass of the two bodies.

$$F = G \frac{Mm}{R^2} \quad .$$

Figure 4.16 is a graph showing how the **force of gravity** (commonly called **weight**) changes with distance measured from the centre of the earth. *To be truly 'weightless' (experience no force of gravity) an object would have to be an infinite distance from any other mass!* According to the Law of Universal Gravitation, as $R \rightarrow \infty$, $F \rightarrow 0$. Obviously, *true* **weightlessness** is not likely to be achieved! When people talk about 'weightlessness', they almost always are referring to **apparent weightlessness**. *Apparent weightlessness is experienced when one feels zero force from supporting structures (your seat, the floor, or the surface of the earth). This will happen when your supporting structure has the same acceleration as you have!* Of course, if there is no supporting structure (as when you jump off a cliff or a ladder, or when you are in the middle of a jump) you will also experience apparent weightlessness.

Examples of Apparent Weightlessness

Figure 4.17(a)   Figure 4.17(b)

(1) A Falling Elevator

Imagine a person standing on a scale in an elevator, as in **Figure 4.17(a)**. When the elevator is standing still, the scale will give the *true* weight of the person, which is the force of gravity exerted by Earth on the person ($F = mg$). Imagine now that the cable breaks, as in **Figure 4.17(b)**. The elevator will accelerate down at rate $a = g$. The person in the elevator will also fall, accelerating at rate $a = g$. The scale, placed in the elevator by the person (who just happens to be both a physicist and a boy scout), will read the *apparent* weight of the person, which is **zero**.

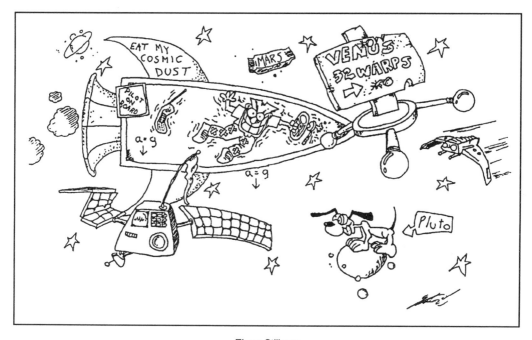

Ehren Stillman

Figure 4.18

(2) The Orbiting Astronaut

The astronaut in an orbiting space vehicle (**Figure 4.18**) feels weightless for the same reason as the person in a falling elevator! Both the astronaut and the vehicle he or she occupies are in 'free fall'. The astronaut feels no resistance from any supporting structure, so he or she feels 'weightless'.

(3) Momentary Weightlessness

You experience brief sensations of weightlessness during everyday activities. If you are running, you will experience apparent 'weightlessness' during those intervals when both feet are off the ground, because you are in a momentary 'free fall' situation. Jumping off a diving board or riding your bike swiftly over a bump, you will experience brief moments of apparent weightlessness.

Exercises

1. Why would a BMX rider feel momentarily 'weightless' during a jump?

2. A 70.0 kg girl is in an elevator which is accelerating downward at a rate of 1.0 m/s². What is her *apparent weight?*

3. How fast would the earth have to move at the equator before a person standing on the equator felt 'weightless'? Earth's radius is 6.37 x 10⁶ m.

4. The earth is in 'free fall' toward the sun. Why do you not feel 'weightless', when you are an occupant of this satellite of the sun?

5. An acrobat does a complete loop at the end of a rope attached to a horizontal bar. The distance from the support to the acrobat's centre of gravity is 3.0 m. How fast must she move at the top of her loop to feel 'weightless' at that point?

6. A motocross rider travelling 20.0 m/s feels 'weightless' as his bike rides over the peak of a mound. What is the radius of curvature of the mound?

4.8 Satellites in Circular Orbits

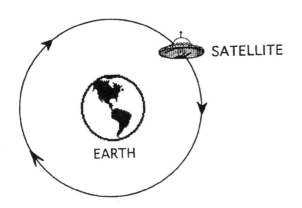

SATELLITE

EARTH

Figure 4.19

Orbital Velocity

What orbital (tangential) speed must a space vehicle have to achieve a circular orbit at a given altitude? Since the **centripetal force** (mv^2/R) is provided by **gravity**, we can write:

$$\frac{mv^2}{R} = \frac{GMm}{R^2}.$$

Therefore,

$$v^2 = \frac{GM}{R}, \text{ and}$$

$$V_{orbital} = \sqrt{\frac{GM}{R}},$$

where M is the mass of the earth, R is the distance from the centre of the earth to the space vehicle, and G is the universal gravitation constant.

Exercise

What **orbital speed** is required by an earth satellite in orbit, 1.0 x 10³ km above the earth's surface? Does it make a difference what the mass of the satellite is? Explain your answer. [Earth's mass = 5.98 x 10²⁴ kg Earth's radius = 6.37 x 10⁶ m]

4.9 Gravitational Potential Energy

Newton's Law of Universal Gravitation tells us the force between a space vehicle and planet earth at any distance R from the centre of mass of the earth:

$$F = G\frac{Mm}{R^2},$$

where M is the mass of the earth, m is the mass of the space vehicle, and R is the distance from the centre of the earth to the space vehicle.

If a space vehicle is to travel to other parts of the solar system, it must first escape the grasp of Earth's gravitational field. How much energy must be supplied to the vehicle to take it *from the earth's surface* (where $R = R_E$) to a distance where the gravitational force due to the earth is 'zero' ($R \rightarrow \infty$)?

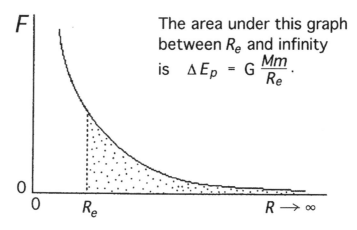

The area under this graph between R_e and infinity

is $\Delta E_p = G\dfrac{Mm}{R_e}$.

Figure 4.20

The force on the space vehicle is continually changing. **Figure 4.20** shows how the force changes with distance. *To get the vehicle out of the earth's gravitational field, enough energy must be supplied to the space vehicle to equal the amount of work done against the force of gravity over a distance between the earth's surface and 'infinity' (where the force approaches zero).*

The amount of work which must be done to escape Earth's gravitational field is equal to the **area underneath the graph of force vs distance, between** $R = R_E$ and $R \rightarrow \infty$. See **Figure 4.20**. Using calculus, it can be shown that the area under the graph (shaded portion) is equal to GMm/R_E. This area represents the change in gravitational potential energy of the vehicle as it moves from distance R_E out to 'infinity'.

$$\Delta E_p = G\frac{Mm}{R_E}$$

In routine, earth-bound problems involving gravitational potential energy, we often arbitrarily take the 'zero' level of potential energy to be at the earth's surface. In situations involving space travel, it is conventional and convenient to the let the 'zero' of E_p be at 'infinity'.

Since the change in E_p between $R = R_E$ and $R \to \infty$ is $+ G \dfrac{Mm}{R_E}$, the E_p at the surface of the earth is **negative.**

$$E_p \ (at \ R = R_E) = - \ G \frac{Mm}{R_E} \ .$$

Escape Velocity

How fast must a spaceship travel to escape the gravitational bond of the planet Earth? In order to escape Earth's gravitational pull, the space vehicle must start with enough **kinetic energy** to do the **work** needed to bring its **potential energy** to the zero level. Sitting on the launch pad, the **total energy** of the space vehicle is

$$E_p \ = \ -G \frac{Mm}{R_E} \ .$$

If the space vehicle is to escape the earth's field, it must be given sufficient kinetic energy so that:

$$- G\frac{Mm}{R_E} + E_k = 0$$

$$- G\frac{Mm}{R_E} + \frac{1}{2} mv^2 = 0$$

$$\frac{1}{2} mv^2 = G\frac{Mm}{R_E} \ .$$

Therefore
$$v^2 = 2G\frac{M}{R_E} \ .$$

This means that $v_{escape} = \sqrt{\dfrac{2GM}{R_E}}$ is the minimum speed the space vehicle must be given in order to escape the earth's gravitational pull.

This minimum speed for escape is called the **escape velocity** for planet Earth. **It depends only on the earth's mass and the earth's radius.** Obviously different planets or moons would have different escape velocities, as the following exercises will show.

Exercises

$$G = 6.67 \times 10^{-11} \ Nm^2/kg^2 \quad M_E = 5.98 \times 10^{24} \ kg \quad R_E = 6.37 \times 10^6 \ m$$

1. Substitute values for G, M_E, and R_E in the formula for escape velocity and calculate the escape velocity for planet Earth. Does the mass of the space vehicle make a difference? Explain.

2. Calculate 'escape velocities' for the sun, the moon and Mars, given the following information.

	Mass	Radius
Sun	2.0×10^{30} kg	7.0×10^8 m
Moon	7.4×10^{22} kg	1.7×10^6 m
Mars	6.4×10^{23} kg	3.4×10^6 m

3. Travelling to other planets involves not only the earth's gravitational field but also that of the sun and the other planets. Would it be easier to travel to Venus or to Mars? (Which would require the lower escape speed?)

Chapter Review Questions $G = 6.67 \times 10^{-11} \ Nm^2/kg^2$

1. How much centripetal force is needed to keep a 43 kg object revolving with a frequency of 0.20 Hz in an orbit of radius 4.8 m?

2. What centripetal force must be exerted by the ice on a hockey player of mass 72 kg who cuts a curve of radius 3.0 m while travelling 5.0 m/s?

3. A 1.25 kg steel puck is swung in a circle of radius 3.6 m at the end of a cord of negligible mass, on a frictionless ice surface. The period of one revolution is 1.6 s. Calculate (a) the speed of the puck; (b) the centripetal acceleration of the puck; and (c) the centripetal force on the puck.

4. A satellite is orbiting Earth 1.00×10^2 km above the surface. At this altitude, $g = 9.5 \ m/s^2$. If earth's radius is 6.4×10^3 km, what is the period of revolution of the satellite?

5. (a) A 1.2×10^3 kg car rounds a curve of radius 75 m travelling 25 m/s. How much centripetal force is needed to take the car around this curve safely?
(b) If the road is not 'banked', what is the minimum coefficient of kinetic friction needed?

6. How much centripetal force is needed to keep a 10.0 kg object revolving with a frequency of 1.5 Hz in an orbit of radius 2.0 m?

7. A 45 kg ape swings through the bottom of his arc on a swinging vine, with a speed of 3.0 m/s. If the distance from the supporting tree branch to his centre of gravity is 4.0 m, calculate the **total tension** in the vine.

8. Why does the moon not fall to Earth?

9. A 1440 N football player, who missed a tackle in a very important high school game, is sent by his coach on a spaceship to a distance of four earth radii from the centre of the earth. What will the force of gravity on him be at that altitude?

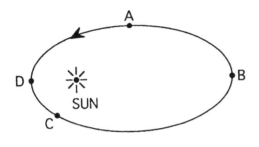

Figure 4.21

10. **Figure 4.21** shows the orbit of a comet around the sun. Where on the diagram will the comet be moving fastest? Explain in terms of **Kepler's Second Law.**

11. Earth's elliptical orbit around the sun brings it closest to the sun in January of each year and farthest in July. During what month would Earth's (a) speed and (b) centripetal acceleration be greatest?

12. The earth orbits the sun once a year, so its period of revolution is 1.0 a. If a space probe orbits the sun with an orbital radius nine times that of Earth, what is the space probe's period of revolution?

13. What is the force of gravity on a 70.0 kg man (a) here on Earth? (b) on an asteroid of mass 1.0×10^9 kg and radius 4.5×10^4 m?

14. What is the force of gravity on a 52 kg astronaut orbiting the earth 25,600 km above the earth's surface?

15. Why does an astronaut *feel* 'weightless' in an orbiting space shuttle?

16. What is the speed of a satellite orbiting the earth at a distance of 9.0×10^5 m above the earth's surface?

17. What is the acceleration of a satellite orbiting the earth in a circle of radius 7.30×10^6 m?

18. What is the altitude above Earth's surface of a satellite which has an orbital speed of 6.5 km/s?

19. What is the period of revolution of a planet which is 5.2 times as far away from the sun as Earth?

20. How far must you travel from the earth's surface before g is reduced to one-half its value at earth's surface?

21. (a) What speed must a satellite have to complete a circular orbit just grazing the earth's surface?
    (b) How does the earth's escape velocity compare with the speed needed to simply orbit the earth at the lowest possible altitude?

22. The earth is 1.49 x 10^8 km from the sun, and its period of revolution is 1.0 a. Venus is 1.08 x 10^8 km from the sun, on average. Use Kepler's Third Law to calculate the length of a 'Venus year' in 'earth years' (a).

23. With what speed does Earth orbit the sun? The mass of the sun is 2.0 x 10^{30} kg and Earth's orbital radius is 1.5 x 10^{11} m.

24. The 'bump' on the motocross track in **Figure 4.22** is part of a circle of radius of 50.0 m. What is the maximum speed at which a motorbike can travel over the highest point of the bump without leaving the ground?

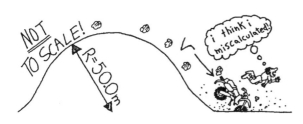

Ehren Stillman

Figure 4.22

25. At what distance from Earth, on a line between the centre of Earth and the centre of the moon, will a spacecraft experience zero net gravitational force?

Earth's mass is 6.0 x 10^{24} kg.

Moon's mass = 7.4 x 10^{22} kg.

Distance from Earth centre to moon centre = 3.8 x 10^8 m

26. Halley's comet is a satellite of the sun. It passed Earth in 1910 on its way around the sun, and passed it again in 1986.
    (a) What is the period of revolution of Halley's comet, in years (a)?
    (b) What is the mean orbital radius of Halley's comet?
    (c) The mean orbital radius equals the average of the orbiting comet's closest and farthest distances from the sun. If the closest Halley's comet gets to the sun is 8.9 x 10^{10} m, what is its farthest distance from the sun?
    (d) When Halley's comet is at its farthest distance from the sun, where is it located in relation to the orbits of the outer planets?

27. The acceleration due to gravity at the surface of a planet of radius 3.5 x 10^6 m is 3.2 m/s^2. What is the mass of the planet?

Brain Busters

28. A Snowbird jet aircraft travelling 600.0 km/h pulls out of a dive. If the centripetal acceleration of the plane is 6 *g's,* what is the radius of the arc in which the plane is moving?

29. Draw a vector diagram showing the forces acting on a car rounding a curve on a frictionless road, which is banked at angle θ. Prove that the correct angle of banking, θ, appropriate for speed *v* and radius *R* is given by: $\tan \theta = \dfrac{v^2}{gR}$.

30. If a satellite requires 2.5 h to orbit a planet with an orbital radius of 2.6×10^5 m, what is the mass of the planet?

31. Calculate the mass of the sun, using Kepler's constant $K = 3.35 \times 10^{18}$ m³/s², and $G = 6.67 \times 10^{-11}$ m³/kg·s².

32. Show that for a spherical planet of uniform density, $g = \frac{4}{3} \rho \pi G R$, where ρ is the density of the planet and R is the radius of the planet.

Ehren Stillman

Test Yourself!

Multiple Choice

1. If an object is in uniform circular motion, what can be said of the *magnitudes* of the object's velocity (v), acceleration (a) and centripetal force (F)?

   A. Only v is constant.
   B. Only a is constant.
   C. Only F is constant.
   D. The *magnitudes* of v, a, and F are all constant.
   E. The *magnitudes* of v, a and F all vary.

2. If the gravitational force of attraction between a boy and a girl 1.00 metre apart is **F**, what will it be when they move closer so they are only 0.25 m apart?

   A. $\frac{1}{4}F$
   B. $4F$
   C. $16\ F$
   D. $\frac{1}{16}F$

3. Observations of a satellite in orbit can be used to calculate the mass of the planet around which the satellite is revolving. The satellite has mass m, is at a distance R from the centre of the planet, and has an orbital period T. The universal gravitation constant is G. What is the *minimum information* one needs to make the calculation of the planet's mass M?

   A. m and R
   B. G and m
   C. R and T
   D. G, R, m and T
   E. G, R and T

4. In what units might gravitational field strength be measured?

   A. N
   B. kg·m/s
   C. J/kg
   D. N/kg

5. On the moon's surface, the force of gravity exerted by the moon on a certain camera is 2.4 N. What will the force of gravity exerted by the moon on the same camera be when it is placed in orbit with an orbital radius equal to twice the moon's radius?

   A. 2.4 N   B. 0.60 N   C. 0.40 N   D. 1.2 N E. 0 N

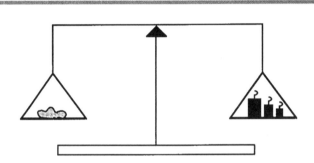

6. According to the above equal-arm balance, a gold sample has a mass of 60 g on earth. If the same sample and balance are transported to the moon, where g is only 1.6 m/s², what will the balance read for the mass of the gold sample there?

   A. 0 g   B. 10 g   C. 60 g   D. 360 g

Open-Ended Questions

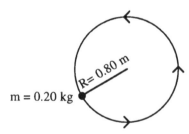

m = 0.20 kg
R= 0.80 m

7. In the above diagram, a 0.20 kg air puck on the end of a string is moving in a horizontal circular path of radius 0.80 m.
   (a) If the tension in the string is 25 N, what is the period of revolution of the air puck?
   (b) If the period of the revolving air puck is reduced by one half, and the radius is kept the same, what will the tension in the string have to be?

8. A 2.0 x 10⁴ kg satellite orbits a planet in a circle of radius 2.2 x 10⁶ m. Relative to zero at infinity, the gravitational potential energy of the satellite is - 6.0 x 10⁹ J. What is the mass of the planet?

9. Ganymede, one of Jupiter's moons, is larger than planet Mercury! Its mass is 1.54×10^{23} kg, and its radius is 2.64×10^{6} m.
   (a) What is the gravitational field strength, g, on Ganymede?
   (b) What is the escape velocity for a space vehicle trying to leave Ganymede?

Gertrude's mass
m = 45 kg

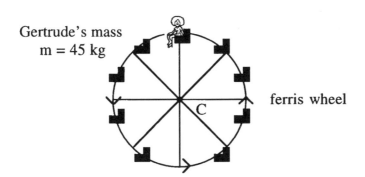

ferris wheel

10. Gertrude has a mass of 45 kg. She is riding on a ferris wheel, so her seat travels in uniform circular motion. The centripetal force on Gertrude is 75 N. What is the upward force exerted by the seat on Gertrude (a) when she is at the top of the wheel? and (b) when she is at the bottom of the wheel?

11. An earth satellite orbits the earth in a circular orbit at a distance of 1.5×10^{4} km from the centre of the earth.

   (a) What is the speed of the satellite?

   (b) What is the gravitational field strength of earth at this altitude?

   (c) If the satellite's mass is increased from m to $10m$, how will this affect the answers to (a) and (b)?

12. A certain space station is shaped like a large bicycle wheel, and the occupants live out in the 'tube' of the wheel, at a radius of 96 m. The 'wheel' is rotated so that the centripetal acceleration simulates a gravitational field of 6.0 m/s². What is the period of rotation required to accomplish this?

Chapter 5 Electrostatics

5.1 Review: Static Electric Charges

If your hair is dry, and you comb it briskly, your comb will attract not only your hair but bits of dust, paper or thread. The comb is probably made of plastic, but many kinds of material will produce the same effect. As long ago as 600 B.C., the Greeks observed the 'attracting power' of **amber** when it was rubbed with cloth. Amber is a fossilized resin from trees, and was used by the Greeks for decoration and for barter. Of course, magnets have a similar 'attracting power', but they only attract certain elements such as iron, nickel, and cobalt, and some of their alloys. Amber, if rubbed with cloth, will attract small bits of just about anything.

The Englishman **Dr. William Gilbert (1544-1603)** was curious about this interesting property of amber, and he did many experiments with it and other materials. Gilbert discovered that many materials, if rubbed with appropriate fabrics, could be **electrified**. Words like *electrified, electricity, electron* and *electronics* originate with the Greek word for *amber,* which was **elektron**.

Charles du Fay (1698-1739), a French scientist, was probably the first person to figure out that there were *two kinds of electricity.* He observed that if two glass rods were rubbed with silk and brought near each other, they would **repel** one another. Two amber rods rubbed with fur would also **repel** one another. If, however, an 'electrified' amber rod was brought close to an 'electrified' glass rod, the two rods would **attract** each other. Du Fay correctly deduced that there must be two kinds of electricity. His names for them were **vitreous** (meaning glassy) and **resinous** (referring to amber). Later in the eighteenth century **Benjamin Franklin (1706-1790)** coined the labels **positive electricity** and **negative electricity**.

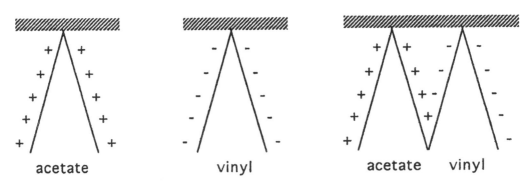

Figure 5.1: Two charged acetate plastlc strips (+), allowed to hang freely from a supporting rod, will repel each other. Two charged vinyl strips (-) will also repel each other. A charged acetate strip will, however, attract a charged vinyl strip.

A glass rod rubbed with silk is, by convention, said to have a **positive charge**. An amber rod rubbed with wool or fur has a **negative charge**.

In classroom experiments, a good way to get a positive charge is to rub an acetate plastic strip with cotton. A negative charge is easily obtained by rubbing a vinyl plastic strip with wool or fur.

Since the electric charges on 'electrified' objects are not moving, they are referred to as **static** (stationary) **charges** or **static electricity**.

A charged object will *attract* any uncharged (neutral) body. It will also attract an oppositely charged body, but it will *repel* another body carrying the same charge.

Bodies with the same charge repel each other. Bodies with opposite charges attract one another. A neutral body is attracted to either a positively charged body or a negatively charged body.

Elementary Atomic Structure

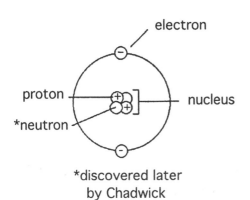

*discovered later
by Chadwick

Figure 5.2

John Dalton's famous **atomic theory (1808)** assumed that all matter was made up of *indivisible particles.* A very important experiment by **Sir Ernest Rutherford (1871-1937)** showed that the atom actually had some internal structure to it. He was able to show that the atom had a **nucleus**, in which **positive charge** was concentrated. Since the atom as a whole is neutral, there must be negatively charged matter somehow distributed around the nucleus. Negatively charged **electrons** were first identified by English physicist **J. J. Thomson**.

A simplified view of the atom as pictured in Rutherford's 'planetary' model shows the nucleus of the atom with its positive charge, surrounded by negatively charged **electrons**. The positively charged particles in the nucleus are **protons**. **Figure 5.2** also shows **neutrons**, but these were not discovered until 1932. An English physicist named **James Chadwick**, a contemporary of Rutherford, added this particle to the list of **subatomic particles**. Neutrons carry no electric charge, and their mass is just slightly greater than that of protons. Electrons are far less massive than protons or neutrons. The mass of a proton is now known to be **1.67×10^{-27} kg**, which is 1836 times as massive as an electron!

The smallest atom is that of hydrogen. It has the simplest possible nucleus — one proton! Its radius is approximately 10^{-15} m, compared with the radius of the hydrogen atom as a whole, which is approximately 10^{-10} m. Rutherford thought that the hydrogen nucleus might be the fundamental unit of positive charge, and it was he who first used the label **proton** for the hydrogen nucleus.

The normal state for an atom to be in is neutral. But atoms can gain or lose electrons, in which case they become electrically charged atoms, called **ions.** Since the protons are safely locked away in the nucleus of an atom, it is only electrons that are transferred from one body to another during the 'electrification' of normal objects.

Explaining Electrification of Objects

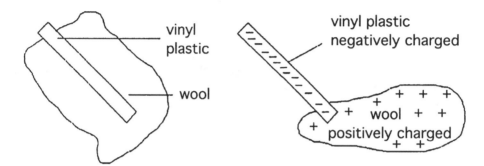

Figure 5.3

When a glass rod is rubbed with silk, the silk appears to have a greater affinity for electrons than glass does. Electrons are transferred from the glass onto the silk. This leaves the glass with a *shortage* of electrons. Its overall charge is now **positive.** The silk has an excess of electrons, so its overall charge is negative. (See **Figure 5.3.**)

Similarly, if amber is rubbed with wool, the wool loses electrons to the amber, so the amber becomes negatively charged while the wool becomes positively charged.

There is no 'creation' or 'destruction' of electric charge during electrification. All that happens is a transfer of electrons from one body to another.

Law of Conservation of Charge

All experiments show that electric charge is never created and never destroyed. Electric charge, like momentum and total energy, is a conserved quantity.

Conductors and Insulators

Conductors are materials that allow charged particles to pass through them easily. Metals such as silver, copper and aluminum are excellent conductors of electricity, but all metals conduct to some extent. Atoms of metals have one or more outer electrons which are very loosely bound to their nuclei — so loosely attached that they are called **free electrons.**

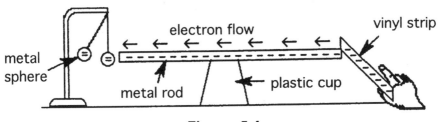

Figure 5.4

In **Figure 5.4**, a metal rod is supported by a plastic cup. Plastic does not conduct electricity. A negatively charged vinyl strip is allowed to touch one end of the metal rod. When the vinyl touches the metal, a few excess electrons are conducted to the rod, so it becomes negatively charged as well.

The negatively charged strip repels excess electrons to the far end of the metal rod. An initially neutral metal sphere, hanging from a silk string, is attracted to the charged rod. When the sphere touches the negatively charged rod, some of the excess electrons are conducted on to the sphere. Since the sphere is now the same charge as the rod, it is repelled from the rod.

Now both the rod and the sphere have an excess of electrons. If the vinyl strip is taken away, the rod and the sphere will retain their negative charge and the sphere will remain in its 'repelled' position. (On a dry day, it may stay there for many hours!)

If the metal rod is replaced with a glass or plastic rod of similar dimensions, no reaction of the metal sphere is evident. This is because glass and plastic are **insulators**. Insulators are materials that resist the flow of charged particles through them. Plastics, rubber, amber, porcelain, various textiles, mica, sulfur and asbestos are a few very good insulators. Carbon in the form of diamond is an excellent (but slightly expensive) insulator; carbon in the form of graphite is a good conductor!

Non-metals such as silicon and selenium find many uses in transistors and computer chips because of their 'semiconductor' behaviour.

It is easy to place a **static** charge on an insulator, because electrons are transferred only where the two objects come in contact. When an excess of charge builds up at a point on an insulator, it will not flow away; it remains 'static'.

Exercises

1. Sir William Gilbert found that he could 'electrify' materials such as glass, amber, ebonite, quartz, etc. He called these materials 'electrics'. He was unable to electrify metal rods by rubbing them with other materials, so he called metals 'non-electrics'. Explain why he could not 'electrify' metals by rubbing them with other materials while holding the metal objects in his hand.

2. If the vinyl strip in **Figure 5.4** was replaced with a positively charged acetate strip, describe what would happen and why.

3. Outline a method by which you could determine, with certainty, whether the charge on your comb (after you comb your hair) is positive or negative.

Charging by Conduction (Touch)

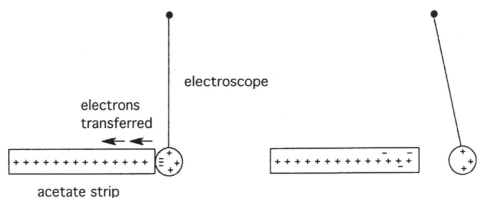

Figure 5.5

If a positively charged acetate strip is brought close enough to touch a neutral, metal-coated sphere of an **electroscope** (a device designed to detect excess electric charge), as in **Figure 5.5**, free electrons on the surface of the conducting sphere will be attracted to the positively charged acetate plastic. The acetate will gain a few electrons, but its overall charge will remain overwhelmingly positive. The sphere, however, now has a positive charge, so it is repelled by the acetate strip. We say the sphere has been charged by contact or by **conduction**. You could just as easily charge the sphere negatively by touching it with a charged vinyl strip.

Charging by Induction

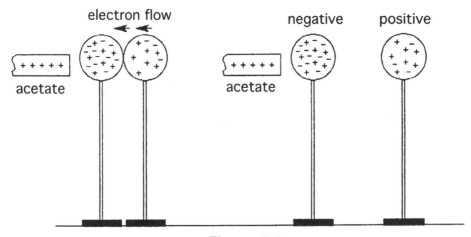

Figure 5.6

Objects can be charged without being touched at all, in which case we call it **charging by induction**. There are many ways to do this. **Figure 5.6** shows one way. Two metal spheres are on insulated stands, and are touching each other. A positively charged acetate strip is brought **near** the two spheres, **but does not** *come in contact with them.* Free electrons from the right hand sphere are attracted toward the left sphere by the positive acetate strip. Now the right sphere is pushed away (using the insulated support stand). Tests with an electroscope will show that the right sphere has been charged **positively** by **induction**; the left sphere is charged **negatively** by **induction**.

Note that charge has not been 'created' during this procedure. All that has happened is this: a few electrons have been transferred from the right hand sphere to the left hand sphere. The total charge is still the same as it was before the charging by induction was attempted. (The net charge is still zero.)

5.2 The Electric Force

The force exerted by one charged body on another can be measured. French scientist **Charles Coulomb (1736-1806)** used an apparatus much like the Henry Cavendish gravitational force apparatus to work out the relationship among these variables: force, distance and quantity of charge.

In *Investigation 5-1,* you will do an experiment that is similar in principle to the one used by Coulomb, but different in design.

Investigation 5-1   Coulomb's Law   **(Demonstration)**

Purpose: **To investigate how the force between two electrically charged spheres varies with the distance between the centres of the two spheres.**

(a)   (b)

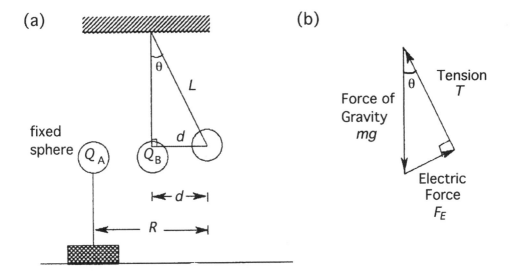

Figure 5.7

Introduction

Direct measurement of the force exerted by two charged spheres on each other is difficult, but an indirect method can be used to compare forces at different distances. **Figure 5.7(a)** shows a small graphite-coated sphere, mounted on an insulating stand. This sphere is given a charge by touching it with a charged acetate strip. A movable, suspended sphere is also charged by the acetate strip. The charges placed on the spheres (Q_A and Q_B) should remain constant throughout the experiment.

In **Figure 5.7(a)**, R is the distance between the centres of the spheres, and d is the displacement of the movable ball from its starting position.

Figure 5.7(b) shows the three forces acting on the movable sphere when it is repelled by the similarly charged fixed sphere. Vectors representing the force of gravity, the electric force and the tension in the string form a right-angled triangle. Note that this force triangle is **similar** to the displacement triangle in **Figure 5.7(a)**. Since the triangles are similar,

$$\frac{F_E}{d} = \frac{mg}{L}.$$

Therefore,

$$F_E = \frac{mg}{L}\, d.$$

Since m, g, and L are constant during the experiment, one can write that

$$F_E = \text{constant} \cdot d,$$

$$\text{or } F_E \propto d.$$

Since F_E is proportional to d, we can use d as a measure of the **electric force** between the two charged spheres at different distances R.

Procedure

1. The apparatus for this experiment is set up on the stage of an overhead projector. Images of both spheres are projected on a screen or a blackboard. Mark the position of the suspended ball before charging the spheres.

2. Charge both spheres by contact with a charged acetate strip. Do several practice runs, bringing the mounted sphere closer to the movable sphere and recording R and d simultaneously. (If a graph grid is projected on the screen, measurements can be made in arbitrary units from the grid.) Practice is important. You must take your measurements very quickly, especially if humidity is high, since the charge may leak from the spheres to the air. Note: On the screen, the values of R and d will be larger than the true values, but both quantities are magnified by the same amount by the projector.

3. When you have mastered the technique of doing the measurements of R and d quickly, carry out the experiment and record your data in a table. Try to obtain at least five readings.

4. Plot a graph of d vs R. Examine its shape, and make a reasonable guess at the nature of the relationship that exists between d and R. Plot a second graph of d vs R^n, where n is the exponent you think is most likely to produce a straight line graph.

Concluding Questions

1. What relationship does your graph suggest might exist between the electric force F_E (which is proportional to d) and the separation distance R?

2. Careful experiments by Charles Coulomb (1736-1806) lead to his conclusion that the electric force between two **point charges** (very tiny charged bodies) varied as the inverse of the square of the separation between the point charges. In the ideal case, a graph of F_E (or d) vs R^{-2} would be straight. Discuss sources of error in your experiment which might account for deviations from the 'ideal' result.

Coulomb's Law

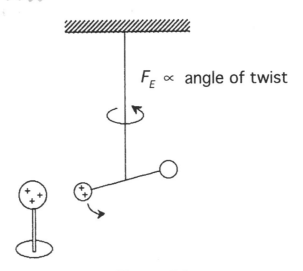

$F_E \propto$ angle of twist

Figure 5.8

Coulomb investigated the nature of the electrical force between charged bodies using an apparatus quite similar to the one used by Cavendish to check Newton's Law of Universal Gravitation. A torque caused by the repulsion of two similarly charged spheres caused a length of vertical wire to twist through an angle. The amount of twist was used to calculate the force of repulsion between the two charged spheres. The apparatus is called a **torsion balance**.

Coulomb was unable to measure the charges on the spheres directly. One can change the *relative* amount of charge, however, in the following way:

If you have one sphere with an unknown charge Q on it, and the other identical sphere has zero charge, and you touch the two spheres together, then both spheres will have charge $\frac{1}{2} Q$. (This assumes that the excess charge on the original sphere will be shared equally with the second, identical sphere.) This sharing of excess charge could be repeated several times, to obtain spheres with charges of $\frac{1}{4} Q$, $\frac{1}{8} Q$, and so on.

Experiments by Coulomb and others lead to the conclusion that **the force of attraction or repulsion between two point charges depends directly on the product of the excess charges on the bodies, and inversely on the square of the distance between the two point charges.** This is known as **Coulomb's Law**, and is written symbolically like this:

$$F = \text{constant} \cdot \frac{Q_1 Q_2}{R^2}, \text{ or}$$

$$F = k \cdot \frac{Q_1 Q_2}{R^2}.$$

The magnitude of the **proportionality constant** depends on the units used to measure the excess charge. If the measuring unit is the **elementary charge** (as on one electron or one proton), then Q would be measured in elementary charges, and the constant k in $F = k \cdot \frac{Q_1 Q_2}{R^2}$ has a magnitude of:

$$k = 2.306 \times 10^{-28} \text{ N·m}^2/(\text{elem. ch})^2.$$

If the measuring unit for excess charge is the **coulomb** (named after Charles Coulomb), then Q would be measured in coulombs (**C**) and the constant k becomes

$$k = 8.988 \times 10^9 \text{ N·m}^2/\text{C}^2.$$

The value of k was worked out after Coulomb's time. At the time he did his experiments, there was not yet a unit for 'quantity of charge'. When scientists decided on an appropriate measuring unit for charge, they named it after Coulomb.

In the wording of Coulomb's Law (above), reference is made to 'point charges'. Coulomb's Law applies to **very small charged bodies**. If the charged bodies are large relative to the distance between them, it is difficult to know what value of R to use. If the bodies are uniform spheres over which the charge is evenly spread, then one can use the distance between their centres. If two large, conducting spheres approach each other, forces between the charges will cause excess charges to re-arrange themselves on the spheres in such a way that the 'centres of charge' may not coincide with the 'centres of mass'. How would this affect your measurements of d and R in **Investigation 5-1**?

The Coulomb and the Elementary Charge

It is now known that a coulomb of charge is equivalent to the amount of charge on 6.2422 x 10¹⁸ electrons (if the charge is negative) or the same number of protons (if the charge is positive). The charge on one electron or one proton, called the elementary charge, is

$$\text{1 elementary charge (e)} = \frac{1}{6.2422 \times 10^{18}/C} = \textbf{1.602 x 10}^{-19}\textbf{ C.}$$

Officially, the coulomb is defined in a way that makes it much easier to measure.

One coulomb of charge is the amount of charge that will pass a point in a conductor in one second when the electrical current is one ampere.

In other words, $1\,A = 1\,C/s$, or $\textbf{1 C} = \textbf{1 A·s.}$

Examples

1. What force would be exerted by a 1.00 C positive charge on a 1.00 C negative charge that is 1.00 m away?

   Solution:

   $$F = k\frac{Q_1 Q_2}{R^2} = \frac{(8.988 \times 10^9 \text{Nm}^2/C^2)(1.00C)(-1.00C)}{(1.00\text{ m})^2} = -8.99 \times 10^9 \text{ N.}$$

   As you can see, a +1.00 C charge would attract a − 1.00 C charge one metre away with a force of nearly ten billion newtons! The Coulomb is actually a *very* large amount of charge!

2. The force of repulsion between two identically charged small spheres is 4.00 N when they are 0.25 m apart. What amount of charge is on each sphere? Express your answer in **microcoulombs (µC)**. ($1\mu C = 10^{-6}$ C.) Use $k = 9.0 \times 10^9$ Nm²/C².

   Solution:
   $$F = k\frac{Q_1 Q_2}{R^2} = k\frac{Q^2}{R^2}.$$

   $$Q^2 = \frac{FR^2}{k} = \frac{(4.0 \text{ N}) (0.25\text{m})^2}{9.0 \times 10^9 \text{ Nm}^2/C^2} = 2.78 \times 10^{-11} \text{ C}^2 = 27.8 \times 10^{-12} \text{ C}^2$$

   Therefore, $Q = \sqrt{27.8 \times 10^{-12} \text{ C}^2} = 5.3 \times 10^{-6}$ C, and $Q = 5.3$ µC.

3. Three tiny spheres with identical charges of +5.0 μC are situated at the corners of an equilateral triangle with sides 0.20 m long. What is the net force on any one of the charged spheres?

Solution:

The net force on one of the charges will be the vector sum of the two repulsive forces exerted by the other two identical charges.

Let the three charges be A, B and C. **Figure 5.9** shows their locations on the triangle, and vectors representing forces exerted on A by charges B and C.

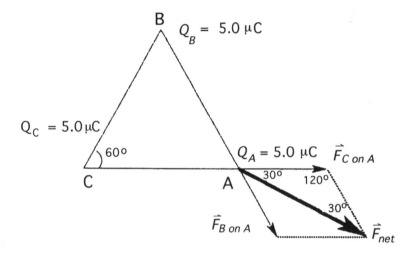

Figure 5.9

First, calculate the **magnitude** of the force exerted by charge C on charge A. **Note!** The value of Coulomb's constant, k, is rounded off to **9.0 x 10⁹ Nm²/C²** for this and most problems.

$$F = k\frac{Q_C Q_A}{R^2} = \frac{9.0 \times 10^9 \text{ Nm}^2/\text{C}^2 (5.0 \times 10^{-6} \text{ C})(5.0 \times 10^{-6} \text{ C})}{(0.20 \text{ m})(0.20 \text{ m})} = 5.63 \text{ N}.$$

The **magnitudes** of $F_{C \text{ on } A}$ and $F_{B \text{ on } A}$ are the same, but their **directions** are not. The two forces are vectors, and their resultant can be found by using **vector addition**, as in **Figure 5.9**.

$$F_{net} = F_{C \text{ on } A} + F_{B \text{ on } A} \qquad \text{(Vector sum!)}$$

You can solve for the net force several ways. You could use a scale diagram. You cannot use Pythagoras's Theorem directly, because the vector triangle is not a right-angled triangle. (You could break it up into two right-angled triangles by drawing a line bisecting the 120° angle!) The easiest solution is to use the **sine law** on the force triangle in **Figure 5.9**, as follows:

$$\frac{F_{net}}{\sin 120°} = \frac{F_{C\ on\ A}}{\sin 30°}$$

$$F_{net} = \sin 120°\cdot\frac{F_{C\ on\ A}}{\sin 30°} = \frac{(0.866)(5.63N)}{(0.500)} = 9.80\ N\ .$$

The **direction** of the net force is on a line bisecting angle A.

Exercises

Use $k = 9.0 \times 10^9$ Nm^2/C^2 1 elementary charge $= 1.60 \times 10^{-19}$ C   1 C $= 6.24 \times 10^{18}$ elementary charges

1. What will happen to the magnitude of the force between two charges Q_1 and Q_2 separated by a distance R if:
   (a) one of the charges is doubled?
   (b) both charges are doubled?
   (c) separation distance is doubled?
   (d) separation distance is tripled?
   (e) both charges are doubled and separation distance is doubled?
   (f) both charges are doubled and separation distance is halved?

2. What force would be exerted on a 1.00 μC positive charge by a 1.00 μC negative charge 1.00 m away from it?

3. What is the force of repulsion between two bodies carrying 6.0 μC of charge and separated by 1.0 μm?

4. What is the force of attraction between a proton and an electron in a hydrogen atom, if they are 5.00 x 10^{-11} m apart?

5. One electron has a mass of 9.1 x 10^{-31} kg. How many coulombs of charge would there be in 1 kg of electrons? How much force would this charge exert on another 1 kg of electrons 1.0 km away? (This is strictly an imaginary situation!)

6. Two small spheres are located 0.50 m apart. Both have the same charge on them. If the repulsive force is 5.0 N, what charge is on the spheres, in μC?

7. Three charged objects are located at the 'corners' of an equilateral triangle with sides 1.0 m long. Two of the objects carry a charge of 5.0 μC each. The third object carries a charge of -5.0 μC. What is the resultant force acting on the -5.0 μC object? Assume all three objects are very small.

8. Imagine you could place 1 g of electrons 1.0 m away from another 1 g of electrons. Calculate what would be
   (a) the **electrical force** of repulsion between the two charge collections;
   (b) the **gravitational force** of attraction between them; and
   (c) the **ratio** of the electrical force to the gravitational force.
   Discuss the 'practical' aspects of this fictitious situation.

9. Discuss whether you think gravity would play a major part in holding atoms together. Refer to your results in **Exercise 8**. Calculate the gravitational force between a proton and an electron 5.00×10^{-11} m apart, and compare this force with the electrical force calculated in **Exercise 4**.

10. Two protons repel each other with a force of 1.0 piconewton (10^{-12} N). How far apart are the protons?

5.3 Electric Field Strength

You will recall that the **gravitational field strength, g,** due to a massive body like the earth is defined by $g = F/m$, where both g and F are vectors. The value of g changes as you move the 'test mass' m away from the earth. In fact, g varies inversely as the square of the distance between m and the earth's centre of mass.

While gravitational field strength is the force per unit mass, **electric field strength, E,** is the **force per unit charge**.

Electric Field Strength $E = \dfrac{F}{Q}$.

Electric field strength is measured in **newtons per coulomb (N/C).**

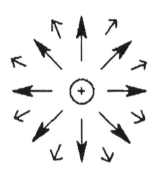

There are two ways to represent an **electric field.** One is with a **field vector diagram.** In a field vector diagram, vectors are drawn showing the direction of the field and its magnitude at various distances from a fixed charge. The direction of the vectors is the direction that the force would tend to move a **positive test charge** in that region of the field. **Figure 5.10** shows the field near a fixed positive charge.

Figure 5.10

The idea of the **electric field** originated with **Michael Faraday (1791-1867),** but he used a different way of representing the field. He used **lines of force,** which showed *the direction in which a positive test charge would tend to move if placed anywhere in the field.* **Figure 5.11** shows the lines of force around (a) a fixed positive charge and (b) a fixed negative charge. **Figure 5.12** shows the lines of force near (a) two oppositely charged bodies and (b) two similarly charged bodies (both positive).

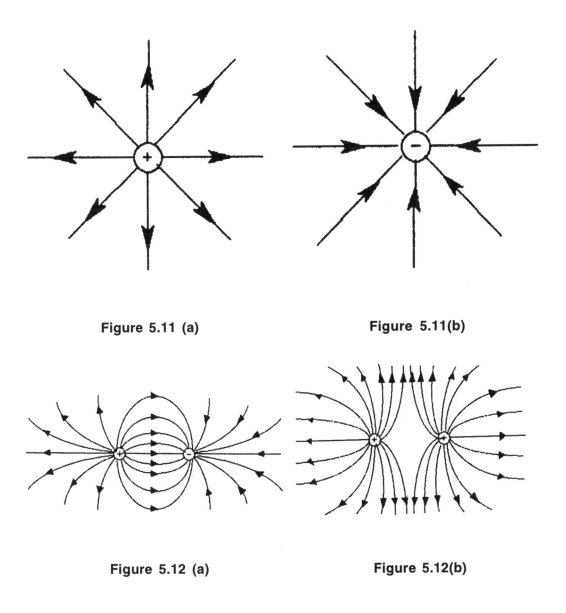

Figure 5.11 (a)   **Figure 5.11(b)**

Figure 5.12 (a)   **Figure 5.12(b)**

Figure 5.13 shows photographs of electric field patterns in a number of situations. An insulating liquid was placed in the dish with the various charged objects, and celery seed was dispersed in the liquid. The celery seed lines itself up in the electric field in such a way that it gives a visual representation of the shape of the electric field. Notice that the lines of force originate on the positively charged objects and terminate on negatively charged objects. The lines do not cross each other, and they always meet the surfaces of the objects at right angles. If the lines are spreading out, this means the field is getting weaker. The 'line density' indicates relative strength of the field in different regions of the field.

Electric Field Patterns Formed by Celery Seeds

**(a) Lines of force around a
single charged rod**

**(b) Lines of force around two
oppositely charged rods**

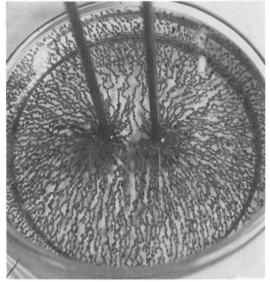

**(c) Lines of force between
two like-charged rods**

**(d) Lines of force between two
oppositely charged plates**

Figure 5.13

Special Activity

Obtain some very fine sawdust from a woodwork shop. You can make electric field lines 'visible' using fine sawdust, just the way you can make magnetic field lines 'visible' using iron filings.

On a dry day (low humidity) rub a cylindrical ebonite rod with fur, to charge the rod negatively. Dip the charged rod into a dish of fine sawdust. The small pieces of dust will tend to line up along lines of force, allowing you to see the 'shape' of the electric field around the rod. Charge a second ebonite rod. Dip it into the sawdust and bring it close and parallel to the first charged rod. Sketch the lines of force as seen from one end of the rods. The two rods have the same charge (negative), so they will repel each other.

Charge an acetate strip positively by rubbing it with cotton. Dip it into the sawdust and examine the electric field 'shape' around a flat piece of acetate. Dip another charged acetate strip into the sawdust and hold the two like-charged strips parallel with one another. Note the shape of the field between the two like-charged flat surfaces.

Charge a vinyl plastic strip negatively by rubbing it with fur or wool. Dip it in sawdust. Bring it close and parallel to (a) another negatively charged vinyl strip and (b) a positively charged acetate strip. Sketch the shapes of the electric fields between (a) two like-charged, parallel flat surfaces and (b) two oppositely charged, parallel flat surfaces.

In an **oscilloscope**, a beam of electrons is made to pass between two parallel plates which are oppositely charged. Sketch what the electric field between the plates would look like.

Electric Field and Voltage

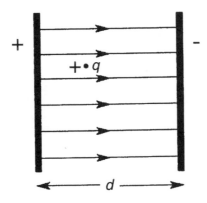

Figure 5.14

Consider a test charge q located between two oppositely charged plates a distance d apart. (**Figure 5.14**) This test charge will experience the same electric force F anywhere between the two plates, because the electric field E is the same anywhere between the two large parallel plates. (See the crude 'proof' on the next page.)

Recall that the **electric field strength** (sometimes called **electric field intensity**) is the force per unit charge. ($E = \dfrac{F}{Q}$.) Imagine that the positive test charge q is moved from the negatively charged plate to the positively charged plate, through distance d. This will require that an amount of work W be done, given by $W = Fd$. The charge q will gain **electrical potential energy**, E_p, equal to Fd.

The change in potential energy per unit of charge as it moves between two points is called the **potential difference** *or the* **voltage** *between the two points.* The symbol for potential difference or voltage is V.

Now since $V = \dfrac{Fd}{q}$, and $E = \dfrac{F}{q}$, then $V = \dfrac{F}{q} d = E d.$

Therefore the electric field strength can be calculated as follows:

$$E = \frac{V}{d} \cdot$$

Since **potential difference (voltage)** has the dimensions of 'energy per unit charge', it could be measured in J/C. However, the **volt (V)** is the standard unit for measuring voltage. This means that electric field strength can be expressed in **volts per metre (V/m)** as well as in **newtons per coulomb (N/C)**. Dimensionally, they are the same thing.

Note that $1\,\dfrac{V}{m} = 1\,\dfrac{J/C}{m} = 1\,\dfrac{Nm/C}{m} = 1\,\dfrac{N}{C} \cdot$

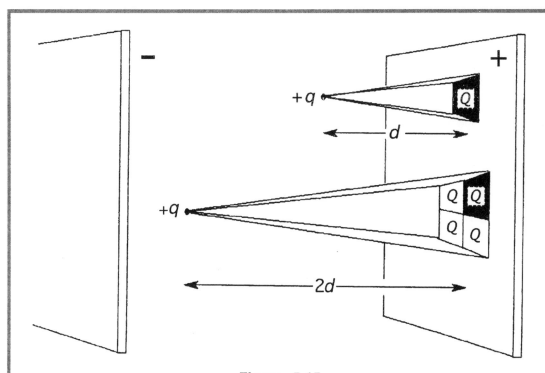

Figure 5.15

The Force Field Near a Large, Uniformly Charged Flat Surface Is Constant.

Consider a small test charge q, which is a distance d from a large, flat plate, over which a charge is uniformly distributed. Looking toward the large plate from q through an imaginary rectangular 'cone', one can 'see' an area of the large plane, with an amount of charge Q on it.

The test charge q is now moved twice as far away to distance $2d$. What happens to the electric force on the test charge?

Looking at the plane again from twice the distance through the same imaginary 'cone', one would 'see' four times the area on the plane, and therefore four times the charge $(4Q)$.

In the first instance, the force on q was $F = k\dfrac{Qq}{d^2}$. *(Coulomb's Law)*

At the new position twice as far away, $F = k\dfrac{(4Q)q}{(2d)^2} = k\dfrac{Qq}{d^2}$.

Since the **force** on test charge q has not changed, neither has the **electric field strength** F/q! It can be shown that the electric field strength between two large parallel plane surfaces is *uniform anywhere between the plates.* (The field near the edges is not uniform.)

Examples

1. A downward force of 6.4 x 10^{-3} N acts on a charge of +3.2 μC. What is the magnitude and direction of the electric field at the location of the charge?

Solution: $E = \dfrac{F}{Q} = \dfrac{(6.4 \text{ x } 10^{-3} \text{ N})}{(3.2 \text{ x } 10^{-6} \text{ C})} = 2.0 \text{ x } 10^3$ N/C.

Since the charge is positive and it is being pushed downward, the direction of the field must be **down.**

2. Two oppositely charged plates are separated by a distance of 2.4 mm. What voltage must be applied to them to create an electric field of 2.0 x 10^4 N/C?

Solution: $E = \dfrac{V}{d}$, therefore

$V = Ed = $ (2.0 x 10^4 N/C) (2.4 x 10^{-3} m) = 4.8 x 10^1 Nm/C = 48 J/C = 48 V.

3. An electron has a mass of 9.1 x 10^{-31} kg and a charge of 1.6 x 10^{-19} C. Placed in an electric field of 1.0 x 10^3 V/m, what is its acceleration?

Solution: $E = \dfrac{F}{Q}$, therefore

$F = EQ = $ (1.0 x 10^3 N/C) (1.6 x 10^{-19} C) = 1.6 x 10^{-16} N.

$a = \dfrac{F}{m} = \dfrac{(1.6 \text{ x } 10^{-16} \text{ N})}{(9.1 \text{ x } 10^{-31} \text{ kg})} = $ 1.8 x 10^{14} m/s^2.

Compare this acceleration with the acceleration due to gravity at the earth's surface, which is 9.8 m/s^2!

Exercises

1. An electron carries a charge of − 1.6 x 10^{-19} C. If a force of 3.2 x 10^{-17} N causes the electron to move upward, what is the magnitude and direction of the electric field?

2. A proton has a charge of +1.6 x 10^{-19} C. If it is in an electric field of strength 9.00 x 10^2 N/C, what force acts on the proton?

3. What is the magnitude and direction of the electric field at a distance of 0.180 m from a fixed charge of 3.60 x 10^{-2} C?

4. A +36 μC charge is 0.80 m away from a +108 μC charge. What is the magnitude and direction of the electric field at a point midway between the two charges?

5. A proton has a mass of 1.67 x 10^{-27} kg. At what rate will it accelerate in an electric field of strength 1.0 x 10^3 N/C?

6. A nichrome wire 30.0 cm long is connected to the terminals of a 1.5 V dry cell. What is the magnitude and direction (relative to the terminals) of the electric field inside the wire?

7. A pair of deflecting plates in an oscilloscope have a voltage of 120 V applied to them. They are separated by a distance of 2.4 mm.

(a) What is the strength of the electric field between the plates?

(b) At what rate will an electron (mass 9.1 x 10^{-31} kg) accelerate at the instant it enters the space between the plates? (The electron is initially moving in a direction perpendicular to the field lines.)

8. A tiny plastic sphere of mass 1.0 x 10^{-15} kg is held suspended between two charged plates by balancing the downward gravitational force with an upward electrical force of equal magnitude.

(a) What is the magnitude of the electrical force acting on the sphere?

(b) If the voltage applied to the plates is 30.0 V, and the plates are separated by a distance of 1.47 mm, what is the amount of excess charge on the sphere?

(c) If the top plate is positively charged, is the charge on the **sphere** positive or negative?

(d) What type of elementary charged particles are on the sphere, and how many of these excess elementary charged particles are there on the sphere?

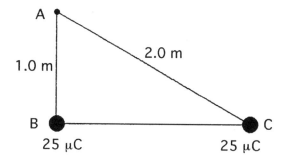

9. What is the resultant electric field strength **E** at point **A** in **Figure 5.16**? Give both the magnitude and the direction.

Figure 5.16

5.4 Electric Fields in a Cathode Ray Tube

A cathode ray tube (CRT) is a special kind of vacuum tube in which a beam of electrons is produced, accelerated, focussed, deflected and displayed (on a fluorescent screen). CRT's are used in oscilloscopes, television sets, radar and computer display terminals. In *Investigation 5-2* you will use a miniature oscilloscope to observe the effect of electric fields on beams of electrons.

How the Beam of Electrons Is Obtained

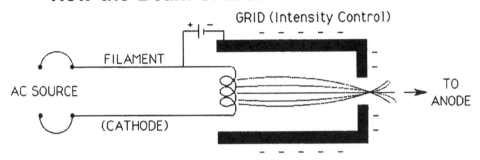

Figure 5.17 The 'Electron Gun'

A small alternating voltage is applied to the **filament** in the **'electron gun'** in **Figure 5.17**, and the resulting current heats the filament to incandescence. When the filament is incandescent, electrons 'boil off' and form a 'charge cloud' around it.

In front of the filament is an electrode called the **grid.** The grid is negatively charged, so electrons are repelled from it. The grid makes electrons converge to a focus point as they pass through a hole in the grid. This 'cross-over' point acts as a point source of electrons. Electrons stream from the point source outward (accelerated by an electric field applied between the grid and the **anode**.) The anode is a positively charged electrode.

The voltage applied to the grid can be changed, allowing more or fewer electrons through the opening. Since this will vary the **intensity** of the beam, which determines the brightness of the beam as seen on the CRT screen, the grid control is called the **intensity control.**

How the Beam Is Focussed and Accelerated

Electrons leaving the grid opening are diverging. A **focussing anode (A_1)** acts as an electronic 'lens', shaping the beam so that when it reaches the screen it will appear as a tiny spot. The **accelerating anode (A_2)** is what accelerates the electrons horizontally. (See **Figure 5.18**) The potential difference (voltage) between the filament and the accelerating anode will be quite high — typically 500 V, 750 V or 1000 V in a classroom model. The high voltage between the filament of the electron gun and the accelerating anode creates the electric field that accelerates the electrons.

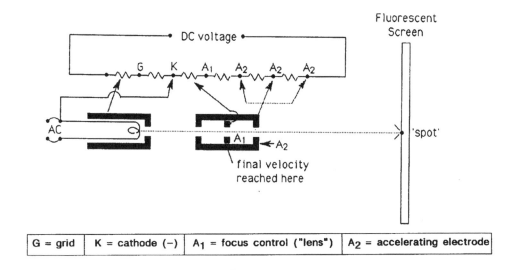

| G = grid | K = cathode (−) | A_1 = focus control ("lens") | A_2 = accelerating electrode |

Figure 5.18

Because of the electric field E, work is done on the electrons, and their electrical potential energy is changed into kinetic energy E_k. The accelerating voltage V_a is a measure of the change in electrical potential energy per unit charge. If the potential energy is changed into kinetic energy of the electrons, then,

$$Va = \frac{E_k}{q} = \frac{\frac{1}{2}mv^2}{q},$$

where V_a is the accelerating voltage (between A_2 and the filament);
        m is the mass of one electron (9.11×10^{-31} kg);
        v is the maximum speed reached by each electron; and
        q is the charge on one electron (1.60×10^{-19} C).

How the Beam Is Deflected

Once the beam is accelerated by V_a and 'up to speed' v, it is made to pass between two mutually perpendicular pairs of deflecting plates. One pair is arranged to deflect the beam in the 'Y' direction. This pair of plates is labelled Y_1 and Y_2. The other pair of plates is arranged to deflect the electron beam in the 'X' direction. These plates are labelled X_1 and X_2. See **Figure 5.19.**

Notice that plates X_1 and X_2 have a small DC voltage, V_δ, applied to them. Both Y_1 and Y_2 are connected to A_2, but only one of the X-plates is connected to A_2. This means that both Y plates are at the same voltage as A_2, so an electron beam passing through the Y-plates 'sees' no difference in potential, and will not be deflected by the Y-plates. However, one of the X-plates does have a slightly different potential than the other X-plate because of the **deflecting voltage** V_δ (δ = 'delta') applied to the X-plates.

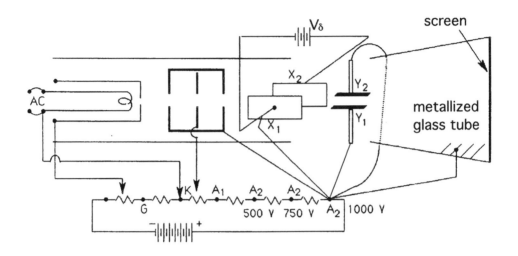

Figure 5.19 Cathode Ray Tube (CRT) with Power Supply (Simplified)

How Does the Amount of Deflection Depend on *E?*

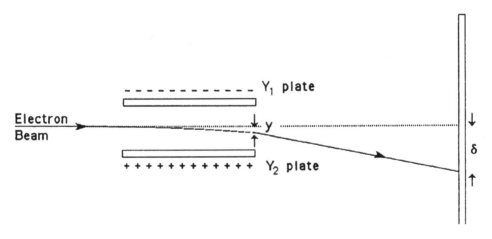

Figure 5.20

Figure 5.20 shows a beam of electrons moving with speed *v* through a pair of parallel deflecting plates. Remember that the electric field between parallel plates is constant anywhere between the plates, therefore the electric force is also constant. Experiencing a constant unbalanced force, the electrons will accelerate at a rate, *a*, (downward in **Figure 5.20**). While passing through the plates in time *t,* the downward acceleration makes the beam 'fall' through displacement *y*. The displacement of the electron beam while it is between the plates is given by

$$y = \frac{1}{2} \, at^2,$$

but since
$$a = \frac{F}{m},$$

therefore
$$y = \frac{1}{2}\frac{F}{m}t^2.$$

Since the electric field $\quad E = \frac{F}{q}$, therefore $F = Eq$, and so

$$y = \frac{1}{2}\frac{Eq}{m}t^2.$$

For a given beam of electrons accelerated by a given accelerating voltage, $\frac{1}{2}$, q, m and t will remain **constant**, and it can be assumed that

$$y = \textbf{constant}\ E, \text{ or that}$$

$$y \propto E.$$

Also, since $E = V_\delta/d$ where d is the distance between the deflecting plates and V_δ is the deflecting voltage, therefore the deflection y is proportional to the deflecting voltage V_δ.

$$y \propto V_\delta.$$

Note: The deflection that you measure on the screen is **not** y. Once the beam leaves the deflecting plates the electrons travel on in a straight line to the fluorescent screen. On the screen, you see the deflection δ. Fortunately, it can be shown that the **screen deflection** δ *is directly proportional to* the **true deflection** y within the plates.*

Since δ is proportional to y and y is proportional to V_δ, therefore

$$\delta \propto V_\delta.$$

This means that the deflection of the beam, as measured on the screen, is a measure of the voltage applied to the deflecting plates. The cathode ray tube (CRT) can therefore be used as a **voltmeter.**

---

* See **Enrichment Material** on the next page.

Showing that δ is proportional to Y:

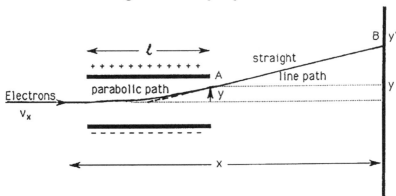

Figure 5.21

Consider an electron entering the deflecting plates with horizontal speed v_x. The electron travels a distance $x = \ell$, in a time t. Time is related to distance and speed as follows: $t = x/v_x$, therefore the time the electron spends between the two plates is ℓ/v_x.

Now consider the vertical deflection of the electron as it passes through the deflecting plates. Since the electric field and therefore the force on the electron is uniform, therefore the acceleration is uniform, and $y = \frac{1}{2}at^2 = \frac{1}{2}a[x^2/v_x^2]$. This is the equation for a *parabola.* To find the *slope* of the parabola at the instant the electron reaches **A** (where the deflecting plates end), one must use calculus.

$$\frac{dy}{dx} = 2(\frac{1}{2}a)\frac{x}{v_x^2} = \frac{ax}{v_x^2} = \frac{a\ell}{v_x^2}.$$

Once the electron leaves **A**, it travels in a straight line to **B**, so the slope of its path remains the same as it was at **A**. For **AB**, the slope is

$$\frac{y' - \frac{1}{2}a\ell^2/v_x^2}{x - \ell} = \frac{a\ell}{v_x^2}.$$

So,
$$y' - \tfrac{1}{2}a\ell^2/v_x^2 = a\ell(x-\ell)/v_x^2.$$

Now, when $y' = 0$, $-\tfrac{1}{2}\ell = (x - \ell)$, and $x = \tfrac{1}{2}\ell$.

This means that the straight line path of the electron after it leaves the plates at **A** can be extrapolated back to the exact centre of the plates. This creates two similar triangles, with heights y and y'. The deflection you actually see on the screen is y', and $y' = \delta$. In **Figure 5.21**, the deflection within the plates is y. Similar triangles tell us that $\delta \propto y$!

Investigation 5-2
Deflecting a Beam of Electrons Using an Electric Field

Part 1

Purpose: How does the deflection of a beam of electrons of given speed depend on the *deflecting voltage* applied to the deflecting plates through which the beam passes?

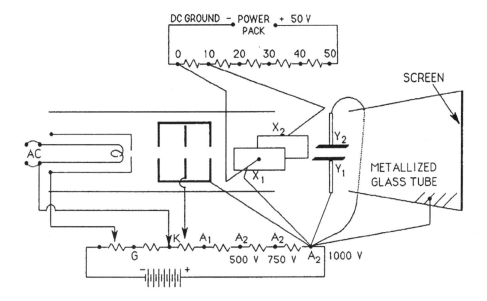

Figure 5.22

Procedure

1. A varying deflection voltage, V_δ, will be applied to the X-plates. Connect X_1, Y_1, and Y_2 to the common binding post at A_2. Use an accelerating voltage V_a of 500 V throughout all of Part 1.

2. To vary the deflecting voltage V_δ, make the following apparatus using your high voltage DC power supply (**Figure 5.23**):

   (a) Connect a wire lead from the DC ground binding post to one end of a string of five identical 10 kΩ resistors. (**Figure 5.23**)
   (b) Connect a second wire lead from the +50 V binding post of the power supply to the other end of the string of resistors.
   (c) Connect a lead from X_1 to the common ground (0 V) side of the resistors. The lead from X_2 can now be connected to any point in the string of resistors, so that you can obtain voltages of 0 V, 10 V, 20 V, 30 V, 40 V or 50 V.

(d) Use a voltmeter to check the exact values obtained at each of the terminals (resistor junctions), and to confirm that this arrangement does give a series of voltages which are multiples of one another.

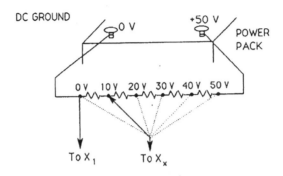

Figure 5.23

3. Put a piece of masking tape on the screen of the CRT so that you can mark the position of the beam when different deflecting voltages are applied. Mark the location of the beam for each of the voltages you use (0 V, 10 V, 20 V, 30 V, 40 V and 50 V if the power supply voltage is 'true').

4. Measure the deflection, δ , in mm and enter the values of V_δ and δ in a suitable table of data.

5. Prepare a graph of δ vs V_δ.

Concluding Questions

1. How does the deflection δ of the electron beam depend on the deflecting voltage V_δ? Write an equation for your graph, including the slope in appropriate units.

2. How does the deflection depend on the electric field strength between the plates? How does your answer follow from the results of this experiment? (Remember how E and V_δ are related.)

Part 2

Purpose: How does the deflection of the beam of electrons depend on accelerating voltage, if a constant deflecting voltage is used?

Instructor Note: See your CRT manual if these instructions for varying V_a do not apply to the model your students have.

Procedure

1. Locate the 'zero' position of the beam as you did in Part 1, and mark it on a fresh piece of masking tape attached to the screen. In Part 1, you used an accelerating voltage V_a of 500 V and varied the deflecting voltage. This time leave the deflecting voltage at a set value such as 50 V throughout all of Part 2. (You will use zero deflecting voltage to locate the 'zero' position, of course.)

2. Mark the position of the electron beam on the screen when the accelerating voltage is 500V. **Turn off the power supply.** Reset the accelerating voltage at 750 V. Turn on the CRT again, re-focus if necessary, and measure the new deflection when V_a = 750 V.

3. **Turn off the power supply.** Change V_a to 1000 V. Turn on the CRT again, re-focus and measure δ.

4. Before analyzing your results, use a voltmeter to check the actual voltages at the three A_2 terminals. Measure the voltage between the filament and each of the A_2 terminals. These are more reliable values to use for V_a than what you read on the apparatus. The labelled values are only approximate voltages.

5. Tabulate your results, then plot a graph of deflection, δ , (y-axis) vs accelerating voltage, V_a (X-axis).

6. Make an educated guess at the **power law relationship** that exists between δ and V_a , and plot a graph that will tell you what the value of n is in $\delta = k \cdot V_a{}^n$.

7. Derive an expression for the deflection within the plates in terms of V_a . Keep in mind that y is proportional to δ. Start with the fact that the deflection within the plates is $y = \dfrac{1}{2} a t^2$.

   Use the fact that the time spent within the plates will be $\dfrac{\ell}{v_x}$.

   The acceleration of the electrons is $a = \dfrac{F}{m} = \dfrac{Eq}{m}$.

   Also, the accelerating voltage $V_a = \dfrac{1}{2} \dfrac{m v_x{}^2}{q}$.

   According to your derivation, how does y (and therefore δ) vary with V_a?

Concluding Questions

1. Write a simple equation relating deflection (δ) and accelerating voltage (V_a). Include a numerical value for the constant of proportionality (slope).

2. If V_a was doubled, what would happen to δ if V_δ was kept the same?

3. If V_δ was doubled and V_a remained the same, what would happen to δ?

4. If **both** V_a and V_δ were doubled, what would happen to δ?

Challenge

What happens if you apply a low (6.3 V) alternating voltage to the X-plates of your CRT? What if you apply AC voltage to the Y-plates and the X-plates simultaneously? Read up on Lissajous' Figures in an electronics book. Use a full-size oscilloscope to display them.

Exercises

1. In a CRT, a voltage of 1.0×10^3 V accelerates electrons from rest to a high speed. Assuming all the work done by the electric field is used to give the electrons kinetic energy $\frac{1}{2}\ mv^2$, what speed do the electrons reach? (The charge on an electron is 1.6×10^{-19} C and the mass of one electron is 9.1×10^{-31} kg.) What fraction of the speed of light ($c = 3.0 \times 10^8$ m/s) is this?

2. If an accelerating voltage of 1.0×10^3 V was used to accelerate protons ($m = 1.67 \times 10^{-27}$ kg), what speed would they reach?

3. A CRT is used with an accelerating voltage of 750 V to accelerate electrons before they pass through deflecting plates, to which a deflecting voltage of 50.0 V is applied.

   (a) What speed do the electrons reach?

   (b) When the electrons travel through the deflecting plates, which are separated by a distance of 2.0 cm, what is the electric field strength between the plates?

   (c) What is the force that will deflect electrons as they pass through the plates?

   (d) At what rate will the electrons accelerate as they pass through the plates?

   (e) The plates have a length of 5.0 cm. For what length of time will the electrons be between the plates?

   (f) What is the deflection in a Y-direction of the electrons as they pass through the plates?

   (g) If the screen is 0.20 m beyond the end of the deflecting plates, what deflection (δ) will you see on the screen?

4. In a CRT, the deflection on the screen is 2.4 cm when the accelerating voltage is 480 V, and the deflecting voltage is 36 V. What deflection (δ) will you see on the screen if the accelerating voltage is 960 V and the deflecting voltage is 18V?

5.5 Electric Potential

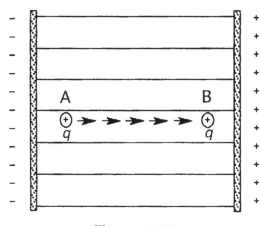

Figure 5.24

The positive test charge q in **Figure 5.24** has **electrical potential energy** E_{pA} at position **A**. It will have more electrical potential energy if it is moved toward the positive plate to position **B**, because **work** must be done to move the positive charge against the repulsive force that exists between two like-charged bodies. At position **B**, the electrical potential energy is E_{pB}.

The **electric potential** (V) at a given point in the electric field is defined as the *potential energy per unit charge.*

For the charge at **A**, $V_A = \dfrac{E_{pA}}{q}$.

When the charge is moved to **B**, $V_B = \dfrac{E_{pB}}{q}$.

The *difference in potential energy per unit charge* between two points **A** and **B** is called the **potential difference,** V_{AB}.

$$V_{AB} = V_B - V_A$$

In **Figure 5.24**, the **potential difference** between points **A** and **B** is equal to the **work done** moving charge q from **A** to **B**. Potential difference could be measured in **joules per coulomb (J/C)**, but this unit is called a **volt (V)**.

Since $V_{AB} = \dfrac{W_{AB}}{q}$, $1\,V = 1\dfrac{J}{C}$.

Potential difference is usually just called **voltage**.

The **potential difference** (V) between two points is defined as *the amount of work required to move a unit of positive charge from the point that is at a lower potential to the point that is at the higher potential* (relative to some arbitrary reference point, such as the positive plate in **Figure 5.24**).

Example

How much work is needed to move 1.0×10^{-6} C of positive charge between two points where the potential difference (voltage) is 12.0 V?

Solution: $V = \dfrac{W}{q}$, therefore $W = Vq = (12.0\,\dfrac{J}{C})(1.0 \times 10^{-6}\,C) = 1.2 \times 10^{-5}\,J$.

Electron Volt

On an atomic scale, the **joule** is a very, very large amount of energy. A smaller unit of energy, the **electron volt (eV)** is used when solving problems about electric potential in situations on the atomic or nuclear scale.

One **electron volt** is defined as the amount of energy gained by one electron when it moves through a potential difference of 1.0 V.

Since the charge on one electron is only 1.6×10^{-19} C, and $W = V q$, one electron volt is only **1.6×10^{-19} J.**

$$1\ eV\ =\ 1.6 \times 10^{-19}\ J$$

Example

If a 750 V CRT is used to accelerate electrons, how much kinetic energy will the electrons gain?

Solution:

Assuming all the work done by the electric field is converted to kinetic energy of the electrons,

$$E_k = W = V q = (750\ V)(1\ e) = 750\ eV.$$

To convert this to joules: $750\ eV = (750\ eV)(1.6 \times 10^{-19}\ J/eV) = 1.2 \times 10^{-16}\ J$.

5.6 Electric Potential of Single Point Charges

The *force* between two point charges Q_1 and Q_2 is given by Coulomb's Law,

$$F = k\frac{Q_1Q_2}{R^2} .$$

The *potential energy* of charge Q_2 at a distance R from Q_1 is found by taking the area under the F vs R graph between R and infinity. (Compare with Gravitational Potential Energy). The result is:

$$E_p = k\frac{Q_1Q_2}{R} .$$

The **electric potential** V, which is the **potential energy per unit charge** relative to infinity, is then

$$V = \frac{E_p}{Q_2} = k\frac{Q_1}{R} .$$

Both electrical potential energy and electric potential are taken to be zero at infinity.

Examples

1. What is the electric potential energy, relative to infinity, of an electron in a hydrogen atom if the electron is 5.0×10^{-11} m from the proton?

    Solution:

    $$E_p = k\frac{Q_1Q_2}{R} = \frac{(9.0 \times 10^9 \text{ Nm}^2/\text{C}^2)\ (+1.6 \times 10^{-19} \text{ C})\ (-1.6 \times 10^{-19} \text{ C})}{(5.0 \times 10^{-11} \text{ m})}$$

    $$E_p = -4.6 \times 10^{-18} \text{ J}.$$

    The potential energy is negative because of the attractive force between the electron and the proton. If you wanted to ionize the hydrogen atom (remove its electron 'to infinity') you would need $+4.6 \times 10^{-18}$ J of energy to do it!

2. How much work is needed to bring a point charge of 1.0×10^{-6} C from infinity to a point that is 3.0 m away from a positive point charge of 1.0×10^{-4} C?

    Solution: E_p at infinity is zero.

    $$\text{Work done } W = E_{pB} - E_{pA} = k\frac{Q_1Q_2}{R_B} - 0$$

    $$W = \frac{(9.0 \times 10^9 \text{ Nm}^2/\text{C}^2)\ (1.0 \times 10^{-6} \text{ C})\ (1.0 \times 10^{-4} \text{ C})}{3.0 \text{ m}} = 0.30 \text{ J}.$$

Exercises

1. How much work is needed to bring a + 5.0 μC point charge from infinity to a point 2.0 m away from a + 25 μC charge?

2. What is the electric potential energy of an electron (relative to infinity) when it is 7.5 x 10^{-11} m away from a proton?

3. How much potential energy would an electron in a hydrogen atom lose if it fell toward the nucleus from a distance of 7.5 x 10^{-11} m to a distance of 5.0 x 10^{-11} m?

4. How much work is done moving a proton from infinity to a distance of 1.0 x 10^{-11} m from another proton?

5. What is the electric potential relative to infinity at a distance of 0.90 m from a point charge of (a) + 50 μC?   (b) – 50 μC?

Chapter Review Questions

1. Two equal charges Q are separated by a distance R. The repulsive force between them is F.

   (a) What will the force be if both charges are doubled?
   (b) What will the force be if the charges remain Q but the distance between them is reduced to $\frac{1}{2}$ R?
   (c) What will the force be if charges are both increased to $4Q$ and the distance between them is reduced to $\frac{1}{4}$ R?

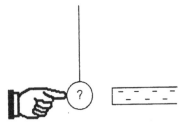

2. A negatively charged rod is brought near a suspended metal sphere. The sphere is 'grounded' by touching it with a finger. The finger and the rod are now removed. What charge will be on the sphere, positive or negative? Describe what happens.

Figure 5.25

3. (a) A tiny plastic sphere is midway between two metal plates, which are 0.050 m apart. When a battery is connected to the plates, the sphere experiences an electric force of 1.2 x 10^{-3} N. How much work is needed to move the charged sphere from one plate to the other?

   (b) If the charge on the sphere is 0.20 μC, what is the battery voltage?

4. What is the repulsive force between two alpha particles which are 1.0 mm apart? (An alpha particle carries an excess of two elementary positive charges, since an alpha particle is a helium ion, He^{2+}.)

5. How far apart are two protons if they repel each other with a force of 1.0 mN?

6. If a body with a charge of 1.0×10^{-3} C experiences a force of 1.0 N in an electric field, what is the electric field strength?

7. A proton is placed in an electric field of strength 5.0×10^3 N/C. At what rate will it accelerate? (proton mass $= 1.67 \times 10^{-27}$ kg; proton charge $= 1.6 \times 10^{-19}$ C)

8. What is the magnitude and direction of the electric field strength midway between a 75 µC charge and a – 25 µC charge, if the charges are 2.0 m apart?

9. The electric field strength between two plates that are 3.0 cm apart is 3.0×10^3 N/C. What is the voltage between the plates?

10. The deflecting voltage applied to the plates in a CRT is 50.0 V. The plates are 1.2 cm apart.

    (a) What is the electric field strength between the plates?

    (b) What force will the field exert on an electron passing between the plates?

    (c) At what rate and in what direction will the electron accelerate? (electron mass $= 9.1 \times 10^{-31}$ kg)

11. An accelerating voltage of 750 V produces a screen deflection of 4.2 cm on a CRT. If the deflecting voltage is kept constant but the accelerating voltage is increased to 1000 V, what will the deflection become?

12. When the accelerating voltage in a CRT is 500 V and the deflecting voltage is 15 V, the beam deflection is 1.2 cm on the screen. If the accelerating voltage is changed to 750 V and the deflecting voltage is changed to 45 V, what will the deflection be?

13. How much work must be done to move a positive charge of +2.0 µC from infinity to a point 1.2 m away from a positive point charge of $+3.0 \times 10^3$ µC?

14. What is the electric potential relative to infinity at a distance of 10^{-11} m from a proton?

15. Two point charges of + 8.0 µC are separated by a distance of 1.0 m. If the force between them is F, what will the force be if 4.0 µC are removed from one point charge and transferred to the other point charge?

Brain Busters

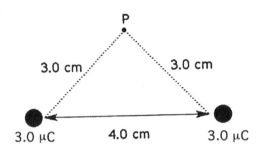

16. Two very small spheres each have a charge of 3.0 µC. They are 4.0 cm apart. What is the potential relative to infinity at point P? P is 3.0 cm from both of the charged spheres.

Figure 5.26

17. Protons are accelerated through a potential difference of 6.0 MV (megavolts) and then make head-on collisions with atomic nuclei with a charge of + 82 elementary charges. What is the closest distance of approach between the protons and the nuclei? Assume the nuclei are stationary.

18. How much work must be done to bring three protons from infinity to a distance of 1.0×10^{-11} m from one another?

Sawdust shows the shape of the electric field around the author's fingers. He is touching the charged dome of an electrostatic generator with the other hand.

Test Yourself!

Multiple Choice

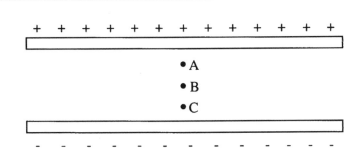

1. What is the *direction* of the electric field at **B**, which is located between a pair of oppositely charged plates?

   A. ↑   B. →   C. ←   D. ↓

2. The electric field strength between the plates is
   A. strongest at A, weakest at B.
   B. strongest at B.
   C. strongest at C, weakest at A.
   D. strongest at A and C, weakest at B.
   E. the same at A, B and C.

• P

(+)
Q_1

(−)
Q_2

3. What is the direction of the electric field at **P** due to point charges Q_1 and Q_2?

   A. ↑   B. →   C. ←   D. ↓

4. Electric field strength can be measured in
   A. N/A.
   B. J/C.
   C. N/A·m.
   D. N/kg.
   E. V/m.

5. The electric field strength at a distance of 1.0 m from a point charge is
   4.0×10^4 N/C. What will the electric field strength be at a distance of 2.0 m
   from the same point charge?

   A. 1.0×10^4 N/C
   B. 2.0×10^4 N/C
   C. 4.0×10^4 N/C
   D. 8.0×10^4 N/C
   E. 16×10^4 N/C

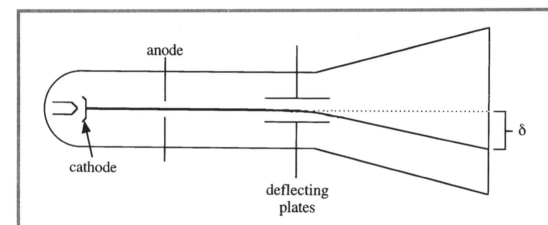

anode

cathode

deflecting
plates

δ

6. A beam of electrons in a cathode ray tube is accelerated toward the anode by an accelerating
   voltage of 100 V. After passing through the anode, the electrons are deflected as they pass
   through two oppositely charged parallel deflecting plates. On the screen, the observed
   deflection is δ. If the accelerating voltage is increased to 400 V, what deflection will be
   observed on the screen?

         A. δ B. ¼ δ C. ½ δ D. 2 δ E. 4 δ

7. An atom carrying an excess charge of 1.60×10^{-19} C is accelerated from rest by a potential
   difference of 750 V. It reaches a peak speed of 8.50×10^4 m/s. What is the mass of the atom?

   A. 1.67×10^{-27} kg
   B. 3.32×10^{-26} kg
   C. 4.84×10^{-20} kg
   D. 9.11×10^{-31} kg

8. What increase in electrical potential energy occurs when an alpha particle with a charge of
   3.2×10^{-19} C is brought from infinity to a distance of 5.0×10^{-10} m of a stationary charge of
   7.5×10^{-18} C?

   A. 4.3×10^{-17} J
   B. 8.6×10^{-8} J
   C. 5.8 J
   D. 1.4×10^2 J

Open-Ended Questions

9. Calculate the electrostatic force of attraction between a positive charge of 8.0×10^{-6} C and a negative charge of 5.0×10^{-6} C, when they are 0.30 m apart.

10. When a charged object is accelerated through a potential difference of 500 V, its kinetic energy increases from 2.0×10^{-5} J to 6.0×10^{-5} J. What is the magnitude of the charge on the object?

11. How fast will an electron be moving if it is accelerated from rest, in a vacuum, through a potential difference of 200 V?

12. Two parallel plates are 4.0 mm apart. If the potential difference between them is 200 V, what is the magnitude of the electric field strength between the plates?

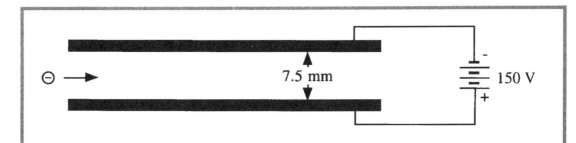

13. An electron enters the space between two oppositely charged, parallel plates. What is the magnitude and direction of the electrostatic force that acts on the electron when it is between the two plates?

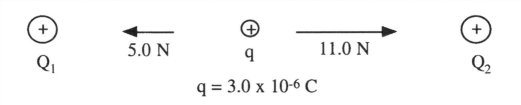

14. The 3.0×10^{-6} C charge, q, experiences opposing forces exerted by Q_1 and Q_2 of 5.0 N and 11.0 N respectively. What is the magnitude and direction of the electric field strength at the location of q?

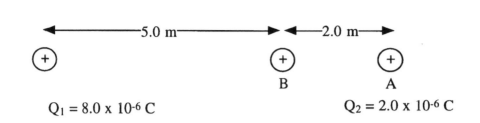

$Q_1 = 8.0 \times 10^{-6}$ C

$Q_2 = 2.0 \times 10^{-6}$ C

15. How much work must be done to move charge $Q_2 = 2.0 \times 10^6$ C from A to B? The other charged object has a charge $Q_1 = 8.0 \times 10^6$ C.

16. What is the electric potential, relative to infinity, of an electron located 5.3×10^{-11} m from the proton in a hydrogen atom?

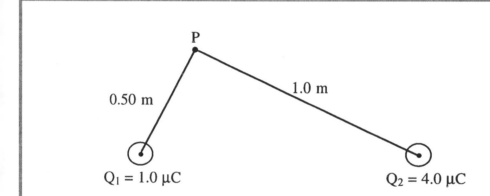

17. What is the electric potential at **P** due to charges Q_1 and Q_2?

Chapter 6   Resistor Circuits

6.1 Current Events in History

Until 200 years ago, the idea that one could produce a steady current of electricity and put it to use was nonexistent. The discovery of a way to produce a flow of electric charges was, in fact, accidental. In the year 1780, at the University of Bologna, Italian professor of anatomy **Luigi Galvani (1737-1798)** was dissecting a frog. First he noticed that when a nearby static electricity generator made a spark, the frog's legs would jump as its muscles contracted, *if a metal knife was touching the frog's nerves!* Galvani proceeded to look for the conditions that caused this behaviour.* In the course of his investigations, Galvani discovered that if two different metal objects (such as a brass hook and an iron support) touched each other, while also touching the frog's exposed flesh, the same contractions of the frog's legs were observed. Galvani thought that the source of the electricity was in the frog itself, and he called the phenomenon 'animal electricity'.

Another scientist, physics professor **Alessandro Volta (1745-1827)**, of the University of Pavia, set about to test Galvani's 'animal electricity' theory for himself. Before long, Volta discovered that the source of the electricity was in the contact of two different metals. The animal (frog) was incidental. Any two different metals, if they are immersed in a conducting solution (acid, base or salt), will produce an electric current. Volta was able to show that some pairs of metals worked better than others. Of course, there were no ammeters or voltmeters to compare currents and voltages in those days. (One way that Volta compared currents was to observe the response of muscle tissue of dead frogs.)

Volta actually invented the first practical electric battery. Zinc and silver disks, separated by paper pads soaked with salt water, acted as electric cells. Stacked one on top of another, these cells became a 'battery' which yielded more current than a single cell.

6.2 Cells and Batteries

There are many types of electric cell in existence today. Usually when you purchase a 'battery' in a store, you are actually buying a single **cell.** Strictly speaking, a battery is two or more cells connected together. Nine-volt batteries used in transistor radios, tape recorders, calculators and smoke alarms are true 'batteries'. If you open up a discarded 9 V battery, you will see six small 1.5 V cells connected together, one after the other (in series).

---

*Neither Galvani nor Volta explained this observation. (There is no truth to the rumour that the frog's leg jumped because 1780 was a 'leap year'.) Many years later it was learned that **radio waves** generated by the sparking generator induced a current in the metal scalpel that was penetrating the frog, even though the scalpel was some distance from the generator!

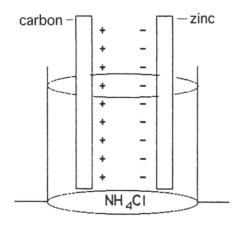

carbon — || — zinc

NH$_4$Cl

Figure 6.1

Figure 6.1 shows one type of **voltaic cell** (after Volta). The two rods (**electrodes**) are made of carbon and zinc, as in the traditional **'dry cell'**, but they are immersed in a solution of ammonium chloride (NH$_4$Cl). In a real dry cell, a paste containing NH$_4$Cl, sawdust and other ingredients is used. The chemistry of voltaic cells will be left to your chemistry courses. The reaction that occurs, however, has the effect of **removing electrons** from the carbon electrode (making it **positive**) and adding them to the zinc (making the zinc negative). In a real dry cell, the whole outer casing of the cell is made of zinc. The zinc is dissolved away as the cell is used, and may eventually leak its contents.

There are many kinds of cells and batteries. Rechargeable 'batteries' may use nickel and cadmium, or molybdenum and lithium, or lead and lead oxide (as in the standard car battery). There are many kinds of cells on the market today, but they all produce electric current when connected to a conducting path!

6.3 Electromotive Force (emf)

In a carbon-zinc dry cell, forces resulting from the chemical reaction within the cell drive charges to the terminals, doing work to overcome the repulsive forces. The work done on the charges increases their potential energy. The difference in potential energy between the terminals amounts to 1.5 J for every coulomb of charge separated. We say the **potential difference** (P.D.) is 1.5 J/C, or 1.5 V. For a cell or battery which is not supplying current, the potential difference is at its peak value, which is called the **electromotive force (emf)**. It is given the symbol $\mathcal{E}$.

For a dry cell, the emf is 1.5 V. A nickel-cadmium cell is usually labelled 1.2 V or 1.25 V, but a freshly charged nickel-cadmium battery will have an even higher emf than its labelled rating. The cells in a lead storage battery have emf's of 2 V each. Six of these cells connected in series within the battery give a total emf of 12 V.

6.4 Electric Current

Definition of Electric Current

When electric charges *flow*, we say a **current exists.** A current will exist as long as a continuous conducting path is created for charges to flow from and back to a source of emf. See **Figure 6.2.**

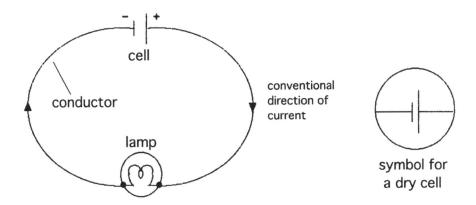

Figure 6.2

Electric current is defined as the amount of electric charge that passes a point in a circuit in one second. If an amount of charge Q passes a point in a circuit in a time t, then the average current I through that point is $I = \dfrac{Q}{t}$.

Current could quite logically be measured in **coulombs per second (C/s)**, but this unit is called the **ampere (A)** after **André Ampère (1775-1836)**, a French physicist.

$$1\,A = 1\ C/s$$

One ampere is the sort of current that exists in a 100 W lightbulb in a lamp in your home. (A 100 W lamp in a 110 V circuit would draw approximately 0.9 A.) In terms of electrons,

$$1\,A = 6.24 \times 10^{18}\ \text{electrons/s.}$$

Current Direction

The direction of current was defined *arbitrarily* by André Ampère to be *the direction that positive charges would move between two points where there is a difference of potential energy.* In many simple circuits we now know it is **negative** charges (**electrons**) that actually move. In solid conductors the positive charges are locked in the nuclei of atoms, which are fixed in their location in the crystal. Loosely attached electrons can move through the conductor from atom to atom. In liquids and gases, however, the flow of charges *may* consist of positively charged ions as well as negatively charged ions and electrons.

Throughout this book, we shall use **conventional current direction**: *the direction that positive charges would move between two points where there is a potential difference between the points.*

Drift Velocity

How fast do electrons move in a wire carrying a current of, say 1 A? When a switch is closed in a circuit, the effect of the current can be detected immediately throughout the entire circuit. This might lead one to conclude that the electric charges (usually electrons) travel at very high velocity through the circuit. In actual fact, this is not so! The average **'drift velocity'** of electrons in a given set of circumstances can be calculated.

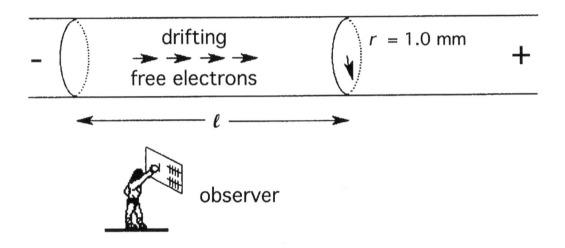

Figure 6.3

Within a length of metal wire there are many, many loosely attached electrons (sometimes called 'free electrons') which move about much like the molecules in a container of gas might move. Silver is an excellent conductor. Let us assume there is one free electron for every silver atom in a piece of wire. When the wire is connected to a source of emf, the potential difference (voltage) will cause electrons to move from the negative terminal of the source of emf toward the positive terminal. This movement is *superimposed* upon the random motion of the electrons which is going on all the time with or without a source of emf.

The trip the electrons make from the negative to the positive terminal is not a smooth one (as it was, for example, in the vacuum of a CRT). Electrons in the metal wire collide with positive silver ions on the way, and transfer some of their kinetic energy to the silver ions. The increased thermal energy of the silver ions will show up as an increase in temperature of the silver conductor.

Assume the current in the silver wire in **Figure 6.3** is **1.0 A**. Then there are 6.24×10^{18} electrons passing the 'observer' each second. This is because

$$1.0 \text{ A} = 1.0 \text{ C/s} = 6.24 \times 10^{18} \text{ e/s.}$$

To calculate the average **drift velocity** of the electrons, we start by again assuming that there is *one free electron for every silver atom,* a reasonable assumption, since chemists tell us that silver usually forms ions with a charge of +1.

All we need to know is what **length** of the silver wire in **Figure 6.3** would contain 6.24 x 10^{18} silver atoms (and therefore 6.24 x 10^{18} **free electrons**). We can find this out in three steps, as follows:

(1) The **mass** of silver needed to have 6.24 x 10^{18} free electrons is:

$$\textbf{mass} = \frac{6.24 \times 10^{18} \text{ atoms}}{6.02 \times 10^{23} \text{ atoms/mole}} \times 108 \text{ g/mole} = 1.12 \times 10^{-3} \text{ g.}$$

(2) The **volume** of silver wire needed to have 6.24 x 10^{18} free electrons is:

$$\textbf{volume} = \frac{\text{mass}}{\text{density}} = \frac{1.12 \times 10^{-3} \text{ g}}{10.5 \text{ g/cm}^3} = 1.07 \times 10^{-4} \text{ cm}^3.$$

(3) The radius of the silver wire in **Figure 6.3** is 1.0 mm, or 1.0 x 10^{-1} cm. Its cross-sectional area is πr^2, so the **length**, ℓ, can be found as follows:

$$\textbf{length, } \ell = \frac{\text{volume}}{\text{area}} = \frac{1.07 \times 10^{-4} \text{ cm}^3}{\pi\{1.0 \times 10^{-1} \text{ cm}\}^2} = 3.4 \times 10^{-3} \text{ cm .}$$

Since a length of 3.4 x 10^{-3} cm contains 6.24 x 10^{18} electrons, and this many electrons pass the observer in 1 s, the **average drift velocity** of the **conducting electrons** is 3.4 x 10^{-3} cm/s, or 0.034 mm/s! This is true only for the stated conditions, of course. If the amount of current, the nature of the material in the conductor, or the dimensions of the conductor change, then the drift velocity will change accordingly.

When you turn on a switch to light a lamp using a battery, the change in the electric field may travel at the speed of light, but the electrons themselves drift ever so slowly through the wire, under the influence of the electric field.

Investigation 6-1
Measuring Current Using Electroplating

Purpose: To measure current by counting copper atoms deposited on a carbon rod in a measured amount of time.

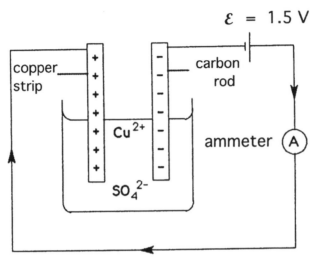

Figure 6.4

Introduction

A solution of copper II sulfate contains two kinds of ions: Cu^{2+} ions, which give the solution its blue colour, and SO_4^{2-} ions, which are colourless. If two electrodes are immersed in the copper II sulfate solution, and connected to a source of emf, the electrode connected to the positive terminal of the cell will attract SO_4^{2-} ions, and the electrode connected to the negative terminal of the cell will attract Cu^{2+} ions.

Cu²⁺ ions attracted to the negative electrode pick up two electrons, and deposit themselves on the negative electrode as **copper atoms, Cu⁰.**

$$Cu^{2+} + 2e^- \rightarrow Cu^0$$

Meanwhile, at the positive electrode, which is made of copper, copper atoms *lose* two electrons and become copper ions, thus replenishing the Cu^{2+} ions in the solution.

$$Cu^0 \rightarrow Cu^{2+} + 2e^-$$

The two electrons return to the source of emf, the cell.

In this experiment, you allow the copper atoms to **plate** on to a negatively charged carbon electrode. If you measure the **increase in mass** of the carbon electrode after, say, twenty minutes of copper-plating, you can calculate the mass of copper plated, thus the number of copper atoms plated, and from this the number of electrons that were transferred in the twenty minutes. Finally you can calculate the **current** in amperes. You can also compare your calculated current with the current measured with an ammeter placed in the same circuit.

Procedure

1. Measure as precisely as you can the **mass** of a dry, clean carbon rod.

2. Set up the circuit in **Figure 6.4.** Make sure the carbon rod is connected to the negative terminal of the dry cell or other DC power source. The red binding post of the ammeter should be connected to the positive terminal of the cell, and an appropriate current range chosen as quickly as possible when the current is turned on. *Let the current run for a carefully measured time, such as 20 minutes.* Record current frequently, and *average* it.

3. As soon as the current is turned off, carefully remove the carbon electrode. Dip it in a beaker of methyl hydrate, and allow it time to dry. A heat lamp can be used to speed drying.

Caution! Methyl hydrate is both highly toxic and flammable!

---

4. Measure the mass of the plated carbon rod precisely, and calculate the amount of **copper** that has plated on its surface. Record the mass of copper.

5. To remove the copper, set up the circuit once more, but *reverse the connections to the cell* so that the copper plates back on to the copper strip.

Concluding Questions

1. One mole of copper atoms (63.5 g) contains 6.02×10^{23} atoms. Using this information and the mass of copper plated on the carbon rod, calculate
   (a) the *number of copper atoms plated;*
   (b) the *number of electrons transferred;* and
   (c) the *number of coulombs transferred in 20 min.*

2. If 1 A = 1 C/s, what was the current in A?

3. Compare your calculated current with the measured current, by calculating the percent difference between the two currents.

Exercises

1. If the current in a wire is 5.0 A, how many coulombs of charge pass a point in the wire in one minute?

2. What is the current if 6.0×10^3 C pass a point in a circuit in 10.0 min?

3. If the current in a circuit is 12 A, how many electrons pass a point in one hour?

4. The drift speed of electrons in a copper wire running from a battery to a light bulb and back is approximately 0.020 mm/s. The battery is at the front of a classroom and wires run around the perimeter of the room to the light bulb. The total length of wire is 40.0 m. How long would it take a single electron to drift from the negative terminal of the battery back to the positive terminal? Express your answer in days.

5. How much copper would be plated by a current of 1.5 A in a time of 1.0 h?

6. How much silver is deposited by a current of 1.000 A in 1.000 h? The mass of one mole of silver atoms is 107.9 g.

$$Ag^+ \; + \; 1e^- \; \rightarrow \; Ag^0$$

6.5 Ohm's Law

Georg Simon Ohm (1787-1854) experimented with current in wires using variations in voltage to produce different currents in the wires. He found that for **metal conductors** at a given temperature, the current was directly proportional to the voltage between the ends of the wire.

$$(I \propto V.)$$

Therefore, $\dfrac{V}{I}$ = constant.

For example, if the potential difference (**voltage**) between the ends of a wire is 1.50 V and the current is 2.00 A, then if the potential difference is increased to 3.00 V, the current will also double and be 4.00 A.

The **constant of proportionality** is called the **resistance** (R) of the length of wire. The relationship among current, voltage and resistance is written:

$$\frac{V}{I} = R,$$

---

where R is the **resistance**, in **ohms** (Ω). This is called **Ohm's Law.** Ohm's Law can be written in two other forms, but all three forms are equivalent.

$$\frac{V}{I} = R \qquad\qquad V = IR \qquad\qquad I = \frac{V}{R}$$

Example

The current in a portable stove's heating element is 12.0 A when the potential difference between the ends of the element is 120 V. What is the resistance of the stove element? (or, "How many ohms on the range?")

Solution: $\qquad R = \dfrac{V}{I} = \dfrac{120 \text{ V}}{12.0 \text{ A}} = 1.0 \times 10^1 \ \Omega$.

Exercises

1. A resistor allows 1.0 mA to exist in it when a potential difference of 1.5 V is applied to its ends. What is the resistance of the resistor, in kilohms? ($1 \text{ k}\Omega = 10^3 \Omega$)

2. If a 10.0 Ω kettle element is plugged into a 120 V outlet, how much current will it draw?

3. A current of 1.25 mA exists in a 20.0 kΩ resistor. What is the potential difference between the ends of the resistor?

Resistors

Under normal circumstances, every conductor of electricity offers some resistance to the flow of electric charges, and is therefore a **resistor.** In any resistor, electrical energy is transformed into thermal energy. (There are some materials which, if cooled to temperatures approaching 0 K, offer no resistance to the flow of charges. These materials are called **superconductors.**) Usually when we use the term resistors we refer to devices manufactured specifically to control the amount of current in a circuit.

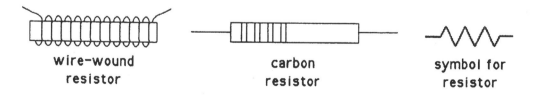

| wire-wound resistor | carbon resistor | symbol for resistor |

Figure 6.5

There are two main kinds of resistor: (1) **wire-wound resistors**, made of a coil of insulated, tightly wound fine wire and (2) **carbon** resistors. See **Figure 6.5**. Carbon resistors consist of a cylinder of carbon, with impurities added to control the amount of resistance. Metal wire leads are attached to each end of the carbon cylinder, and the whole assembly is enclosed in an insulating capsule.

Table 1   Resistor Colour Code

Band Colour	Number	Multiplier	Tolerance
black	0	10^0	
brown	1	10^1	
red	2	10^2	
orange	3	10^3	
yellow	4	10^4	
green	5	10^5	
blue	6	10^6	
violet	7	10^7	
gray	8	10^8	
white	9	10^9	
gold			5 %
silver			10 %
(No colour)			20 %

Resistor Colour Code

Resistors are either labelled with their resistance or colour-coded with four coloured bands, each of which has significance. The first coloured band gives the **first digit.** The second coloured band gives the **second digit.** The third coloured band gives the **power of ten multiplier** *(the number of zeros following the first two digits).* See **Table 1**. If there is no fourth coloured band, the manufacturer's tolerance is 20%. If the fourth band is gold, the tolerance is 5%. If the fourth band is silver, the tolerance is 10%.

Example

A resistor has the following coloured bands: brown, black, red, gold. What is the manufacturer's rating of this resistor?

Solution: Consulting **Table 1**, the reading Is 1 000 $\Omega \pm 5\%$. The manufacturer claims that the resistor has a resistance somewhere in the range between 950 Ω and 1050 Ω.

Exercises

Use **Table 1** to figure out the resistance rating of the following colour-coded resistors:
  (1) red, red, red, silver   (2) brown, black, orange, gold
  (3) brown, green, green, silver   (4) yellow, violet, yellow

Limitations of Ohm's Law

Ohm's Law applies to metal resistors and metal-like resistors such as those made of compressed carbon. The ratio of potential difference to current, that is **resistance,** is constant for this class of material providing the temperature of the material remains constant. One cannot apply Ohm's Law to just any conductor in a circuit. For example, Ohm's Law would **not** apply to a conducting solution or to a gas discharge tube. Ohm's Law only applies to metallic or metal-like conductors at a specific temperature.

6.6 Joule's Law

James Prescott Joule (1818-1889)   did experiments to measure the amount of heat released by various resistors under different conditions. He found that, for a particular resistor, *the amount of thermal energy released in a unit of time by a resistor is proportional to the square of the current.* Since the rate at which energy is released with respect to time is called **power**, Joule's results can be expressed as follows:

$$P \propto I^2$$

$$\text{or, } P = \text{constant} \cdot I^2$$

The constant in this equation will have units with the dimensions W/A², since constant = P/I^2. Consider the following simplification of these measuring units (W/A²):

$$1\ \frac{W}{A^2} = 1\ \frac{J/s}{C^2/s^2} = 1\ \frac{J/C}{C/s} = 1\ \frac{V}{A} = 1\,\Omega$$

The **ohm** (Ω) is the unit for **resistance!** In fact then, the constant of proportionality in the relationship discovered by Joule is the same constant of proportionality that is in Ohm's Law. The ratio P/I^2 is the **resistance** of the resistor.

Joule's Law can be written as follows: $P = R \cdot I^2$.   By combining Joule's Law with Ohm's Law for resistors, other expressions for electrical power can be derived.

$$P = RI^2 = \frac{V}{I} \cdot I^2 = VI.$$

$$\text{Also,} \quad P = VI = V \cdot \frac{V}{R} = \frac{V^2}{R}.$$

In summary,

$$P = RI^2 = VI = \frac{V^2}{R}$$

Examples

1. What is the resistance of the element of a 1500 W kettle, if it draws 12.5 A?

Solution $R = \dfrac{P}{I^2} = \dfrac{1500 \text{ W}}{\{12.5 \text{ A}\}^2} = 9.6 \, \Omega.$

2. How much thermal energy is released by a 1500 W kettle in 5.0 minutes?

Solution

Thermal energy released $= Pt = 1500 \dfrac{J}{s} \cdot 5.0 \text{ min} \cdot 60.0 \dfrac{s}{\text{min}} = 4.5 \times 10^5 \text{ J.}$

Exercises

1. What is the resistance of a 60.0 W lamp, if the current in it is 0.50 A?

2. A 600 W coffee percolator is operated at 120 V.

   (a) What is the resistance of the heating element of the percolator?

   (b) How much thermal energy does it produce in 6.0 min?

3. When you pay your electricity bill, you are charged not for power but for the energy used. The unit for measuring the energy used is the kilowatt·hour (kW·h).

   (a) How many joules are there in one kW·h?

   (b) How much energy, in kW·h, does a 400 W TV set use in a month (30 days), if it is used an average of 6.0 h each day?

   (c) If electrical energy costs $0.06 /kW·h, what will it cost you to operate the TV set for one month?

4. How many kW·h of energy does a 900 W toaster use in 3.0 min?

5. A 1.0 kΩ resistor is rated ½ W. (It will be destroyed if the rate of heat dissipation is greater than ½ W.) What is the maximum voltage you can apply to this resistor without risking damage to it?

6.7 EMF, Terminal Voltage and Internal Resistance

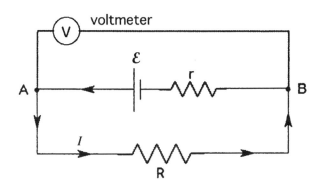

Figure 6.6

In **Figure 6.6** the dry cell has a rated emf of 1.50 V. If you use a high quality voltmeter to measure the potential difference between the terminals **A** and **B** of the cell, when essentially no current is being drawn from the cell other than a tiny amount going through the voltmeter itself, the voltage between the terminals will be nearly equal to the ideal value of the emf. That is, *with no current, the terminal voltage of the battery,* V_{AB}, will equal the emf, $\mathcal{E}$.

If, however, the cell is connected to a resistor R so that a current I exists in the simple circuit *including the cell itself,* then it will be observed that the terminal voltage is *less than* the cell emf.

$$V_{AB} < \mathcal{E}$$

This is because the cell itself has an **internal resistance** of its own, symbolized by r. According to Ohm's Law, the loss of potential energy per coulomb between the terminals is Ir. The measured terminal voltage of the cell will be less than the ideal emf by an amount equal to Ir.

$$V_{AB} = \mathcal{E} - Ir$$

Example

A dry cell with an emf of 1.50 V has an internal resistance of 0.050 Ω. What is the terminal voltage of the cell when it is connected to a 2.00 Ω resistor?

Solution

Apply Ohm's Law to the circuit as a whole, and consider the internal resistance r to be in series with the external resistance, R.

$$I = \frac{\mathcal{E}}{R + r} = \frac{1.50 \text{ V}}{2.05 \text{ Ω}} = 0.732 \text{ A}$$

Now the terminal voltage $V_{AB} = \mathcal{E} - Ir$.

$$V_{AB} = 1.50 \text{ V} - (0.732 \text{ A})(0.050 \text{ Ω}) = 1.50 \text{ V} - 0.037 \text{ V} = 1.46 \text{ V}.$$

Exercises

1. A dry cell with an emf of 1.50 V and an internal resistance of 0.050 Ω Is 'shorted out' with a piece of wire of resistance only 0.20 Ω. What will a voltmeter read if it is connected to the terminals of the dry cell at this time?

2. A battery has an emf of 12.50 V. When a current of 35 A is drawn from it, its terminal voltage is 11.45 V. What is the internal resistance of the battery?

3. A battery with an emf of 6.00 V has an internal resistance of 0.20 Ω. What current does the battery deliver when the terminal voltage reads only 5.00 V?

6.8 Resistors in Series

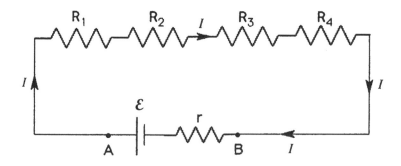

Figure 6.7

In **Figure 6.7**, four resistors are connected end-to-end so that there is one continuous conducting path for electrons coming from the source of emf, through the resistors and back to the source. Electrons move through the resistors, one after the other. The same current exists in each resistor. Resistors arranged like this are said to be **in series** with each other. **Figure 6.7** shows a typical **series circuit**.

Within the cell, the gain in potential energy per unit charge is equal to the emf, $\mathcal{E}$. When a current I exists, energy will be lost in resistors R_1, R_2, R_3, R_4 and r. The loss of potential energy per unit charge in each resistor is the voltage, V, across that resistor. From Ohm's Law we know that $V = IR$. The Law of Conservation of Energy requires that the total **gain** in energy in the cell(s) must equal the total **loss** of energy in the resistors in the circuit. It follows that *the total gain in energy per unit charge ($\mathcal{E}$) must equal the total loss of energy per unit charge in the circuit.*

$$\mathcal{E} = Ir + IR_1 + IR_2 + IR_3 + IR_4$$

$$\therefore \mathcal{E} - Ir = IR_1 + IR_2 + IR_3 + IR_4.$$

Recalling that **terminal voltage** $V_{AB} = \mathcal{E} - Ir$,

$$V_{AB} = IR_1 + IR_2 + IR_3 + IR_4 = V_S,$$

where V_S is the *sum of voltages across the resistors in the external part of the circuit*.

Another way of writing this is:

$$V_{AB} = V_1 + V_2 + V_3 + V_4 = V_S$$

Equivalent Resistance

What is the total resistance of a series circuit like the one in **Figure 6.7?** In other words, what single resistance (called the **equivalent resistance, R_s**) could be used to replace R_1, R_2, R_3 and R_4 **without changing current I?**

If $V_s = IR_s$,   and $V_s = IR_1 + IR_2 + IR_3 + IR_4$,   then

$$IR_s = IR_1 + IR_2 + IR_3 + IR_4 \ .$$

$$\therefore \ R_s = R_1 + R_2 + R_3 + R_4$$

Summary: For a Series Circuit:

(1) **Current (I) is the same everywhere throughout the circuit.**

(2) **The net gain in potential energy per coulomb in the circuit equals the net loss of potential energy per coulomb in the circuit. That is, for a circuit like the one in Figure 6.7, with a single source of emf,**

$$V_{AB} = V_1 + V_2 + V_3 + V_4 + ... + V_n \ .$$

(3) **The equivalent resistance of all the resistors in series with each other is equal to the sum of all their resistances.**

$$R_s = R_1 + R_2 + R_3 + R_4 + ... + R_n \ .$$

6.9 Resistors in Parallel

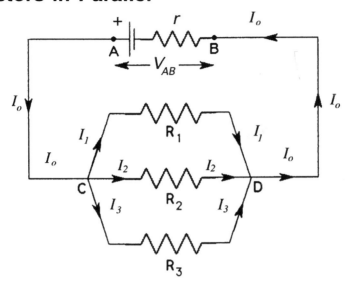

Figure 6.8

The resistors in **Figure 6.8** are in **parallel.** The current divides into three branches. Electrons coming from the cell take one of three paths, which meet at a **junction** where the electrons all converge to one path again and return to the battery.

Electric charge is a conserved quantity. The electrons do not get 'created' or 'lost' during their epic journey through the parallel network of resistors. The number of electrons entering a junction (such as D) per second will equal the number of electrons leaving that junction per second. Likewise, the number of electrons entering junction C per second will equal the number of electrons leaving C per second. (The direction of electron flow is opposite to the conventional current direction shown on **Figure 6.8**.) If we express current in C/s or in A, as is normally the case,

$$I_0 = I_1 + I_2 + I_3 .$$

The net gain in potential energy per unit charge in the cell, which is V_{AB}, is equal to the loss in potential energy per unit charge between C and D. If you think of C as an extension of terminal A, and D as an extension of terminal B of the cell, you can see that the difference in potential between C and D is the same no matter which of the three paths the electrons take to get from one terminal to the other. In fact,

$$V_{AB} = V_1 = V_2 = V_3 .$$

where V_{AB} is the terminal voltage of the cell, and V_1, V_2 and V_3 are the voltages across resistors R_1, R_2 and R_3 respectively.

Since the voltages are the same in each branch, we shall use the label V_p for the voltage in **any** branch of the parallel network.

Equivalent Resistance

What single resistance could be used in place of the parallel network of resistors, and draw the same total current? Call this the **equivalent resistance**, R_p .

If the voltage across the parallel network is V_p , and the equivalent single resistance is R_p , we can apply Ohm's Law as follows to find the total current I_0 entering the network:

$$I_0 = \frac{V_p}{R_p} \ .$$

However, $I_0 = I_1 + I_2 + I_3$.

Using Ohm's Law again, $\qquad \dfrac{V_p}{R_p} = \dfrac{V_p}{R_1} + \dfrac{V_p}{R_2} + \dfrac{V_p}{R_3}$.

Eliminating V_p, $\qquad \dfrac{1}{R_p} = \dfrac{1}{R_1} + \dfrac{1}{R_2} + \dfrac{1}{R_3}$.

Summary: For a Parallel Circuit Network:

(1) Voltage is the same between the ends of each branch of a parallel network.

(2) The total current entering a junction of a parallel network is equal to the total current leaving the same junction. As a result, the total current entering a parallel network of resistors or leaving the same network is equal to the sum of the currents in the branches.

(3) The reciprocal of the single equivalent resistance that will replace all the resistance in a parallel network, and draw the same current, is equal to the sum of the reciprocals of the resistances in the branches.

$$\frac{1}{R_p} = \frac{1}{R_1} + \frac{1}{R_2} + \frac{1}{R_3} + ... + \frac{1}{R_n}.$$

6.10 Combined Series and Parallel Circuits

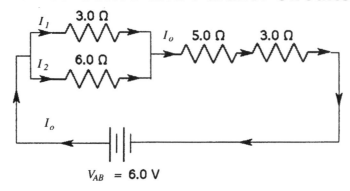

$V_{AB} = 6.0$ V

Figure 6.9

Figure 6.9 shows a combined **series-parallel** circuit. The rules you have learned for series and parallel circuits can be applied to this problem. A logical approach for finding the equivalent resistance and current for the circuit in **Figure 6.9** is to first reduce the parallel network to a single equivalent resistance, then treat the circuit as a series circuit.

Example

(a) What is the equivalent resistance of the circuit in **Figure 6.9**?
(b) What is the voltage across the 6.0 Ω resistor?

Solution:

First, reduce the parallel network to an equivalent single resistance.

$$\frac{1}{R_p} = \frac{1}{3.0\ \Omega} + \frac{1}{6.0\ \Omega} = \frac{2 + 1}{6.0\ \Omega} = \frac{3}{6.0\ \Omega} = \frac{1}{2.0\ \Omega}\ ;$$

$$\therefore\ R_p = 2.0\ \Omega.$$

Next, add the three resistances that are in series with one another.

$$R_s = 2.0\ \Omega + 5.0\ \Omega + 3.0\ \Omega = 10.0\ \Omega$$

Thirdly, find the current using Ohm's Law with the total equivalent resistance and the battery terminal voltage.

$$I_o = \frac{V_{AB}}{R_s} = \frac{6.0\ \text{V}}{10.0\ \Omega} = 0.60\ \text{A}\ .$$

Finally, the voltage across the parallel network is found by using Ohm's Law on the parallel network by itself.

$$V_p = I_o R_p = (0.60\ \text{A})(2.0\ \Omega) = 1.2\ \text{V}.$$

The voltage across both branches of the network is 1.2 V.

Exercises

1. (a) Draw a circuit showing a 6.0 V battery with an internal resistance of 0.50 Ω, connected to a parallel network consisting of a 25.0 Ω resistor in parallel with a 6.25 Ω resistor.
   (b) Calculate the current in the battery.

2. Calculate the equivalent resistance of each of the following networks of resistors.

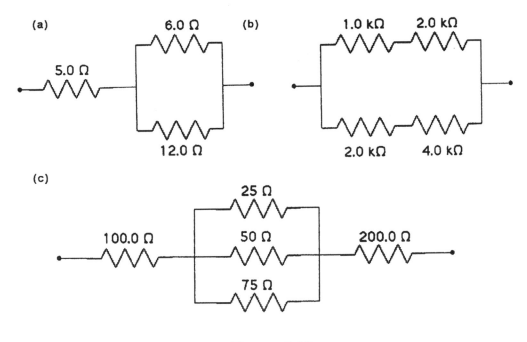

Figure 6.10

3. Calculate the current in the cell in this circuit.

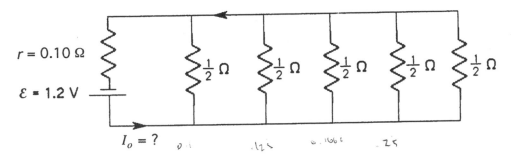

Figure 6.11

4. A wire has length ℓ and resistance R. It is cut into four identical pieces, and these pieces are arranged in parallel. What will be the resistance of the parallel network thus created?

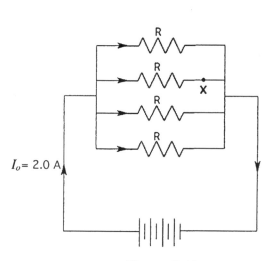

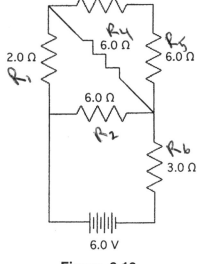

$I_o = 2.0$ A

Figure 6.12

Figure 6.13

5. Four identical resistors are connected in parallel, as in **Figure 6.12**. The current is 2.0 A with all four resistors in the circuit. What will the current be if the wire at X is cut?

6. (a) What is the equivalent resistance of the network of resistors in **Figure 6.13**?
   (b) What current exists in the 3.0 Ω resistor?

6.11 Kirchhoff's Laws for Electric Circuits

So far we have looked at series and parallel circuits from the points of view of (a) conservation of energy, (b) conservation of charge and (c) Ohm's Law. Most simple circuits can be analyzed using the rules worked out for series and parallel circuits in **Sections 6.8** and **6.9**. For more complicated circuits, a pair of rules called **Kirchhoff's Rules** (also called **Kirchhoff's Laws**) may be applied.

Kirchhoff's Current Rule

At any junction in a circuit, the sum of all the currents entering that junction equals the sum of all the currents leaving that junction.

Kirchhoff's Current Rule follows from the Law of Conservation of Electric Charge. Charged particles do not get 'lost' or 'created' in a circuit. Charged particles (usually electrons) that enter a junction point will leave that junction point.

Kirchhoff's Voltage Rule

The algebraic sum of all the changes in potential around a closed path in a circuit is zero.

Kirchhoff's Voltage Rule is really a restatement of the Law of Conservation of Energy.

In *Investigation 6-2*, you will examine several circuits from the point of view of **Kirchhoff's Laws.**

Investigation 6-2   Kirchhoff's Laws for Circuits

Purpose: To examine several circuits from the point of view of Kirchhoff's Laws.

Part 1   A Series Circuit

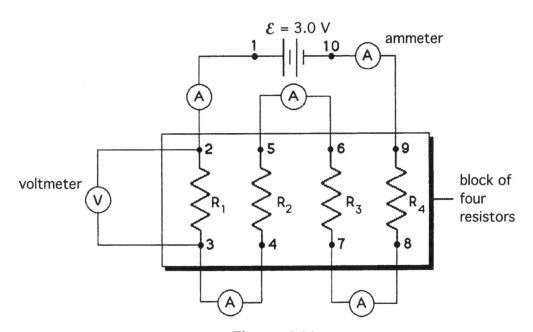

Figure 6.14

Procedure

1. To check Kirchhoff's Current Law, wire the series circuit in **Figure 6.14** and insert your ammeter in *each* of the locations, in turn, where the symbol **A** for ammeter is shown in the diagram. Record each current in your notebook (possibly on a diagram like **Figure 6.14**).

I_{12} = _____ I_{34} = _____ I_{56} = _____ I_{78} = _____ I_{9-10} = _____

2. To check Kirchhoff's Voltage Law, measure the terminal voltage of the battery or power supply, V_{1-10}. Then measure the voltages between the ends of each resistor. Remember that the **voltmeter** is not in the same conducting path as the circuit. *The voltmeter is always connected in parallel with the circuit component whose voltage you are measuring*. An example is shown in **Figure 6.14**, where the voltmeter is connected correctly across the ends of resistor R_1. The symbol for the voltmeter is **V**. Record all the voltages in your notebook.

V_{1-10} = _____ V_{23} = _____ V_{45} = _____ V_{67} = _____ V_{89} = _____

Concluding Questions

1. Do your current readings support Kirchhoff's Current Law? How would you describe the current at various junctions in your series circuit?

2. Compare the potential *gain* in the battery (terminal voltage) with the potential *drop* in the resistors in the circuit. Do your results suggest that $\Sigma V = 0$?

3. What are some **sources of error** in this investigation? For example, how might the ammeter itself affect the results for current, and how might the voltmeter affect the results for voltage?

4. Calculate the resistance of each resistor using Ohm's Law and the current and voltage readings for each individual resistor. Compare your calculated resistances with the manufacturer's ratings. (See **Resistor Colour Code**.) Organize your results in a table, as follows:

	R_1	R_2	R_3	R_4
Measured Voltage, V	V	V	V	V
Measured Current, I	A	A	A	A
Calculated Resistance, R	Ω	Ω	Ω	Ω
Colour Code Rating, R	Ω	Ω	Ω	Ω

5. Calculate the equivalent resistance R_s of the whole series circuit by using Ohm's Law and dividing the terminal voltage of the battery or power supply by the current in the battery. Compare this value with the sum of the individual calculated resistances.

What is the **percent difference** between R_s and $\Sigma [R_1 + R_2 + R_3 + R_4]$?

Part 2   A Parallel Circuit

Procedure

1. Set up the circuit in **Figure 6.15.** To simplify recording of your data, copy the diagram into your notebook. When you measure the current at each point labelled **A**, record the current right on the diagram in the ammeter circle.

2. Measure the voltage of the battery (V_{1-18}) and also the voltage across each resistor. Record the voltages in your notebook.

V_{1-18} = _____ V_{34} = _____ V_{78} = _____ V_{11-12} = _____ V_{15-16} = _____.

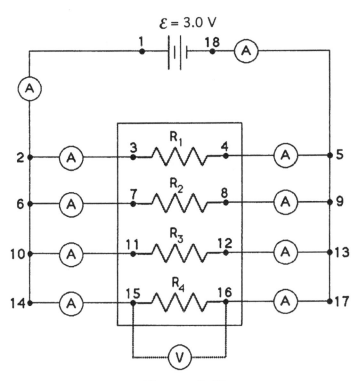

Figure 6.15

Concluding Questions

1. Examine the currents at each of the eight junctions of the parallel network of resistors. Do your results confirm Kirchhoff's Current Law?

2. Compare the potential **gain** in the battery (terminal voltage) with the potential **drop** across **each** branch of the circuit, in turn. Do your measurements seem to confirm Kirchhoff's Voltage Law?

3. What are some **sources of error** in this experiment?

4. Use the measured voltage across each resistor, and the measured current in each resistor, to calculate R_1, R_2, R_3 and R_4. Calculate the resistance of the parallel network using

$$\frac{1}{R_p} = \frac{1}{R_1} + \frac{1}{R_2} + \frac{1}{R_3} + \frac{1}{R_4} .$$

Organize your data in a table like the following one:

	R_1	R_2	R_3	R_4
Measured Voltage, V	V	V	V	V
Measured Current, I	A	A	A	A
Calculated Resistance, R	Ω	Ω	Ω	Ω

(a) R_p calculated in **Procedure 4** =		Ω
(b) R_p calculated from $\dfrac{V_{1-18}}{I_o}$ =		Ω
Percent difference between (a) and (b) =		%

5. Calculate the equivalent resistance of the parallel network by dividing the terminal voltage of the battery by the current in the battery. What is the percent difference between this R_p and the result from **Procedure 4**?

Challenges

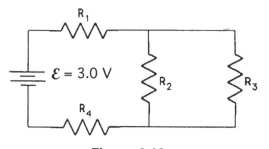

Figure 6.16

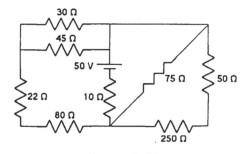

Figure 6.17

1. Set up a series-parallel circuit like the one in **Figure 6.16**. Test out Kirchhoff's two laws for this circuit.

2. In the circuit in **Figure 6.17**,
   (a) What is the equivalent resistance of the entire circuit?
   (b) What current is drawn from the battery?
   (c) What is the current in the 50 Ω resistor?
   (d) What is the voltage across the 22 Ω resistor?

Chapter Review Questions

1. What is the difference between the terminal voltage of a battery and its emf?

2. What current exists in a wire if 2.4×10^3 C of charge pass through a point in the wire in a time of 6.0×10^1 s?

3. The current through an ammeter is 5.0 A. In one day, how many electrons will pass through the ammeter?

4. How much silver will be electroplated by a current of 0.255 A in one day?

5. A mercury cell has an emf of 1.35 V and an internal resistance of 0.041 Ω. If it is used in a circuit that draws 1.50 A, what will its terminal voltage be?

6. A set of eight decorative light bulbs is plugged into a 120 V wall receptacle. What is the potential difference across each light bulb filament, if the eight light bulbs are connected (a) in series? (b) in parallel?

7. What is the resistance of a resistor if a potential difference of 36 V between its ends results in a current of 1.20 mA?

8. What is the potential difference (voltage) between the ends of a resistor if 24.0 J of work must be done to drive 0.30 C of charge through the resistor?

9. The coloured bands on a resistor are brown, black, yellow and gold. What is the manufacturer's rating of the resistance of the resistor?

10. You need a 4.7 MΩ resistor from a box of miscellaneous resistors. What coloured bands should you be looking for in your collection?

11. A 2.2 kΩ resistor is rated at '½ W'. What is the highest voltage you could safely apply to the resistor without risking damage to it from overheating?

12. What current will a 1500 W kettle draw from a 120 V source?

13. A toaster draws 8.0 A on a 120 V circuit. What is its power rating?

14. A 60.0 W light bulb and a 40.0 W light bulb are connected in parallel in a 120 V circuit. What is the equivalent resistance of the two light bulbs?

15. A branch circuit in your house has the following appliances plugged into it: a 1500 W kettle, a 150 W light, and a 900 W toaster. The branch circuit is protected by a 20 A circuit breaker. If house voltage is 120 V, will the circuit breaker be activated? Explain your answer.

16. How many kW·h of energy will a 400 W television set use in one month, if it is turned on for an average of 5.0 h per day? What will it cost you at $0.06/kW·h?

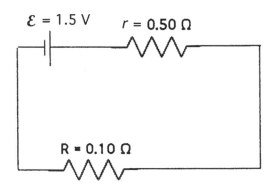

17. The cell in **Figure 6.18** is short-circuited with a wire of resistance 0.10 Ω. What is the terminal voltage under these conditions?

18. A storage battery has an emf of 12.0 V. What is the terminal voltage if a current of 150 A is drawn just as the starter motor is turned on, if the internal resistance is 0.030 Ω?

Figure 6.18

19. What is the equivalent resistance of resistors of 8.0 Ω, 12.0 Ω and 24.0 Ω if they are connected (a) in series? (b) In parallel?

20. A resistor is intended to have a resistance of 60.00 Ω, but when checked it is found to be 60.07 Ω. What resistance might you put in parallel with it to obtain an equivalent resistance of 60.00 Ω?

21. A 12.0 Ω resistor and a 6.0 Ω resistor are connected in series with a 9.0 V battery. What is the voltage across the 6.0 Ω resistor?

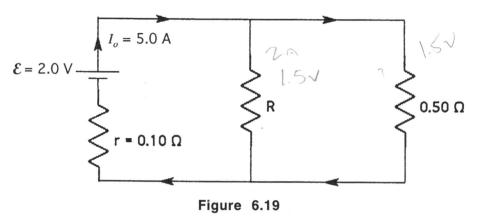

Figure 6.19

22. What is the value of the resistance R in **Figure 6.19**, if the current through the battery is 5.0 A?

23. You have three 6.0 kΩ resistors. By combining these three resistors in different combinations, how many different equivalent resistances can you obtain with them? (All three must be used.)

24. For each circuit, find (i) the equivalent resistance of the entire circuit and (ii) the current at the point marked '*I*'.

(a)

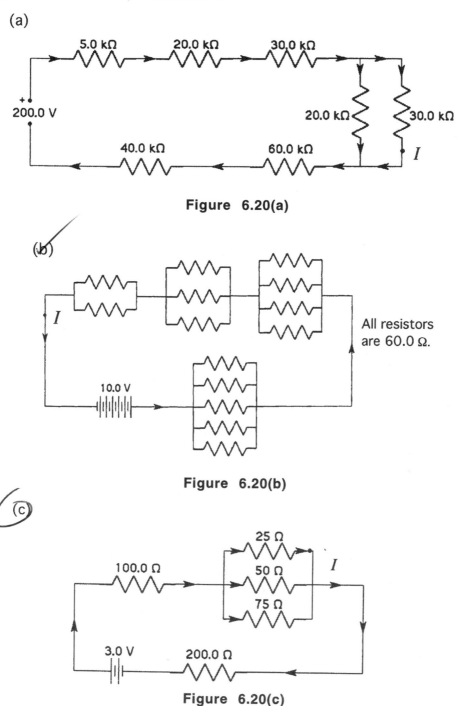

5.0 kΩ   20.0 kΩ   30.0 kΩ

200.0 V   20.0 kΩ   30.0 kΩ

40.0 kΩ   60.0 kΩ   *I*

Figure 6.20(a)

(b)

I

All resistors are 60.0 Ω.

10.0 V

Figure 6.20(b)

(c)

25 Ω

100.0 Ω   50 Ω   *I*

75 Ω

3.0 V   200.0 Ω

Figure 6.20(c)

Brain Busters

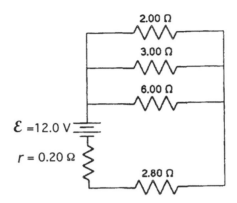

Figure 6.21

(25) What is the voltage across the 6.0 Ω resistor in **Figure 6.21**?

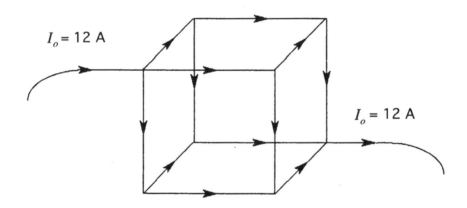

Figure 6.22

26. Twelve identical pieces of resistance wire, each of resistance 1.0 Ω, are formed into a cubical resistance network, as in **Figure 6.22.** If a current of 12 A enters one corner of the cube and leaves at the other corner, what is the equivalent resistance of the cube between the opposite corners? Use Kirchhoff's Laws!

Test Yourself!

Multiple Choice

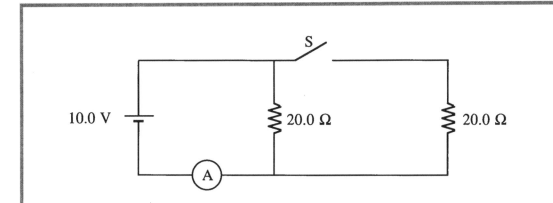

1. The current through **A** is 0.50 A when the switch S is open. What will the current through **A** be when the switch S is closed?
   A. 0 A
   B. 0.25 A
   C. 0.50 A
   D. 1.0 A

2. Which one of the following arrangements of four identical resistors will have the least resistance?

   A

   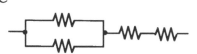

   B

   C

   D

   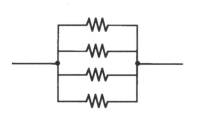

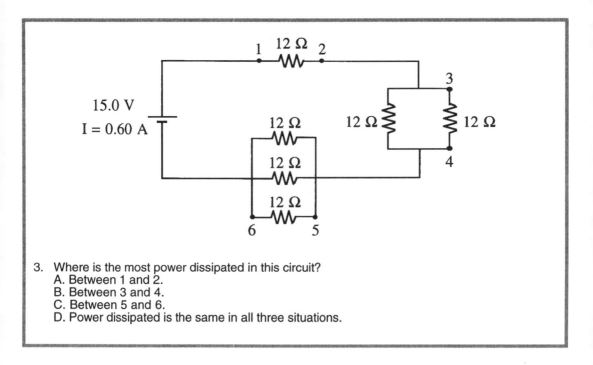

3. Where is the most power dissipated in this circuit?
   A. Between 1 and 2.
   B. Between 3 and 4.
   C. Between 5 and 6.
   D. Power dissipated is the same in all three situations.

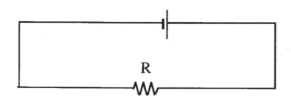

R

4. In this circuit, if you wish to measure the current through resistor R and the voltage between the ends of resistor R, where should the ammeter and voltmeter be placed?

	ammeter	voltmeter
A	in series	in series
B	in series	in parallel
C	in parallel	in parallel
D	in parallel	in series

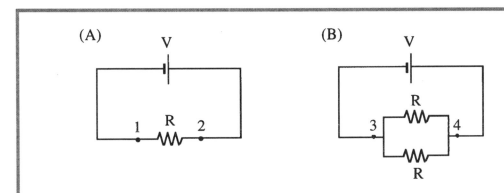

5. The power dissipated in circuit **(A)** in resistor R between 1 and 2 is P. In circuit **(B)** the same source voltage is used, but an identical resistor R is added in parallel with the first resistor. How much power will be dissipated between 3 and 4?

A. ¼ P B. ½ P C. P D. 2 P E. 4 P

Open-Ended Questions

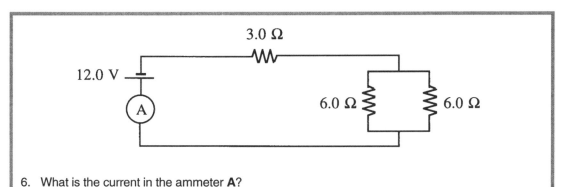

6. What is the current in the ammeter **A**?

7. A 1500 W kettle is connected to a 110 V source. What is the resistance of the kettle element?

8. A flashlight contains a battery of two cells in series, with a bulb of resistance 12.0 Ω. The internal resistance of each cell is 0.260 Ω. If the potential difference across the bulb is 2.88 V, what is the EMF of *each* cell?

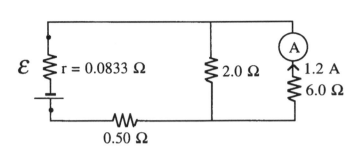

9. What is the EMF of the battery if the current in **A** is 1.2 A, and the internal resistance of the battery is 0.0833 Ω?

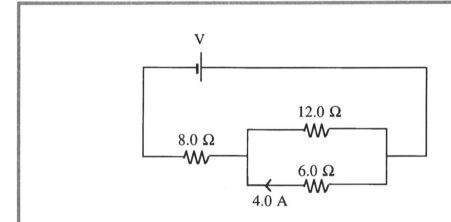

10. What is the voltage *V* of the power supply?

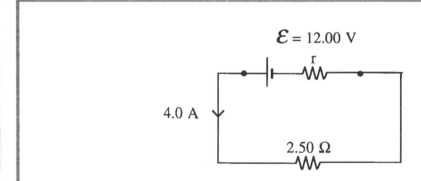

11. What is the internal resistance of the battery?

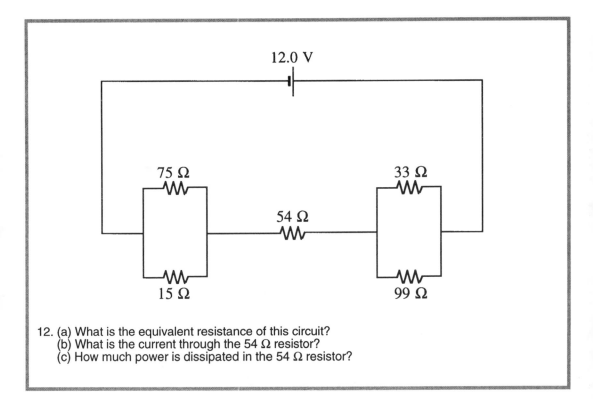

12. (a) What is the equivalent resistance of this circuit?
    (b) What is the current through the 54 Ω resistor?
    (c) How much power is dissipated in the 54 Ω resistor?

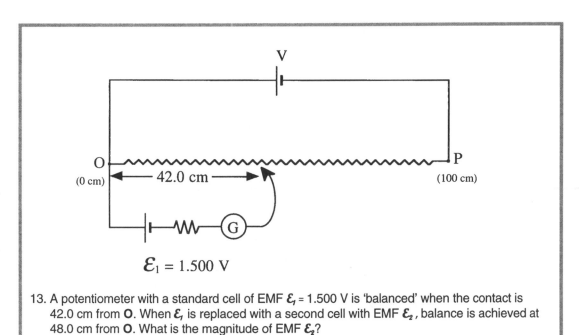

$\mathcal{E}_1 = 1.500$ V

13. A potentiometer with a standard cell of EMF $\mathcal{E}_1 = 1.500$ V is 'balanced' when the contact is 42.0 cm from **O**. When $\mathcal{E}_1$ is replaced with a second cell with EMF $\mathcal{E}_2$, balance is achieved at 48.0 cm from **O**. What is the magnitude of EMF $\mathcal{E}_2$?

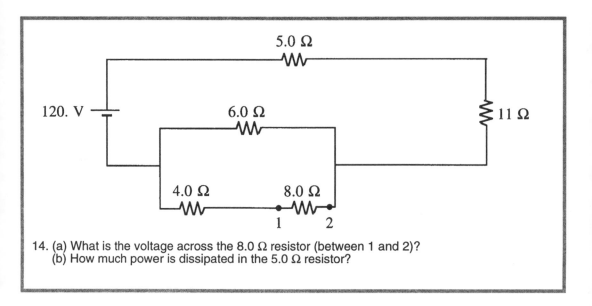

5.0 Ω

120. V

6.0 Ω

11 Ω

4.0 Ω   8.0 Ω

1   2

14. (a) What is the voltage across the 8.0 Ω resistor (between 1 and 2)?
(b) How much power is dissipated in the 5.0 Ω resistor?

Laura Theroux records 'current events' in her physics lab book.

Chapter 7   Magnetic Forces

7.1 Basic Ideas about Magnets

Permanent Magnets

If a magnet is suspended from a string or supported at its centre of gravity so that it is free to rotate, it will turn until one end of it points toward the north. The end that points north is called the **north-seeking** or **north pole**. The opposite end is the **south-seeking** or **south pole**. This property of magnets has been used in compasses for many centuries.

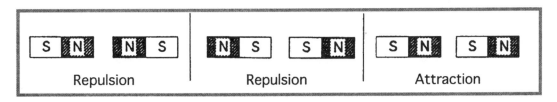

| Repulsion | Repulsion | Attraction |

Figure 7.1

Like poles repel each other; opposite poles attract each other.

Two magnets nearby will exert a force on each other. If two **like** poles are near each other, they will **repel** each other; two **unlike** poles will **attract** each other.

Bar magnets are examples of **permanent** magnets, because they stay magnetized (if handled carefully) for a long time. **Electromagnets** are magnetized only while there is current in them.

Permanent magnets found in school laboratories are usually made of some kind of steel alloy. **Alnico** magnets are especially strong. The alloy of which they are made contains cobalt, nickel, iron and the non-magnetic element aluminum.

Only a few elements are strongly magnetic. The three best-known magnetic elements are iron, nickel and cobalt. These are called **ferromagnetic** elements (after the Latin *ferrum*, which means iron). Less well known ferromagnetic elements include the rare-earth elements neodymium and gadolinium.

The naturally occurring mineral **magnetite**, also called **lodestone** (an iron oxide with the formula Fe_3O_4), is quite strongly magnetic. Its magnetic properties have been known since ancient times.

Magnetic Fields and Lines of Force

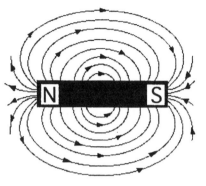

Just as there is a gravitational field around any massive body and an electrical field around a charged body, there is a magnetic field around any magnet. **Figure 7.2** depicts the **magnetic field** around a bar magnet. A series of **lines of force** show the direction of the field at any point. The direction of a magnetic line of force is taken to be the direction that an *isolated north pole* (if such an animal existed) would tend to move in that region of the field. The direction of the field at any point can be determined by using a small compass needle. Its north end will point in the direction of the field at that point.

Figure 7.2

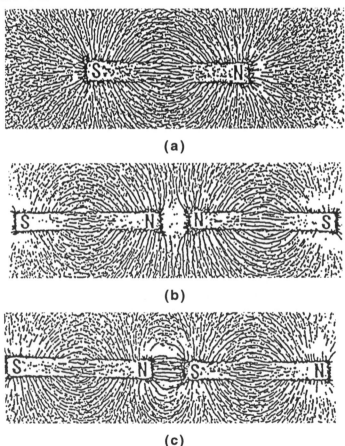

(a)

(b)

(c)

Figure 7.3

If fine iron filings are sprinkled on a piece of white cardboard that sits on top of a magnet, the overall shape of the field can be seen. The tiny iron filings become magnets themselves in the field of the permanent magnet. **Figure 7.3** shows the shape of the field around (a) a single bar magnet, (b) two bar magnets with like poles facing each other and (c) two bar magnets with opposite poles facing each other.

Notice that the lines of force are closest together near the poles, and furthest apart at distances well away from the poles. Iron filings tend to bunch up near the poles, suggesting that the field is strongest near the poles. Another observation you might make from the diagrams is that the lines of force do not cross each other.

Electromagnets

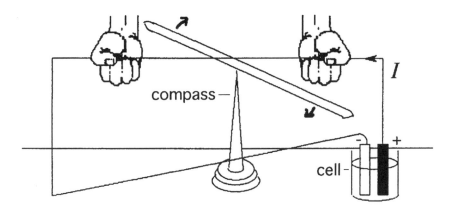

Figure 7.4

In 1820, a Danish physicist named **Hans Christian Oersted (1777-1851)** made a chance observation, which turned out to be one of the most important discoveries ever made by a scientist. He was using a simple electric circuit, consisting of a wire connected to a battery. He happened to notice that a compass needle nearby was deflected from its normal north-south alignment when current existed in the wire. (See **Figure 7.4**) When the battery was disconnected, the compass needle returned to its normal position.

If the needle deflected in one direction when it was held *above* the conducting wire, it would reverse direction when held *below* the wire. Experiments showed that the magnetic field around the conductor appeared to be *circular,* and only existed if there was current in the wire.

André Ampère (1775-1836), a French physicist, quickly followed up on Oersted's discovery by investigating magnetic fields caused by electric currents in conductors of various shapes and sizes. Some of his conclusions will be outlined later in this chapter.

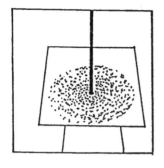

Figure 7.5

In **Figure 7.5**, a piece of heavy gauge copper wire has been poked through a white file card, which sits on a paper cup for support. A high current from a rechargeable battery was passed through the wire, and iron filings were sprinkled on the card. The diagram shows the circular shape of the lines of force in the magnetic field around the wire. Since the filings are most crowded near the wire, and spread out further away from the wire, it would appear that the strength of the field falls off with distance from the wire. Ampère showed that the magnetic field strength near a long straight piece of wire is inversely proportional to the distance from the wire.

(a)

(b)

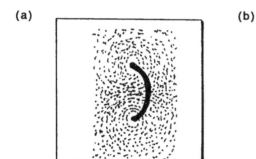 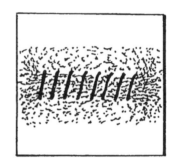

Figure 7.6

If a wire is formed into a single turn, the magnetic field looks like **Figure 7.6 (a)**. When a long coil with many turns is constructed, the coil is called a **solenoid**. **Figure 7.6 (b)** shows the shape of the magnetic field around and inside a solenoid. Notice the strong similarity to the field around a bar magnet (**Figure 7.3**). Inside the solenoid, the lines of force run parallel with each other. The magnetic field inside a solenoid is quite uniform for the entire length of the solenoid.

While iron filings show the *shape* of the field nicely, they do not indicate its *direction.* A small compass needle can be used for that purpose. When the direction of the lines of force around a conductor is established using a compass needle, a definite pattern can be seen, which is best expressed by **Ampère's Rule**, sometimes called the **Right Hand Rule. Figure 7.7** illustrates the Right Hand Rule for a straight conductor.

Right Hand Rule for Straight Conductors

Imagine you are holding the conductor in your right hand, with your thumb pointing in the direction of conventional current (the direction that positive charges would like to move). Then your fingers will curl in the same direction as the magnetic lines of force.

Current
I

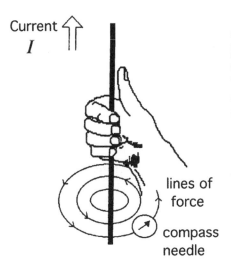

lines of force

compass needle

Figure 7.7

Ampère's Right Hand Rule for a straight conductor will work with a single loop of wire [**Figure 7.8(a)**] or with a single turn of a solenoid [**Figure 7.8(b)**]. Notice that *inside* the solenoid, the lines of force go from south to north. Outside the solenoid, the lines go from north to south, as you observed with a bar magnet.

With either a single loop or a solenoid, there is a north pole and a south pole, as with a bar magnet. It is assumed that within a bar magnet the iron atoms obtain their magnetism from the motion of electrons within them.

The revolution of electrons around atoms produces a magnetic effect in any atom, but the overall effect of the orbiting motions is small, because it is believed there are as many electrons orbiting in one direction as in the other, so that magnetic effects tend to cancel. In most atoms, the *spins* of the electrons, which also produce a magnetic effect, tend to cancel each other's effects as well. In ferromagnetic elements, however, there appears to be an imbalance in the spins which produces a strong magnetic field in their atoms. Ferromagnetism is a complicated subject, which must be left for more advanced courses.

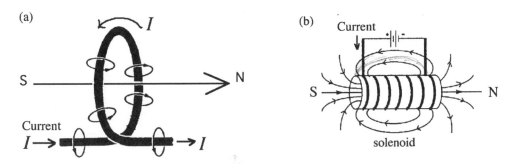

Figure 7.8

If an iron core is placed inside a solenoid, the iron core itself becomes magnetized. When the atoms of iron add their magnetic strength to that of the solenoid, the magnetic field strength of the combination far exceeds that of the solenoid itself. The combination of solenoid and iron core is called an **electromagnet.**

Electromagnets have many, many uses. Every transformer, motor, generator, doorbell, loudspeaker and junkyard lifting magnet has an electromagnet inside it. Since Oersted's discovery in 1820, scientists and engineers have found countless ways of using electromagnetism!

Exercises

1. In **Figure 7.9**, the conductor on the left carries current 'into the page'. The conductor on the right carries current 'out of the page'.

Figure 7.9

(a) Draw sample lines of force around each conductor, showing their direction.
(b) Would these conductors attract each other or repel each other? Explain your answer. (Hint. If you place two bar magnets side by side so that the lines of force of their magnetic fields are in the same direction, how do the magnets affect each other?)

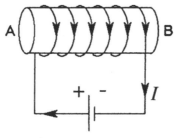

Figure 7.10

2. Which end of the solenoid (**A** or **B**) in **Figure 7.10** will be north?

Challenge!

Find out what these terms mean: **ferromagnetism, diamagnetism,** and **paramagnetism.**

7.2 How Magnetic Fields Affect Moving Charged Particles

Consider a solitary charged particle, perhaps a single electron or proton. In an **electric field**, there will be a force on that charged particle, and it will accelerate due to the electric force on it. The charged particle will be affected by an **electric field** whether the charged particle is initially stationary or already moving.

Curiously, a **magnetic field** has no apparent effect on a *stationary* charged particle. Once a charged particle is *moving,* however, it may experience a force in the presence of a magnetic field. What determines whether there will be a force on a moving charged particle, and what the direction and strength of the force will be? *Investigation 7-1* will look at some of the factors involved. First we shall consider the direction of the force on a moving electron.

Magnetic Force on a Beam of Electrons

Figure 7.11

Figure 7.11 shows a simple **cathode ray tube** (CRT) which allows a narrow beam of electrons to pass through a slit (visible on the left) and strike a fluorescent screen, so that the path of the electrons can easily be seen on the screen. In **Figure 7.11**, the lines of magnetic force due to the bar magnet are directed **out of the page** into the south pole of the bar magnet. As you can see, the electrons are pushed **upward!** The moving charges are *not* attracted to the poles of the magnet, but are deflected in a direction **perpendicular** to the magnetic field.

In the situation in **Figure 7.11**, you will notice that the **velocity,** the **field** and the **force** are all **mutually perpendicular.**

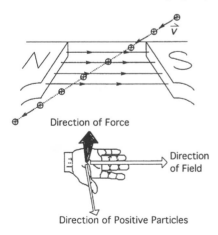

Figure 7.12

Another Rule of Thumb: The Right Hand Motor Rule

If you experiment with the apparatus in **Figure 7.11**, varying the alignment of the bar magnet in every way you can, you will find that the direction of the deflection of the electron beam is predictable.

There is a convenient 'rule of thumb' for predicting in what direction a beam of charged particles will be deflected by a magnetic field. It is called the **Right Hand Motor Rule** (for reasons you will understand better when you look closely at how an electric motor works).

If you wish to predict the direction of the **magnetic force** on moving charged particles, here is what you do:

(1) *Point your thumb in the direction that positively charged particles would move (the direction of conventional current).*
(2) *Point your fingers in the direction of the magnetic field (from N to S).*
(3) *Your palm now faces in the direction that the positive charges would be pushed by the magnetic field.* See **Figure 7.12.**

In **Figure 7.11, electrons** (negatively charged) move from left to right, therefore the direction of conventional current is from right to left. The magnetic field in **Figure 7.11** is 'out of the page'. Use the right hand rule for the situation in **Figure 7.11**, and it should predict a force *upward,* as is the case in the figure.

Investigation 7-1
Deflecting a Beam of Electrons Using a Magnetic Field

Purpose: To investigate the deflection of electron beams by magnetic fields, using a laboratory cathode ray tube.

Introduction

In **Chapter 5,** *Investigation 5-2,* you observed that the deflection, y, of an electron moving in an **electric field**, was proportional to the electric field strength E. The experiment actually showed that y was proportional to the deflecting voltage V_δ, which produces the electric field. Since $E = V_\delta/d$ and d is constant, then $y \propto E$.

In this investigation you will use a solenoid carrying known currents to produce a magnetic field. This magnetic field will be used to deflect electrons moving through a cathode ray tube (CRT). You will also vary the **accelerating voltage** of the CRT to see how changing the speed of the electrons affects the deflection.

Comparing Forces

For any body acted on by a constant, unbalanced force F, there is an acceleration, a, causing a displacement, y, in time t.

$$y = \frac{1}{2} at^2$$

For an electron travelling through a field exerting a constant force F, if the electron is travelling at speed v and the length of the field region is ℓ, and the mass of the electron is m, then

$$y = \frac{1}{2} \frac{F}{m} \cdot \frac{\ell^2}{v^2}.$$

If the same accelerating voltage, V_a, is used throughout an experiment, then speed v will be constant. Since m and ℓ are also constant, this means that

$$y = \text{constant} \cdot F,$$
$$\text{or } y \propto F.$$

If the accelerating voltage is kept constant, you can use the deflection of the beam as a means of comparing magnetic forces.

[Strictly speaking, the magnetic force on an electron moving through a magnetic field *cannot* be constant (except in magnitude) because the direction of the force is continually changing! If, however, the beam deflection is kept *small*, you can assume that the force is essentially constant throughout the field, and assume with little error that $y \propto F$.]

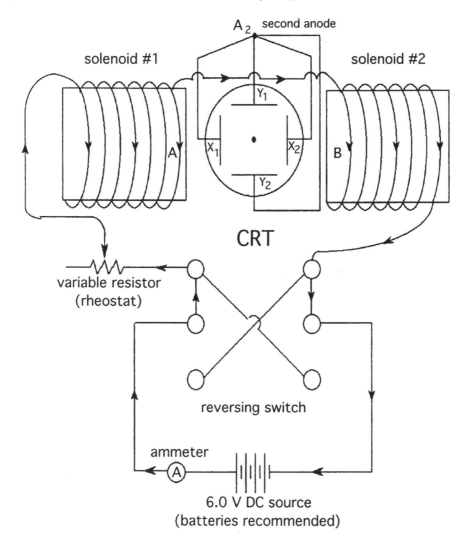

Figure 7.13

General Information

In this investigation the X and Y deflecting plates are not used at all.

All four plates (X_1, X_2, Y_1 and Y_2) should be connected to the second anode A_2 so that they are at the same potential as A_2 and cause no deflection whatever.

To obtain a fairly uniform field, arrange two solenoids in series, as in **Figure 7.13**, so that they can be left in exactly the same position around the base of the CRT throughout this entire experiment. Use a small compass to check that the coils are wired such that if pole A is north, pole B is south (or vice versa). The experiment requires that lines of force run approximately 'straight' through the base of the CRT. Use books or other supporting material to ensure that the solenoids are at the same level as the base of the CRT.

A variable resistance (**rheostat**) is used to vary the current in the solenoids. The **ammeter** measures the current in the solenoids. The **reversing switch** allows you to reverse the direction of the current in the solenoids, which reverses the magnetic field direction and therefore the deflection direction. To measure deflection caused by a given current, pass that current through the solenoids and mark the position of the beam on the screen. Reverse the current and mark the new position. Measure the total change, divide by two, and you have a good measure of the average deflection caused by that particular current in the solenoids. Call this deflection δ.

Part 1

Problem: **How does the deflection of an electron beam depend on the current in the solenoids whose magnetic field is causing the deflection?**

Procedure

1. Set up the apparatus as in **Figure 7.13**. Set the accelerating voltage V_a at 750 V, and leave it there throughout **Part 1**. Make sure that all deflecting plates are connected to A_2.

2. With a current of, say, 1.0 A in the solenoids, mark the position of the beam. Reverse the current with the reversing switch. Mark the new position and measure the distance between the two marks. Divide this distance in two to get the average deflection caused by 1.0 A in the solenoids.

3. Repeat **Procedure 2** with at least four other currents in the solenoid.

4. Prepare a graph of deflection, δ , vs solenoid current, I.

Concluding Questions

1. How does the deflection of the beam depend on solenoid current? Express your answer in an equation, complete with a numerical value for the slope, in appropriate units.

2. If $\delta \propto y$, and $y \propto F$, how does the magnetic force depend on the solenoid current?

Part 2

Problem: How does the deflection of the beam of electrons depend on the accelerating voltage, if the solenoid current is kept constant?

Procedure

1. Set the solenoid current at a fixed value, such as 4.0 A. Do not vary this current throughout this part of the experiment.

> To vary the electron speed, what you do is vary the accelerating voltage, V_a. (Recall from **Chapter 5** that V_a is equal to the gain in kinetic energy per unit charge of the accelerated electrons, so $V_a = \frac{1}{2}mv^2/Q$.) Your CRT is labelled with accelerating voltages of, perhaps, 500 V, 750 V and 1 000 V. These labelled values must be checked with a voltmeter, since they are only approximate.

2. Measure the average deflection δ for at least three different accelerating voltages. (You will probably have to re-focus the beam when you change accelerating voltages.)

3. Plot a graph of average deflection δ vs accelerating voltage, V_a.

4. Make an educated guess at the power-law relation between δ and V_a, and plot a second graph that will give you a straight line.

Concluding Questions

1. Write an equation that describes how deflection varies with accelerating voltage, when an electron moves through a magnetic field. Include a numerical value for your slope, complete with proper units.

2. The accelerating voltage is $V_a = \frac{1}{2} mv^2/Q$. Work out a relationship between beam deflection and electron speed. In other words, how does δ vary with v?

3. In the **Introduction** it was shown that $y = \frac{1}{2} at^2 = \frac{1}{2} \frac{F}{m} \cdot \frac{\ell^2}{v^2}$. Since m and ℓ are constant in Part 2 (Speed v is a variable this time.), we can say that $y \propto \frac{F}{v^2}$, and since $y \propto \delta$, therefore $\delta \propto \frac{F}{v^2}$. How does the magnetic force vary with the electron speed?

4. What is a simple way to tell whether a deflection on a CRT screen is caused by an electric field or a magnetic field?

5. What are some sources of error in this experiment?

Exercises

1. When the solenoid current in the arrangement used in **Investigation 7-1** is 2.2 A, the beam in the CRT is deflected 1.2 cm. What will the deflection be if the solenoid current is increased to 3.6 A?

2. The deflection on a CRT screen is 1.4 cm when the accelerating voltage is 500 V. If the solenoid current is kept constant, what will happen to the magnetic deflection if:
(a) the accelerating voltage is increased to four times its original value?
(b) the electron speed is increased four times?

3. The deflection on a CRT screen is 1.2 cm when the solenoid current is 1.5 A and the accelerating voltage is 500. V. If the solenoid current is changed to 3.0 A, what accelerating voltage is needed to maintain the same deflection?

7.3 Magnetic Field Strength, *B*

Investigation 7-1 suggests, in a roundabout way, that the magnetic force that a charged particle experiences while travelling through a magnetic field depends directly on the speed of the particle. It is a curious fact that the faster a charged particle travels, the greater the force exerted on it by a magnetic field.

$$F \propto v$$

Other experiments show that the magnetic force on a charged particle moving through a magnetic field depends directly on the amount of **charge** on the particle. That is, $F \propto Q$.

If $F \propto v$ and $F \propto Q$, then $F \propto Qv$.

Therefore, $\dfrac{F}{Qv} = $ **constant.**

The constant ratio (F/Qv) can be used as a measure of the **magnetic field strength** (B) at the point in the magnetic field where the moving charge is passing. The dimensions of the units for magnetic field strength will be

$$1 \frac{N}{C\frac{m}{s}} = 1 \frac{N}{Am} = 1\,T.$$

This unit is called the **tesla (T)** after **Nicola Tesla (1856-1943)**. (1 T = 1 N/A·m)

The relationship among magnetic force, magnetic field strength, charge and velocity can be written:

$$F = BQv.$$

In **Investigation 7-1,** the charged particles (electrons) were moving in a direction perpendicular to the direction of the magnetic field. Sometimes the charges do not move perpendicular to the magnetic field. If that is the case, then one must use the **component of B** that **is** perpendicular to **v.** See **Figure 7.14.**

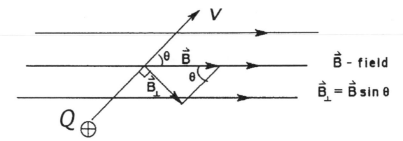

Figure 7.14

In **Figure 7.14**, a particle carrying charge Q is moving through a magnetic field of strength **B,** making an angle θ with the lines of force of the field. Since the component of the magnetic field in a direction perpendicular to the direction of motion is $B \sin \theta$, the force on the moving charge is $F = BQv \sin \theta$.

If the charged particles move in a direction *parallel* with the magnetic field, so that $\theta = 0°$, then $\sin \theta = 0$, and $F = BQv\,(0) = 0$. The particles experience **no force** if they move parallel with the lines of force!

If the charged particles move in a direction *perpendicular* to the magnetic field, so that $\theta = 90°$, then $\sin \theta = 1.000$, and $F = BQv\,(1.000) = BQv$.

The maximum force is experienced when the particles move in a direction that is perpendicular to the magnetic field. In most situations you will encounter in this course, the formula reduces to

$$F = BQv.$$

Exercises

1. An electron travelling with a speed of 2.0 x 10⁶ m/s moves in a direction perpendicular to a magnetic field of strength 2.5 x 10⁻² T.
    (a) What is the force acting on the electron?
    (b) What is the magnitude and the direction of the acceleration?

2. A proton travelling at a speed of 3.0 x 10⁶ m/s travels through a magnetic field of strength 3.0 x 10⁻³ T, making an angle of 45° with the magnetic lines of force. What force acts on the proton?

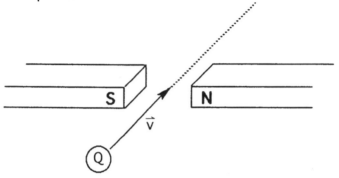

Figure 7.15

3. (a) A beam of alpha particles (He²⁺) is travelling between the magnetic poles in **Figure 7.15**. In what direction will the alpha particles be deflected?
   (b) If the magnetic field strength is 6.4 T and the alpha particles move with a speed of 6.0 x 10⁷ m/s, what will the magnetic force on the alpha particles be?

7.4 The Magnetic Field Strength of a Solenoid

Solenoid variables

N = number of turns
L = length of solenoid
I = current
B = magnetic field strength

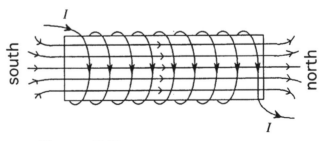

Figure 7.16

André Ampère investigated the magnetic fields associated with solenoids very thoroughly. He observed that the magnetic field inside a long solenoid is uniform, with straight lines of force running parallel with the axis of the solenoid, as in **Figure 7.16.**

The strength, B, of the magnetic field inside a solenoid depends primarily on two factors:

(1) the **number of turns of wire per unit length** of solenoid, N/L, and
(2) the **current** in the solenoid, I.

In symbols,
$$B \propto \frac{NI}{L}, \text{ or}$$

$$B = \text{constant} \cdot \frac{NI}{L}.$$

The constant of proportionality is given the impressive title of the **permeability of free space**. The symbol used for the permeability of free space is μ_0, where

$$\mu_0 = 4\pi \times 10^{-7} \text{ Tm/A}.$$

Ampère's Law for Solenoids is written in either of two forms:

$$B = \mu_0 \frac{NI}{L}, \qquad \text{or}$$

$$B = \mu_0 nI,$$

where n is the **number of turns per unit of length (m^{-1})** of the solenoid.

Ampère's Law for Solenoids will be used to calculate the magnetic field of the solenoids you used in **Investigation 7-1** and will use again in **Investigation 7-2**.

Exercises

1. A solenoid is 15.0 cm long and has 250 turns. What is the magnetic field strength inside the solenoid if the current in the coils is 3.8 A?

2. A solenoid is to be wound on a cardboard form 30.0 cm long. How many turns of wire are needed to produce a magnetic field of 6.28×10^{-3} T, if the maximum allowable current is 5.0 A?

3. A solenoid 40.0 cm long has a magnetic field of 5.0×10^{-3} T when the current in it is 10.0 A. How many turns of wire does it have?

4. What magnetic field strength is needed to exert a force of 1.0×10^{-15} N on an electron travelling 2.0×10^7 m/s?

7.5 Magnetic Force on a Current in a Wire

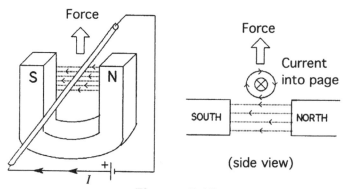

Figure 7.17

Since a wire carrying current has a magnetic field around it, one would expect such a wire to experience a force when placed in the field of an external magnet. A wire carrying current is a wire carrying moving **charges**, which you already know will experience a magnetic force if they move through a magnetic field at an angle greater than 0° with the direction of the field lines.

In **Figure 7.17**, a straight piece of wire is placed between the poles of a large U-magnet. Current is going 'into the page'. The wire segment between the poles of the magnet will experience an upward force (just as individual positive charges would).

The **Right Hand Motor Rule** can be applied here as well as with individual positive charges. *Point your right thumb in the direction of conventional current. Point your fingers straight out in the direction of the magnetic lines of force. The palm of your hand will now be 'pushing' in the direction of the force on the wire segment carrying the current.* Again, the magnetic field, the current, and the magnetic force are *mutually perpendicular.*

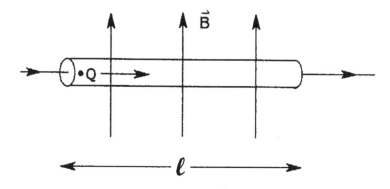

Figure 7.18

Figure 7.18 shows a short segment of wire of length ℓ through which an amount of charge Q travels in time t. Since the segment is perpendicular to the magnetic field lines, one would expect that the force on the charges moving through the wire would be $F = BQv$, where v is the speed of the charges moving in the wire. Now $v = \dfrac{\ell}{t}$, so $F = BQ\dfrac{\ell}{t}$.

Now the current in the segment, which we shall label I_s, is equal to $\dfrac{Q}{t}$. It would be expected then that the **magnetic force** on a segment of wire of length ℓ carrying current I_s would be given by

$$F = BI_s\ell.$$

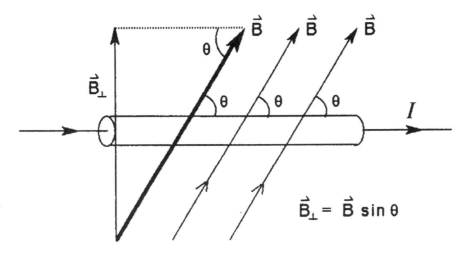

Figure 7.19

If the wire segment is not perpendicular to the lines of magnetic force, then the component of **B** perpendicular to the wire segment must be used. The situation is very much the same as for isolated moving charges moving through a magnetic field (**Figure 7.14**). In **Figure 7.19** the wire segment makes an angle θ with the lines of force.

$$F = BI_s\ell \sin \theta$$

If the segment is perpendicular to the field lines, this reduces to $F = BI_s\ell$. In **Investigation 7-2** you will check whether the force is proportional to I_s.

Investigation 7-2   The Current Balance

Purpose: To measure the magnetic field strength of a solenoid for different solenoid currents, using a current balance.

Introduction

Figure 7.20 shows the essential components of a current balance. A source of emf (6.0 V D.C.) is connected to the large solenoid, with a variable resistance and an ammeter in the solenoid circuit.

A plastic 'teeter totter' is balanced at the opening at one end of the solenoid. A current is passed through a conducting strip which runs around one end of the teeter totter. The magnetic field of the solenoid exerts a net force on the portion of the strip that runs perpendicular with the solenoid's lines of force — the segment ℓ on the diagram.

Current direction in the strip is chosen so that the end of the balance arm (teeter totter) *inside* the solenoid is pushed *downward.* To measure the downward magnetic force on the strip, it is simply balanced by using the force of gravity on known masses added at the other end of the balance.

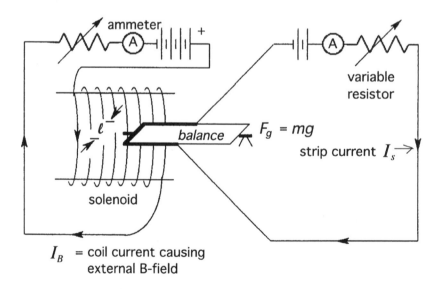

Figure 7.20

Procedure

1. Set the current through the solenoid at 4.0 A or as close to this value as possible. This is current I_B. *Do not change I_B during the first part of the experiment.*

2. With the balance in position on its pivot, send a small current through the strip and check that the magnetic force is pushing *down* inside the solenoid.

> ### Turn off the current while doing Procedure 3.

3. You will need at least five different masses to add to the end of the current balance. Use 10 mg (milligram) standard masses if they are available. If they are not available, prepare a set of standard masses as follows: Measure the mass of a 10 m length of fine transformer wire. Calculate the length of wire needed to have a mass of 10 mg. Cut at least five pieces of wire this length. Calculate the force of gravity on each standard mass by multiplying the mass (10 mg = 1.0×10^{-5} kg) by 9.8 N/kg.

4. Place a standard mass on the free end of the current balance. *Make sure that the standard masses are placed in a position such that they are the same distance from the pivot of the 'teeter totter' as the conducting strip at the other end of the 'teeter totter'.* (Why is this so important?) The free end of the balance arm should now move downward. Turn on the solenoid current I_B and the strip current. Adjust the current in the strip until the magnetic force on the strip just equals the force of gravity on the other end of the balance, and the balance arm remains horizontal. Record the strip current (I_S) and the force of gravity needed to balance the magnetic force.

5. Repeat **Procedure 4** with at least four different masses. Prepare a data table and record the strip currents and forces of gravity used in each situation.

6. Plot a graph of magnetic force (F) vs strip current I_S. (The magnetic force equals the force of gravity needed each time to balance the balance arm. Why?) Calculate the slope of your graph and record this slope in appropriate units.

7. Measure precisely the length of the conducting strip, ℓ, in metres.

8. The slope of your graph of F vs I_S will be $\Delta F/\Delta I_S$. If the graph is a straight line going through (0,0), then $\Delta F/\Delta I_S = F/I_S$. In theoretical discussion before this investigation (Section 7.5) it was predicted that $F = BI_S\ell$, where B is the magnetic field strength of the solenoid. Calculate a predicted value for B using $B = \dfrac{F}{I_S\ell}$.

9. You will now keep the *strip current* constant and vary the solenoid current, I_B. Set the strip current I_S at 2.0 A and leave it there for the remainder of the experiment Turn off the solenoid current. Place a 10 mg mass on the free end of the balance. Turn on the solenoid current and gradually increase I_B until the balance arm remains horizontal. Record I_B and the force of gravity on the 10 mg mass.

10. Repeat **Procedure 9** with at least four other masses. Record all currents and balancing forces as before.

11. Plot a graph of magnetic force F vs solenoid current I_B. Find the slope and express it in appropriate units.

Concluding Questions

1. How does the magnetic force on the strip vary with the current in the strip, if the solenoid current is kept constant?

2. When the solenoid current was 4.0 A, what was the magnetic field strength due to the solenoid current?

3. When the solenoid current is varied and the strip current is kept constant, how does the magnetic force depend on the solenoid current?

4. For *Investigation 7-3* you need to know what the magnetic field strength of your solenoid is for any current in the solenoid. Calculate its *magnetic field strength per ampere of solenoid current* as follows:

   In general, the force on a segment of conductor is $F = BI_s\ell$. When you kept I_s constant and varied I_B, your graph probably indicated that

   $$F = (\text{constant}) \cdot I_B.$$

   Since the 'constant' equals the graph's slope, $F = (\text{slope}) \cdot I_B$.

   Now, since $\qquad\qquad BI_s\ell = (\text{slope}) \cdot I_B,$

   $$\therefore \frac{B}{I_B} = \frac{slope}{I_s\ell}.$$

   Record this important ratio for future reference. It permits you to calculate magnetic field strength of your solenoid for any current you put through it!

5. According to Ampère's Law for Solenoids, the magnetic field strength of a solenoid can be calculated as follows: $B = \mu_o \dfrac{N}{L} \cdot I_B$, where N is the number of turns in the coil, L is the length of the solenoid, I_B is the current in the solenoid, and μ_o is the magnetic permeability of free space.

   $$\mu_o = 4\pi \times 10^{-7} \text{ Tm/A}.$$

   Measure L carefully and find out what N is for your solenoid*. Calculate the ratio, B/I_B, using Ampere's Law. Calculate the percent difference between the ratio you obtained this way and the ratio you obtained from data in **Procedure 4**.

   *If data is not available, and you do not wish to dismantle a solenoid, use $N = 525$ turns if the solenoid is the standard PSSC model.

6. Discuss the major sources of error in this experiment.

Exercises

1. (a) A solenoid 15.0 cm long has 600 turns and carries a current of 5.0 A. What is the magnetic field strength inside this coil?
   (b) A 2.0 cm segment of a current balance arm is balanced inside the solenoid when the current in it is 3.0 A. What is the magnetic force on the segment?

2. A 61 mg mass just balances the balance arm of a current balance when the strip current is 3.0 A. If the strip is 2.2 cm long, what is the magnetic field strength inside the solenoid in which the current balance is located?

3. The magnetic field strength inside a certain solenoid is 0.025 T. If a 3.2 cm conducting strip, which is perpendicular to the magnetic field inside the solenoid, experiences a force of 5.9×10^{-4} N, what is the current in the conducting strip?

4. A conductor 25 cm long carries a current of 50.0 A. It is placed in a magnetic field of strength 49 T. What force is exerted on the conductor if it makes these angles with the magnetic lines of force? (a) 0° (b) 45° (c) 90°

5. (a) A 5.0 cm segment of wire carrying 2.5 A is perpendicular to a magnetic field of 25 T inside a solenoid. What is the magnetic force on the segment?
   (b) If the current inside the solenoid is increased to five times its original value, what will the new magnetic field strength be?

7.6 Magnetic Fields and the Electron

J. J. Thomson (1856-1940) was not the first to observe cathode rays, which we now know are made up of electrons. He is credited with the discovery of electrons because he was the first to make a significant measurement of a property of the cathode rays. What he measured was the **ratio of the charge to the mass** of the particles in the cathode rays. Thomson used a combination of magnetic and electric fields to do this.

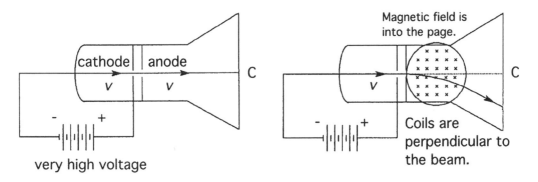

Figure 7.21   **Figure 7.22**

Figure 7.21 shows a simple cathode ray tube (CRT), where electrons (once called cathode rays) are accelerated by a high voltage toward an anode. Electrons passing through the holes in the anode will travel at some speed v to a fluorescent screen, where they will form a spot on the screen at C.

If a magnetic field B is applied perpendicular to the path of the electrons, as in **Figure 7.22**, the beam of negative electrons will be deflected **downward** (Right Hand Motor Rule) and form a spot on the screen at A.

The magnetic field pushes electrons downward with a force $F = BQv = Bev$, where e is the charge on one electron.

The magnetic force is always perpendicular to the velocity of the electron, so it acts as a **centripetal force**. It produces an acceleration toward the centre of a circular path. Therefore,

$$F = Bev = \frac{mv^2}{R} .$$

From these equations, the ratio of charge to mass can be determined to be

$$\frac{e}{m} = \frac{v}{BR} .$$

Both B and R are measurable. Thomson eliminated the need to know v by using a clever technique. If an electric field E is applied to the same beam of electrons, and adjusted so that the electric force ($F = EQ = Ee$) on the electrons is just equal to the magnetic force (**Figure 7.23**), then $Bev = Ee$. When these conditions are fulfilled, then

$$v = \frac{E}{B} .$$

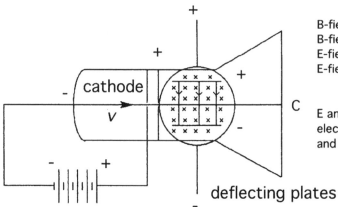

B-field is into the page.
B-field pushes electrons DOWN.
E-field is 'down'.
E-field pushes electrons UP.

E and B are adjusted so that electric force = magnetic force, and deflection = 0.

Figure 7.23

The speed of the electrons is equal to the ratio of the electric field strength to the magnetic field strength, when the electric force just balances the magnetic force to produce zero deflection. When this condition is met, we can substitute this value for speed in the equation for charge-to-mass ratio, and we get

$$\frac{e}{m} = \frac{v}{BR} = \frac{\frac{E}{B}}{BR} = \frac{E}{B^2 R}.$$

Thomson determined the charge-to-mass ratio. The modern value is

$$\frac{e}{m} = 1.76 \times 10^{11} \text{ C/kg} .$$

J. J. Thomson was certain that electrons were subatomic particles, and not just a type of atom. Later on, **Robert A. Millikan (1868-1953)** successfully measured the charge on one electron. He did this with an extremely intricate experiment in which electrically charged oil drops were suspended between parallel charged plates. Electrical forces were used to balance the gravitational forces on the tiny drops. He was able to calculate the charge on the drops, and found that the charge was always a multiple of 1.6×10^{-19} C. No charge smaller than this was ever found in his experiment, so he assumed that this was the **elementary charge,** the smallest charge in nature.

Knowing that $e = 1.6 \times 10^{-19}$ C, and that $\frac{e}{m} = 1.76 \times 10^{11}$ C/kg, the **mass** of one electron could now be calculated.

$$m_{electron} = \frac{1.6 \times 10^{-19} \text{ C}}{1.76 \times 10^{11} \text{ C/kg}} = 9.1 \times 10^{-31} \text{ kg}.$$

This tiny mass of the electron confirmed Thomson's view that the electron was a subatomic particle.

Experiment 7-3 Estimating the Mass of the Electron

Purpose: To measure the approximate mass of an electron, using a tuning-eye diode and a solenoid that was calibrated in *Investigation 7-2.*

Introduction:

When an electron moving at speed *v* passes through a magnetic field *B*, in a direction perpendicular to the magnetic lines of force, the electron is deflected into a circular path of radius *R*. The magnetic force, $F = Bev$, is therefore a **centripetal force**, and we can write the equation,

$$Bev = \frac{mv^2}{R} \cdot \quad (1)$$

Assume the voltage between the cathode and the anode of a vacuum diode tube is V_a. Then V_a is the **work done per unit charge to accelerate electrons from the cathode to the anode.** The work shows up as **kinetic energy** of the electrons, and it reaches a maximum just as the electrons reach the anode.

$$V_a = \frac{1/2\, mv^2}{e} \quad (2)$$

Now Equation (1) assumes that electrons are moving at a constant speed through a magnetic field. In Equation (2), the speed is the **maximum speed** achieved by the accelerating electrons. In the tuning-eye diode tube that you use in this experiment, the design is such that the electrons, although they are accelerating, reach near maximum speed just before they enter the region outside the dark metal cap you see looking down into the tube. Their speed while in your field of view as they move toward the fluorescent anode is, for all practical purposes, constant. This means that we can combine Equations (1) and (2), to derive an expression for the mass of the electron.

From Equation (1), $v = \dfrac{BeR}{m}$. Substituting for *v* in Equation (2),

$$V_a = \frac{1/2\, m}{e} \cdot \frac{B^2 e^2 R^2}{m^2} \cdot$$

Simplifying and solving for *m*,

$$m_{electron} = \frac{B^2 e R^2}{2V_a} \cdot$$

Since all the variables on the right side of the equation are known or are measurable, the mass of the electron can be determined!

Inside the tuning eye diode, electrons accelerate radially from the central cathode toward the fluorescent anode (**Figures 7.24** and **7.25**). Deflecting electrodes cause a fan-shaped shadow to form. With no magnetic field applied, the edges of the shadow are straight, indicating that the electrons are travelling in straight lines from cathode to anode.

When a solenoid is lowered over the tube, so that its magnetic field is perpendicular to the flow of electrons, the electrons are sent into a curved path, which can be seen on the screen.

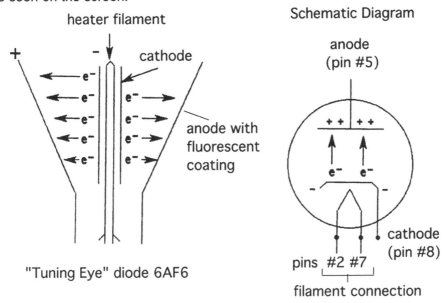

Figure 7.24

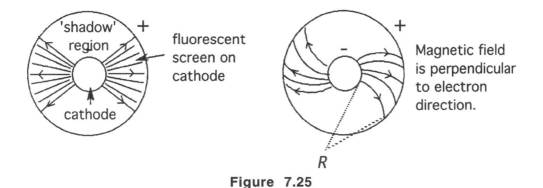

Figure 7.25

Procedure

1. Connect the apparatus as in **Figure 7.26**. Use an anode voltage of 100 V to start.

2. Place an air-cored solenoid (calibrated in **Investigation 7-2**) over the tube. A rheostat and ammeter are in series with the solenoid, which is connected to a 6.0 V D.C. source.

3. Vary the current in the solenoid until the curvature of the edge of the electron beam can be conveniently matched with that of a piece of wood dowelling or a non-magnetic brass cork borer, inserted down through the solenoid. If you now measure the diameter of the dowelling or cork borer, you can calculate the **radius of curvature** of the electron beam. Record this value of R. Also record I_B.

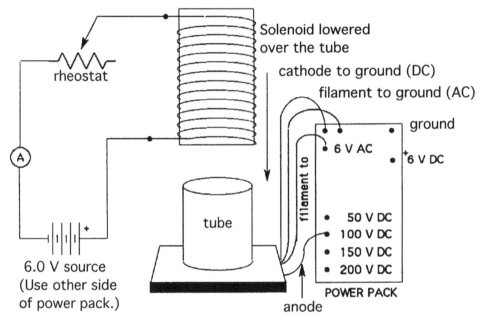

Figure 7.26

4. Consult your data from **Investigation 7-2** (The Current Balance) to see what the magnetic field strength of your solenoid would be for the solenoid current you just used to measure R. (**Investigation 7-2** gave you a value for B/I_B. Multiply B/I_B by I_B to obtain B.)

5. Measure the voltage you are using for the anode voltage, V_a. The power supply label of 100 V may not be reliable.

6. You now know B, R, e, and V_a. Calculate the mass of an electron from

$$m_{electron} = \frac{B^2 e R^2}{2V_a} .$$

7. Do at least two more trials using different solenoid currents and possibly different accelerating voltages. Calculate the mass of the electron in each trial.

Concluding Questions

1. What is the mean value you obtained for the mass of the electron? The accepted value is 9.1 x 10^{-31} kg. What is the percent difference between your value and the accepted value?

2. This method of measuring the mass of an electron is quite crude, but you should be able to obtain a 'ball park' figure for the mass of one electron. What are some of the 'assumptions' made in this experiment that might introduce sources of error?

Exercises

1. A magnetic field of strength 4.34 x 10^{-3} T makes electrons deflect into a circular path of radius 1.1 x 10^{-2} m. The accelerating voltage used to get the electrons up to maximum speed was 200.0 V. If the charge on an electron is 1.6 x 10^{-19} C, what is the mass of an electron?

2. A beam of protons passes through a magnetic field of strength 4.0 x 10^{-3} T, and is deflected into a curved path of radius 1.14 m. If the accelerating voltage was 1.0 x 10^3 V, what is the mass of a proton?

3. If the proton in **Exercise 2** were replaced by deuterium ions that have twice the mass of a proton but carry the same charge, what would the radius of curvature of the magnetically deflected deuterium ions be, in the same circumstances?

4. Protons are accelerated and made to pass through crossed fields where the electric field is perpendicular to the magnetic field, and the protons are moving at such a speed that the magnetic force just equals the electric force, but is in the opposite direction, so that there is no overall deflection of the beam. What speed do the particles have if $B = 0.50$ T and $E = 5.5$ x 10^4 N/C? (Such a device was used by J. J. Thomson when he was measuring the charge-to-mass ratio of electrons. It is called a **velocity selector**.)

7.7 The Mass Spectrometer

x = B-field into page
E-field is perpendicular
to B-field

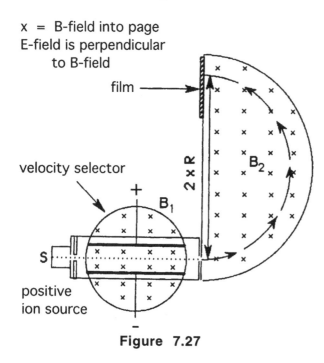

Figure 7.27

The **mass spectrometer** was developed as a tool for measuring the masses of charged atoms. Electric current or heat is used to ionize atoms at the source **S**. Ions pass through a slit into the **velocity selector** where those with a chosen velocity, $v = \dfrac{E}{B}$, will get through the crossed electric and magnetic fields and through the slit that lets them enter a different magnetic field region, where the ions are forced into a circular path ending on a photographic film.

Two different magnetic fields are used in the mass spectrometer. In the velocity selector portion, the field is B_1. The velocity of the charged particles that emerge from the velocity selector will be $v = \dfrac{E}{B_1}$.

The charged particles entering the larger magnetic field region will experience only a magnetic force, and this will accelerate them into a circular path. Since

$$F = B_2 Qv = \frac{mv^2}{R},$$

$$\therefore m = \frac{B_2 QR}{v} = \frac{B_2 QR}{E/B_1} = \frac{B_1 B_2 QR}{E}.$$

Since all the quantities on the right side of the equation are measurable, the mass of an ion can be calculated from this result. You can see that for an atom of a given charge, **the radius traced out in its circular path through the second magnetic field is proportional to its mass.** Isotopes of the same element can be separated in a beautifully simple way using the spectrometer! The mass spectrometer can be used to separate the elements in a mixture, or the isotopes in an element. It can also be used to measure the mass of charged molecules.

Exercises

1. Two isotopes of hydrogen are present in a particle beam issuing through the final slit into the magnetic field outside the velocity selector of a mass spectrometer. Protons and deuterons, both with a charge of +1, are subjected to the same magnetic field strength. Both go into a circular path. If the proton path radius is R, what will the deuteron path radius be? (A deuteron is a deuterium nucleus, which consists of a proton and a neutron.)

2. What is the velocity of ions that pass successfully through a velocity selector, if the electric field has a strength of 1.5×10^5 N/C and the magnetic field in the velocity selector is 0.50 T? What will the radius of the path of these ions be if the bending magnet has a field strength of 0.75 T? Assume the ions have a charge of +e, and an atomic mass of 20 u, where 1 u = 1.67×10^{-27} kg.

7.8 Electric Motors

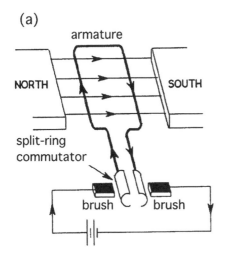

(a)

armature

NORTH

SOUTH

split-ring commutator

brush   brush

(b)

line of force of external magnet

force ⇧

N ⊗   ⊙ S

force ⇩   lines of force
           due to current
           in armature

Figure 7.28

Figure 7.28 shows a simple one-turn coil motor operated on direct current. The coil in a motor is called the **armature.** Of course, a real motor will have many turns of wire. The external or 'field' magnet may also be an electromagnet rather than a permanent magnet. The external magnetic field exerts a torque on the armature, causing it to turn continuously.

Note the importance of the **split-ring commutator.** When the armature makes one-half turn, the split-ring commutator makes the current in the two halves of the coil *change direction* so that the magnetic force (and therefore the torque) is always 'down' on the left side and 'up' on the right side.

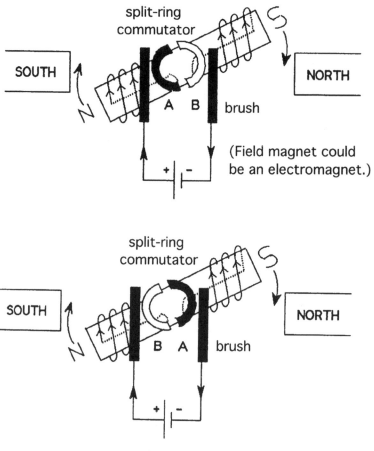

Figure 7.29

Figure 7.29 shows the construction of a typical laboratory demonstration motor (called the **St. Louis Motor**). Current enters the armature at **A**. The contact is called a **brush,** and is made of copper. Commercial motors may use a graphite brush which is spring-loaded to keep it in firm contact with the armature.

The split metal cylinder on the armature is the **split-ring commutator**. Current direction is from the brush at **A** to the left half of the commutator, then to the coil of wire on the armature. Current direction is such that the left end of the armature is an N-pole and the right end is an S-pole. Current leaves the right side of the split-ring commutator at **B** and returns to the battery.

Since opposite poles attract, the external field magnets exert a torque on the armature. When the armature has made one-half a turn, current direction in the armature reverses because of the commutator. Current now enters at **B** and leaves at **A**. The external field magnets keep on turning the armature clockwise as before, because the left side is still an N-pole and the right side is still an S-pole.

Electric motors come in all sizes. Some are very tiny and drive toys; others are huge and drive trains or buses. You will find electric motors in toy trains, automobiles, clocks, wheelchairs, streetcars, can openers, cement mixers, furnace fans, robots and many, many other devices.

The motors described in **Figures 7.28** and **7.29** operate only on direct current. Alternating current motors work on essentially the same principle, but do not use a split-ring commutator. Since the current is already 'alternating', there is no need for a split-ring commutator to reverse the current every half-turn.

Chapter Review Questions

1. Name at least three ferromagnetic elements.

2. If you wanted to accelerate a stationary proton, would you use an electric field or a magnetic field? Explain.

3. Draw a diagram showing a conductor with conventional current moving **into your page**. Draw a few sample lines of magnetic force around the conductor, including their directions.

4. Describe the magnetic field inside a long solenoid.

5. Draw a solenoid with current moving in a direction of your choice. Label the north end of the solenoid.

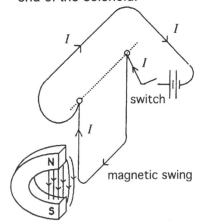

6. When the switch is closed on this 'magnetic swing', will it move 'out' from the poles of the magnet or 'in' toward the magnet? Use the Right Hand Motor Rule.

Figure 7.30

7. An electron moving with a speed of 0.10 c moves through a magnetic field of strength 0.60 T. What force acts on the electron?

$$(c = 3.0 \times 10^8 \text{ m/s}) \qquad (e = 1.6 \times 10^{-19} \text{ C})$$

8. A solenoid is wound with 100 turns per centimetre. What is the magnetic field strength inside the solenoid when it carries a current of 5.0 A? $(\mu_0 = 4\pi \times 10^{-7} \text{ T} \cdot \text{m/A})$

9. A magnetic field from a solenoid is used to deflect a beam of electrons 0.80 cm on the screen of a CRT. If the current in the solenoid is doubled, what will the deflection be then?

10. An electron beam in a CRT is deflected 0.64 cm when the accelerating voltage is 500.0 V. By how much will the beam be deflected if the magnetic field is kept constant but the accelerating voltage is increased to 2000.0 V?

11. What is the magnetic force exerted on a segment of wire 12 cm long in a perpendicular magnetic field of strength 36 T, if the wire carries a current of 6.0 A?

12. If the force on a 5.0 cm piece of wire carrying 12 A is 1.0×10^{-3} N, what is the magnetic field strength of the perpendicular field through which the current passes?

13. A conducting wire 1.0 m long carries a current of 7.5 A. It is placed in a magnetic field of strength 5.0×10^{-5} T. If the wire makes an angle of 60° with the magnetic lines of force, what is the force acting on the wire?

14. A 75 mg mass just balances the strip in a current balance when the current in the strip is 2.5 A. If the strip is 2.0 cm long, what is the magnetic field strength inside the solenoid in which the current balance is located?

15. An alpha particle is accelerated by a voltage of 1.53×10^3 V and is then deflected by a magnetic field of strength 0.020 T into a circular path of radius 0.40 m. If the alpha particles have a charge of 3.2×10^{-19} C, what is their mass?

16. Why does a DC motor need a split-ring commutator?

17. Two parallel wires carry currents in the *same* direction. Will the wires attract or repel each other? Explain with the help of a diagram.

Brain Busters

18. In the velocity selector part of a mass spectrometer, a field of 0.65 T is used for magnetic deflection of a beam of protons travelling at a speed of 1.0×10^6 m/s. What electric field is needed to balance the force due to the magnetic field? If the distance between the plates of the electrical deflection apparatus is 0.50 cm, what voltage must be applied to the plates?

19. What speed must electrons in a beam of electrons going through a velocity selector have, if the beam is undeflected by crossed electric and magnetic fields of strengths 6.0×10^3 V/m and 0.0030 T respectively? If the electric field is shut off, what would the radius of the beam become due to the unbalanced magnetic force?

Test Yourself!

Multiple Choice

X
•

1. At **X**, what is the direction of the magnetic field due to the bar magnet?

   A. into the page
   B. ←
   C. →
   D. ↓
   E. out of the page

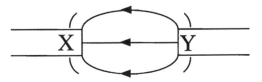

2. Identify the poles of the magnet in the above diagram.

	Pole X	Pole Y
A	south	north
B	south	south
C	north	south
D	north	north

3. A permanent magnet is dipped into a pile of metal scraps. Which type of metal will **not** be picked up by the magnet?
   A. iron
   B. tin
   C. cobalt
   D. nickel

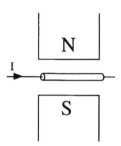

4. What is the direction of the magnetic force on the conductor in the above diagram?
   A. ↑
   B. ↓
   C. into the page
   D. out of the page
   E. →

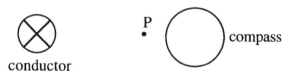

conductor   P   compass

5. The conductor on the left is carrying conventional current into the page. In which direction will a compass needle point if the compass is placed at **P**?

   A. ←   B. ↑   C. →   D. ↓

R   S

fixed   movable
conductor   conductor

6. Two conducting wires, **R** and **S**, run parallel with each other, and both carry current into the page. Conductor **R** is fixed, but conductor **S** can move. In what direction will the magnetic fields due to currents in the wires tend to make conductor **S** move?

   A. ←   B. ↑   C. →   D. ↓

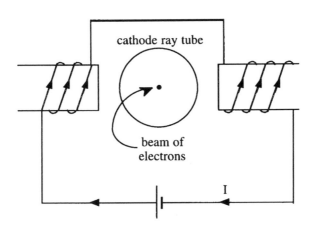

cathode ray tube

beam of
electrons

I

(7-9) Two solenoids are being used to deflect the same beam of electrons in a cathode ray tube.

7. In what direction will the electron beam be deflected?

A. ←   B. ↑   C. →   D. ↓

8. If the magnetic field strength **B** is doubled, the deflection will change from δ to

A. 2.00 δ.
B. 0.500 δ.
C. 0.707 δ.
D. 1.00 δ.
E. 1.414 δ.

9. If the accelerating voltage V_a is doubled, the deflection will change from δ to

A. 2.00 δ.
B. 0.500 δ.
C. 0.707 δ.
D. 1.00 δ.
E. 1.414 δ.

Open-Ended Questions

10. A particle carrying a charge of 0.50 μC enters a magnetic field of strength 0.045 T, with a velocity of 350 m/s. The velocity is perpendicular to the magnetic field. What is the magnetic force acting on the charged particle?

11. A segment of conducting wire 5.0 cm long carrying 5.0 A of current is perpendicular to a magnetic field of 12 T. What magnetic force acts on the segment?

12. A solenoid 0.20 m long has 600 turns of wire. What current must be passed through the solenoid to produce a magnetic field of 2.0×10^{-2} T?

13. (a) A particle of mass m and charge q is moving with speed v in a circular path of radius R in a uniform magnetic field B. How would you calculate the radius from the other information?
(b) An alpha particle, of mass 6.7×10^{-27} kg and charge 3.2×10^{-19} C, is accelerated from rest by a voltage of 2.00×10^{3} V. What will be the radius of curvature of its path in a uniform magnetic field of 0.070 T?
(c) What is the momentum of the alpha particle?

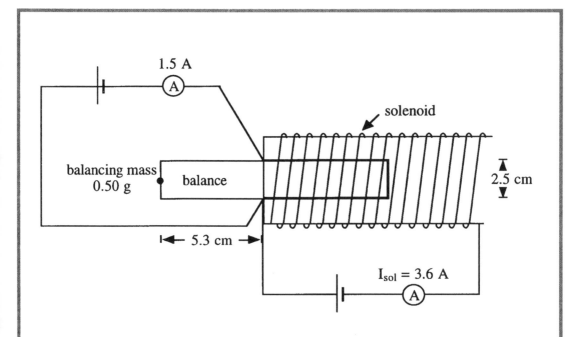

14. What is the magnetic field B inside the solenoid of this current balance, if the force of gravity on the 0.50 gram mass just provides enough torque to balance the torque due to the magnetic force on the current balance?

Chapter 8   Electromagnetic Induction

8.1   Induced Emf

In the previous chapter, you learned that when electric charges move, they produce a magnetic field. Also, a magnetic field will exert a force on moving charges. Early in the nineteenth century, scientists such as **Michael Faraday (1791-1867)** in England and **Joseph Henry (1797-1878)** in the U.S.A. were aware of these properties. Both asked the obvious question, "If a current produces magnetism, might magnetism produce a current?"

Both scientists did discover that magnetism could be used to induce an emf that would produce a current in a circuit. Faraday was the first to publish his discovery, and he studied electromagnetic induction in more detail.

In *Investigation 8-1* you will observe a number of ways in which an emf can be induced using changing magnetic fields. The main purpose of *Investigation 8-1* is to give you some concrete experience with magnetic induction devices, so that the more theoretical discussion of electromagnetic induction that follows will be more understandable.

Investigation 8-1 Electromagnetic Induction

Purpose: To investigate some ways of inducing an emf.

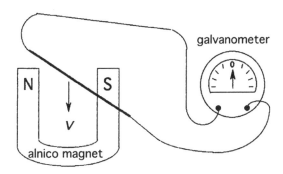

Figure 8.1

Part 1

Procedure

1. Attach the two ends of a 2.0 m length of wire to the terminals of a sensitive galvanometer. See **Figure 8.1**.

2. Move a section of the wire swiftly *downward* between the poles of a strong Alnico horseshoe magnet. Watch the galvanometer scale carefully for a *very small* deflection. Note the **direction** of the deflection. Move the section of wire swiftly *upward* in the opposite direction between the poles of the magnet. Observe the direction of the galvanometer deflection again.

3. Leave the wire stationary and move the magnet instead of the wire.

4. Try moving the wire in a direction parallel with the lines of force of the magnet.

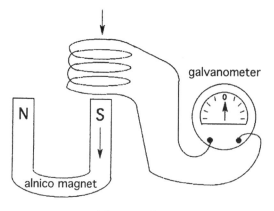

Figure 8.2

5. Form a coil with *one* turn from the wire, and try moving the coil over one pole of the magnet, as in **Figure 8.2.**

6. Experiment with more turns on the coil, and with different speeds. Does it matter whether the coil moves or the magnet? Does the direction of the induced current depend on the direction of motion of the coil relative to the magnet?

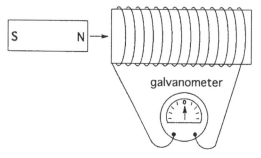

Figure 8.3

7. Connect your galvanometer to a commercial solenoid like the one you used in the **Investigations** in the last chapter. See **Figure 8.3.** Insert the north pole of a bar magnet into the solenoid. Observe the direction of the induced current while the magnet's north pole is (a) *entering* and (b) *leaving* the solenoid.

8. Try inserting the south pole of your bar magnet first. Again, observe the current direction while the magnet is (a) entering and (b) leaving the solenoid.

9. Try using two bar magnets held with 'like' poles side by side. This will approximately double the magnetic field strength.

10. Experiment until you are satisfied that you know what variables contribute to obtaining the highest possible induced current.

11. Draw a diagram showing a bar magnet being inserted N-pole first into a solenoid. Show the direction of the induced current on the diagram. Now use Ampère's Right Hand Rule to determine the magnetic polarity of the end of the solenoid that is nearest the N-pole of the bar magnet.

Concluding Questions

1. Summarize the factors which contribute to a larger induced current when a magnet and a coil are used.

2. When a magnet is moved into or out of a solenoid, a current is induced in the solenoid. This in turn produces a magnetic field in the solenoid. Describe the polarity of the solenoid *relative to the polarity of the permanent magnet* being used to induce the emf in the solenoid (a) when the bar magnet enters the solenoid and (b) when the bar magnet leaves the solenoid.

Part 2

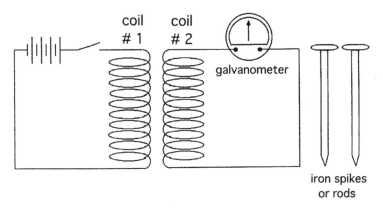

Figure 8.4

Procedure

1. Set up the arrangement in **Figure 8.4**. The battery is connected by way of a switch to the first coil, but not the second. A galvanometer is connected to the second coil.

2. With the two coils very close but not touching, turn on the switch to send current through the first coil. Does the galvanometer indicate current in the second coil? Turn off the current. If you did not see anything happen, try it all again. Watch the galvanometer needle very closely while you are turning the switch on and while you are turning it off.

3. Place a soft iron core (perhaps a few large spikes) inside each of the coils, and repeat **Procedure 2**.

4. If available, use as a second coil a smaller solenoid that will fit inside the first coil. Repeat **Procedure 2** with and without an iron core. Find out what the effect is of varying the number of turns in coil number 1, by inserting coil number 2 only a fraction of the way inside the larger coil.

5. Examine a demonstration induction coil. How is the 'off' and 'on' switching accomplished with this high voltage device?

Concluding Questions

1. Under what conditions is a current induced in the second coil by a current in the first coil? Why do you think there is no induced current when the current in the first coil is constant?

2. Describe the direction of the induced current while the current in the first coil is being turned off, compared with the direction of the induced current when the current in the first coil is being turned on.

Challenge!

Examine a demonstration transformer. This is an excellent example of a device in which an emf is induced. Why does the transformer require no 'on-off' switching mechanism?

8.2 Inducing an 'EMF' in a Straight Piece of Wire

If a length of conducting wire (ℓ) is made to move through magnetic lines of force that are perpendicular to the conductor, as in **Figure 8.5 (a)** and **Figure 8.5 (b)**, an emf will develop between the ends of the conductor. If the conductor is part of a complete circuit, a current will exist in the circuit, as you saw in *Investigation 8-1.*

Consider a quantity of charge Q at one end of the segment of wire. The charge is free to move, since this is a conducting material. For simplicity in applying the Right Hand Motor Rule, let the charge be positive (although you know that in a metal it is really negative electrons that move).

Let the wire be made to move straight down through the perpendicular lines of force in the direction of the arrow labelled *v*, which is the velocity of the wire and therefore is also the vertical velocity of the charge in the wire.

The charges moving downward through the magnetic field will experience a force $F = BQv$, due to the external magnetic field. The direction of this force, according to the **Right Hand Motor Rule**, will be *out of the page*, which means they will be forced to move along the length of the wire, which is also coming *out of the page.*

When a charge Q has been forced to move the length ℓ of the segment of wire in the magnetic field, the amount of work that will have been done on it will be

$$W = Fd = BQv{\cdot}\ell$$

Because of the work done on them, the charges have gained potential energy, and the gain in potential energy per unit charge between the two ends of the segment of wire will be the emf between the ends of the wire.

Induced emf $\quad \mathcal{E} = \dfrac{BQv\ell}{Q} = Bv\ell.$

At first glance, it may seem unlikely that the units for emf in this formula could possibly be volts, so it is worth doing a unit check on this formula!

The units of $Bv\ell$ will be:

$$[T]\,[\frac{m}{s}]\,[m] = [\frac{N}{A\,m}]\,[\frac{m}{s}]\,[m] = \frac{N\,m}{A\,s} = \frac{J}{C} = V.$$

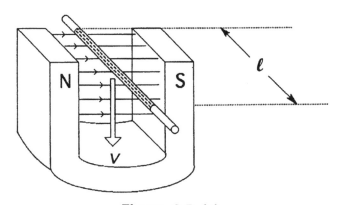

Figure 8.5 (a)

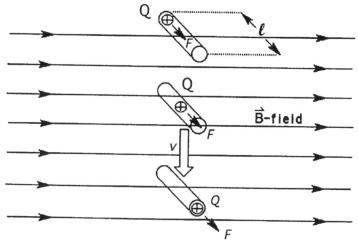

Figure 8.5(b)

Example

How fast must a 25 cm piece of wire be made to move through the poles of a 0.50 T magnet in order to develop a potential difference between its ends of 1.0 V?

Solution:

$$\mathcal{E} = Bv\ell,$$

$$\therefore \quad v = \frac{\mathcal{E}}{B\ell}.$$

$$\therefore v = \frac{1.0 \text{ V}}{(0.50 \text{ T})(0.25 \text{ m})} = 8.0 \text{ m/s}.$$

Exercises

1. An aircraft with a wingspan of 30.0 m travelling 250 m/s dives perpendicular to the lines of force of the earth's magnetic field (5.0 x 10^{-5} T). What emf is induced between the two wing tips?

2. A 15 cm piece of wire is moved through the poles of a 0.40 T magnet with a speed of 5.0 m/s. What is the potential difference between the ends of the wire?

3. How fast would you have to move a 0.50 m wire perpendicular to the earth's magnetic field (5.0 x 10^{-5} T) in order to induce an emf of 1.5 V?

4. In **Figure 8.5 (b)**, in which direction would **electrons** tend to move along the segment of wire? (***Into*** the page or ***out of*** the page?)

8.3 The Generator

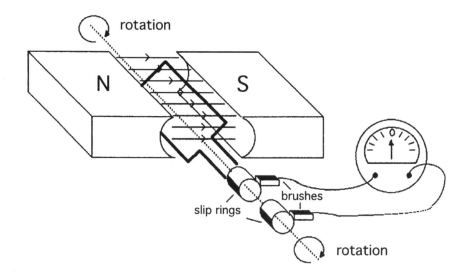

Figure 8.6

The generator was invented by **Michael Faraday**. **Figure 8.6** shows a simple, hand-operated generator with a coil consisting of only one turn (to simplify the explanation).

When the coil is rotated, the two long sides of the coil cut across the lines of force of the magnet, and a varying emf is induced in these two segments.

When the coil is vertical, as in **Figure 8.7(a)**, the two segments of wire in which an emf can be induced are both moving parallel with the lines of force, and *no* emf is induced.

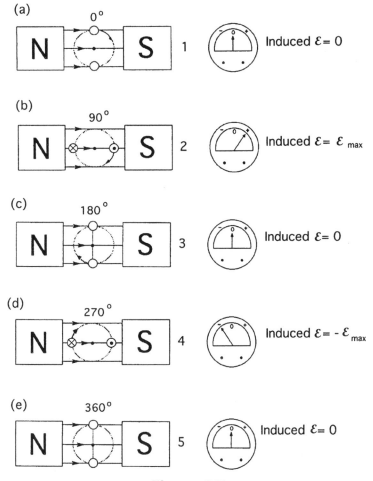

Figure 8.7

When the coil is horizontal, as in **Figure 8.7(b)**, the segments in which an emf can be induced are *perpendicular* to the lines of force through which they are moving, and the induced emf is at its maximum or **peak voltage**.

Figure 8.7 begins with the coil of the generator perpendicular to the lines of force. Consider just the **top segment** of wire. Its length is ℓ and its speed is v. The strength of the magnetic field is B. The angle between the plane of the coil and the vertical position is $\theta = 0$.

At any position of the segment, the induced emf in it is $\mathcal{E} = B \ell v_{\perp}$, where $v_{\perp}$ is the component of v that is perpendicular to the magnetic field lines. When the segment is at the top position, $v_{\perp} = 0$. Therefore, when $\theta = 0$, $\mathcal{E} = 0$.

In the second diagram (**Figure 8.7(b)**), the segment has made one-quarter of a rotation, and now $\theta = 90°$. In this position, the velocity vector is perpendicular to the magnetic field lines. At $\theta = 90°$, $v_{\perp} = v$, and the induced emf is at its maximum.

$$\mathcal{E} = \mathcal{E}_{max} = B\ell v$$

In the third diagram (**Figure 8.7 (c)**), $v_{\perp} = 0$ again, so $\mathcal{E} = 0$ as well. In the fourth position (**Figure 8.7 (d)**) where $\theta = 270°$, the velocity vector has reversed its direction, so the induced emf also reverses. Therefore, at 270°, $\mathcal{E} = - \mathcal{E}_{max}$.

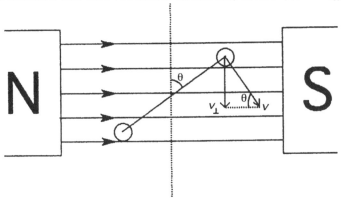

Figure 8.8

At *any* angle θ, $v_{\perp} = v \sin \theta$ (**Figure 8.8**), and $\mathcal{E} = B \ell v \sin \theta$. This is the emf induced in one **segment**. Since the coil has *two segments* whose emf's are additive, their combined emf is $2B \ell v \sin \theta$. For a more realistic generator coil with N turns in it,

$$\mathcal{E} = 2NB \ell v \sin \theta .$$

The maximum value of the induced emf is achieved when $\theta = 90°$ where $\sin \theta = 1$, and when $\theta = 270°$, where $\sin \theta = -1$.

Therefore, $\qquad\qquad\qquad\qquad \mathcal{E}_{max} = \pm 2NB \ell v ,$

and in general, $\qquad \mathcal{E} = \mathcal{E}_{max} \sin \theta$.

Figure 8.9 is a graph showing how the induced emf varies with the angle through which the coil rotates. A graph of **emf vs time** would have the same shape, since the coil will rotate with a constant frequency of rotation under normal circumstances.

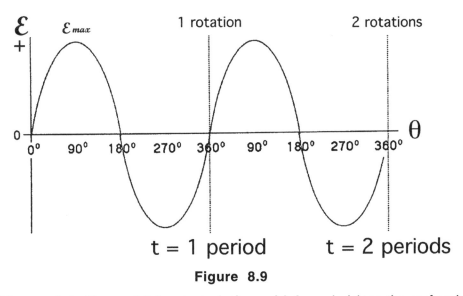

Figure 8.9

The graph in **Figure 8.9** is a typical **sinusoidal** graph (since the emf varies as the sine of the angle). A graph of **current** vs angle (or time) would also be sinusoidal, since current is proportional to emf. The shape of this graph is the familiar shape of **alternating current**. Commercial generators in North America have a frequency of 60 Hz. This means they make one full cycle (360 °) sixty times in one second.

Exercises

1. How might you convert the generator in **Figure 8.6** so that instead of producing alternating emf and current it will produce direct current? Would it be a steady D.C.? Sketch a graph to show how the emf would vary with time.

2. Start with the formula for the induced emf of a generator:

$$\mathcal{E} = 2NB \, \ell \, v \sin \theta.$$

Use the fact that the speed of a segment of the coil can be calculated from $v = 2\pi R/T$, where R is the radius of the circle traced out by the rotating segment, and T is the period of the rotation, to write an equation for the emf induced by a generator in terms of the frequency (f) of rotation of the coil.

3. Assuming the coil in a generator is rectangular, its area would equal its length times its total width; that is $A = 2\ell r$. Rewrite your equation from **Exercise 2** in terms of the *area* of the coil.

4. The armature of a 60 Hz AC generator rotates in a magnetic field of strength 0.48 T. If the area of the coil is 2.4 x 10^{-2} m^2 and it contains 120 loops, what will the peak emf be?

5. List four factors you could change to increase the emf produced by a generator. Tell how you would change them.

8.4 Magnetic Flux and Faraday's Law of Induction

Investigation 8-1 probably convinced you that an essential requirement for inducing an emf in a wire or a coil is a *changing magnetic field*. You obtained a changing field in two ways in that investigation: (1) by moving a permanent magnet relative to a conductor, or vice versa; and (2) by turning a current on or off, causing the magnetic field to build up or collapse in the area of the conductor.

You probably noticed that the faster you changed the field, the more induced current you observed on the galvanometer. Since the current was caused by the induced emf, it would appear that the induced emf is greater when the time duration of the change in the magnetic field is less.

$$(\mathcal{E} \propto 1/\Delta t)$$

Michael Faraday observed that the amount of induced emf depended not simply on the change in magnetic field strength (B), but on the change in **magnetic flux.** The symbol for magnetic flux is ϕ.

Magnetic flux ϕ is defined as the product of (a) the component of the magnetic field strength B that is perpendicular to the plane of the coil, and (b) the area A of the coil. If the angle between B and the **axis** of the coil is θ , then

Magnetic flux $\phi = B_\perp A = BA \cos \theta.$

What **Faraday** found out was that *the amount of induced emf depends on the rate at which the magnetic flux changes with respect to time.*

For a wire loop of one turn (as in **Figures 8.10** and **8.11**), if the magnetic flux changes from ϕ_1 to ϕ_2 , the change in magnetic flux will be $\Delta\phi = \phi_2 - \phi_1$ in a time interval of Δt . The induced emf will be

$$\mathcal{E} = - \frac{\Delta\phi}{\Delta t}.$$

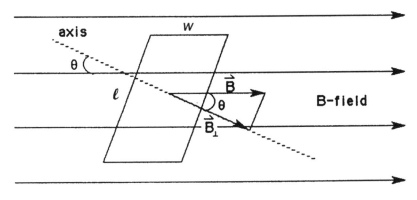

Figure 8.10

For a wire loop with N turns,

$$\mathcal{E} = -N \frac{\Delta\phi}{\Delta t}.$$

This general rule for magnetic induction is called **Faraday's Law Of Induction**.

Units for Magnetic Flux

The measuring unit for magnetic flux ϕ could be T·m², since flux is the product of magnetic field and area, but for historical reasons this unit is called the **weber (Wb)**.

$$1 \text{ Wb} = 1 \text{ T·m}^2$$

It is worthwhile doing a unit check on the formula for Faraday's Law.

$$\mathcal{E} = -N \frac{\Delta\phi}{\Delta t} = -N \frac{\Delta\{BA\cos\theta\}}{\Delta t}.$$

$$1\left[\frac{Wb}{s}\right] = 1\left[\frac{T\,m^2}{s}\right] = \left[1\frac{\frac{N}{A\,m}\cdot m^2}{s}\right] = 1\left[\frac{N\,m}{A\,s}\right] = 1\left[\frac{J}{C}\right] = 1\ [V].$$

Since emf should be in volts, the units 'check out'!

Why the Minus Sign?

When a changing flux causes an emf to be induced, the induced emf in turn produces an **induced current**. The induced current causes a magnetic field to be produced around itself. This induced magnetic field **opposes** the magnetic flux that produced the induced emf in the first place!

(a)

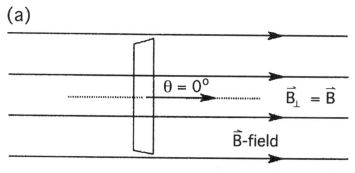

magnetic flux $\Phi = BA \cos \theta = BA$

(b)

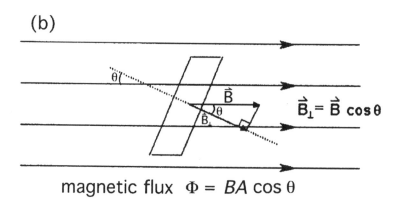

magnetic flux $\Phi = BA \cos \theta$

(c)

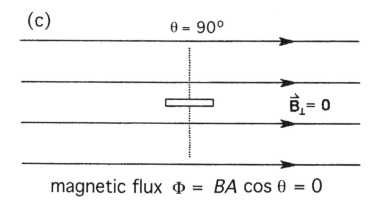

magnetic flux $\Phi = BA \cos \theta = 0$

Figure 8.11

Lenz's Law

The polarity of the induced emf will always be such that it will produce a current whose magnetic field opposes the changing flux that produced the emf.

This observation is called **Lenz's Law**, after **Heinrich Lenz (1804-1865)** who first made it.

Lenz's Law is really a special case of the of **Law of Conservation of Energy**. To obtain energy from a generator, mechanical energy must be used to obtain the electrical energy. Work must be done to overcome the repulsive or attractive forces that exist between the permanent magnet's field and the induced magnetic field which results from the induced current.

Examples: Applying Faraday's Law of Induction

1. A circular loop of wire of radius 2.5 cm is in a magnetic field of 0.40 T. If the loop is removed from the field in a time of 0.050 s, what is the average induced emf? (The axis of the loop is parallel with the field.)

Solution: $\mathcal{E} = -N \cdot \dfrac{\Delta\phi}{\Delta t} = -N \cdot \dfrac{\Delta\{B_\perp A\}}{\Delta t} = -NA \cdot \dfrac{\{B_{\perp 2} - B_{\perp 1}\}}{\Delta t}$.

$$\mathcal{E} = \dfrac{-(1)(\pi)(2.5 \times 10^{-2}\ m)^2 (0 - 0.40\ T)}{(0.050\ s)} = 1.6 \times 10^{-2}\ V .$$

2. A square coil of wire 5.0 cm on a side has 100 turns. It lies between the poles of a magnet of field strength 0.020 T. If it is rotated through 90° in a time of 2.0×10^{-3} s, what is the average induced emf?

Solution: $\mathcal{E} = -N \cdot \dfrac{\Delta\phi}{\Delta t} = -N \cdot \dfrac{\Delta\{B_\perp A\}}{\Delta t} = -NA \cdot \dfrac{\{B_{\perp 2} - B_{\perp 1}\}}{\Delta t}$.

$$\mathcal{E} = -\dfrac{(100)(0.050\ m)^2 (0 - 2.0 \times 10^{-2}\ T)}{(2.0 \times 10^{-3}\ s)} = 2.5\ V .$$

Exercises

1. A square loop with sides 12 cm by 12 cm has 25 turns of wire and is in a magnetic field of strength 4.2 x 10⁻² T with its axis perpendicular to the direction of the field. If it is rotated in 0.15 s so that its axis is parallel to the field, what is the average induced emf during this quarter turn of the loop?

2. The magnetic flux in a coil of 50 turns changes from − 0.56 Wb to + 0.14 Wb in a time of 7.0 ms. What is the average induced emf?

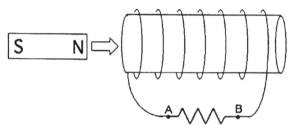

Figure 8.12

3. When the magnet in **Figure 8.12** is moved to the right toward the inside centre of the solenoid, in what direction will current in the resistor move? Explain.

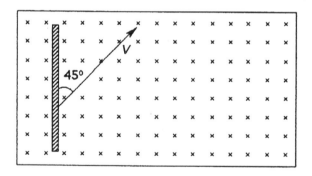

Figure 8.13

4. (a) A wire 7.8 cm long moves with a velocity of 2.4 m/s through a magnetic field of strength 0.68 T, which is directed *into the page* on the above diagram. The velocity vector makes an angle of 45° with the wire. What is the magnitude of the induced emf in the wire?

   (b) Which end of the wire will become positively charged?

   (c) What is the magnitude and direction of the **electric** field in the wire?

8.5 Counter EMF ('Back EMF') in a Motor

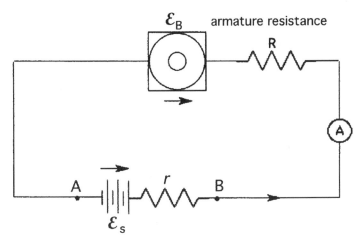

Figure 8.14

An electric motor has essentially the same design as a generator. The generator changes mechanical energy into electrical energy, whereas the motor does the exact opposite. It changes electrical energy into mechanical energy. When current exists in the armature of a motor, the armature turns in the magnetic field of the motor. This causes the motor to produce an induced emf which *opposes* the voltage of the source making the motor turn!

The motor cannot help itself! It automatically becomes a generator as soon as its armature turns. Consistent with Lenz's Law, the induced emf acts counter to the source emf, so it is called **counter emf** or **'back emf'**. The 'back emf' increases when the motor armature frequency increases, as would be expected of a generator.

Kirchhoff's Law applies in this situation. If the source emf is $\mathcal{E}_s$, then

$$\mathcal{E}_s \ = \ Ir \ + \ IR + \ \mathcal{E}_B$$

where I is the current, r is the internal resistance of the source, R is the resistance of the armature of the motor, and $\mathcal{E}_B$ is the 'back emf'.

$$\mathcal{E}_B \ = \ \mathcal{E}_s \ - \ Ir \ - \ IR$$

$$\mathcal{E}_B = V_{AB} \ - \ IR$$

where V_{AB} is the **terminal voltage** of the source.

Investigation 8-2   Back EMF of an Electric Motor

Purpose: To investigate electromagnetic induction in an electric motor.

Procedure

1. Connect a small DC motor to a galvanometer. Turn the shaft with your fingers and watch the galvanometer. Turn the shaft in the opposite direction. Try turning the shaft faster.

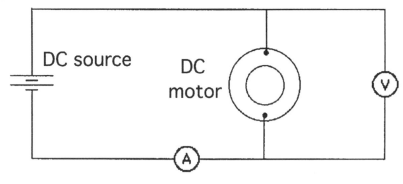

Figure 8.15

2. Set up the circuit in **Figure 8.15**. Choose a battery or power supply voltage that will make the shaft turn at its top speed. (Instructions with the motor will say what the maximum safe operating voltage is.)

3. You will need to know the **resistance** of the armature of the motor. To find out what it is, do the following: (a) Stop the shaft of the motor from turning by holding it with your fingers. (b) Measure the voltage across the motor and the current through the motor. (c) Calculate the armature resistance by using Ohm's Law: $R = V/I$.

4. Measure the **'back emf'** of your motor while it is running at full speed. To do this, measure V across the motor, which is equal to the terminal voltage of the power supply or battery. Measure I, then calculate $\mathcal{E}_B = V - IR$.

5. Let the motor run, but brake the shaft slightly with your fingers. What happens to the current? What happens to the 'back emf'?

6. To find out how the 'back emf' varies with the frequency of rotation of the motor shaft, the arrangement in **Figure 8.16** is used. A thread approximately 1.5 m long is attached to an enlarged spindle on the motor shaft, and a small mass (washer) is attached to the other end of the thread. This mass will provide a **load** which will slow down the motor's frequency.

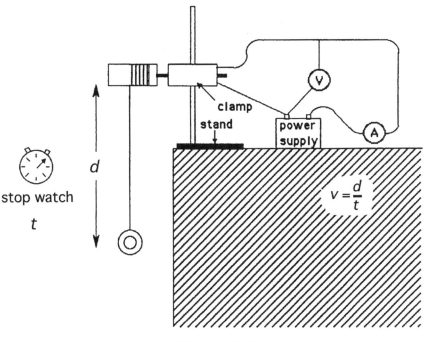

Figure 8.16

7. With a load of 1 washer on the thread, turn on the motor and measure the time it takes the motor to lift the load a measured distance (perhaps 1.00 m). Calculate the speed at which the washer rises ($v = d/t$). Repeat the same procedure with one washer, but record V and I, and calculate $\mathcal{E}_B = V - IR$. Copy **Table 1** and record your data.

Table 1   Data for Back EMF vs Speed

Load	d	t	v	I	V	R	$\mathcal{E}_B$
washers	m	s	m/s	A	V	Ω	V
1							
2							
3							
4							
5							

8. Repeat **Procedure 7**, but with loads of 2, 3, 4 and 5 identical washers. Record your data in your copy of **Table 1**.

9. Plot a graph of $\mathcal{E}_B$ vs v using your data from **Procedures 7 and 8**.

Concluding Questions

1. When a current exists in an electric motor, magnetic torque makes the armature rotate. What limits the speed at which the shaft can rotate? (Why does it not accelerate indefinitely?)

2. How do you know that the induced current in a motor opposes the current that makes the motor turn in the first place?

3. How does the frequency of rotation of the motor's armature depend on the speed at which the motor lifted the washers? **Hint!** $v = 2\pi R/T = 2\pi Rf$.

4. How does the **'back emf'** depend on the **frequency of rotation** of the motor?

5. Could the **'back emf'** ever equal the **terminal voltage** of the source? Explain.

Exercises

1. An electric motor is operated from a 6.0 V supply. When the armature is held still, the current in it is 4.0 A. When the armature is allowed to turn freely, the current is 2.4 A.
   (a) What is the resistance of the armature?
   (b) What is the 'back emf' of the motor at this frequency of rotation?
   (c) If the load on the motor is increased so that its frequency is reduced to three quarters of what it was, what will the 'back emf' be then?

2. A motor has an armature resistance of 1.8 Ω. Running at full speed, it draws a current of 0.50 A when connected to a 12.0 V source. What is the 'back emf'?

3. In **Exercise 2**, what will the 'back emf' be if the motor runs at half its normal frequency?

4. The 'back emf' of a motor is 4.2 V when operated from a 6.0 V source. When held stationary, the current in the motor's armature is 5.0 A.
   (a) What is the resistance of the armature?
   (b) What current will exist in the armature when it is rotating at normal speed?

5. Why might overloading a motor actually destroy the armature of the motor?

6. The input power for a motor is IV, where I is the current and V is the source voltage. The power lost as heat in the armature is I^2R. The power output of the motor is therefore $IV - I^2R$. The **efficiency** of the motor equals the ratio of power output to power input. Show that this ratio reduces to $\mathcal{E}_B/V$.

7. Is an electric motor more efficient at high frequency or low frequency? Explain.

8.6 Transformers

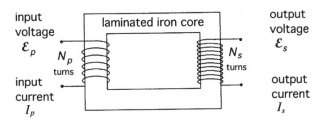

Figure 8.17

A **transformer** is designed specifically to alter the voltage in an alternating current (AC) circuit. Electricity is transmitted over long distances at very high voltages, because it is more economical to do so. (The reasons for this will be discussed later.) The electricity delivered into your house is at a much lower voltage (120V or 240V). Your doorbell system might operate at approximately 18V. A **transformer** can change a low voltage to a high voltage *or* a high voltage to a low voltage.

The transformer has two coils in it, called the **primary coil** and the **secondary coil**. In an iron-core transformer such as the one in **Figure 8.17**, the coils are linked magnetically by a laminated, soft iron core. A magnetic field produced by the primary coil will also engulf the secondary coil.

If an AC voltage $\mathcal{E}_p$ is applied to the primary coil of the transformer, the AC current in the primary will produce a changing magnetic field, and therefore a changing magnetic flux. If the rate of change of flux with respect to time is $\Delta\phi/\Delta t$, then the emf induced in the secondary coil will be of magnitude

$$\mathcal{E}_s = - N_s \frac{\Delta\phi}{\Delta t}.$$

The changing flux simultaneously induces a counter-emf in the primary coil which (if resistance is negligible in the primary circuit) just equals the applied voltage. *(**This is consistent with Kirchhoff's Voltage Law applied to the primary circuit.**)*

$$\mathcal{E}_p = - N_p \frac{\Delta\phi}{\Delta t}.$$

If the two equations are divided, then

$$\frac{\mathcal{E}_s}{\mathcal{E}_p} = \frac{N_s}{N_p}.$$

This is a very fundamental transformer equation. What it says is this:
If you want to step up the voltage, use more turns in the secondary coil than in the primary coil. (This is what a '**step up transformer**' does.) *If you want to step down the voltage, use fewer turns in the secondary coil than in the primary coil.* (This is what a '**step down transformer**' does.)

Transformers can be very **efficient**. In other words, the power output at the secondary coil is very nearly equal to the power input at the primary coil. (An efficiency of 99% is not uncommon.) If we assume that $P_p = P_s$,

then
$$I_p \mathcal{E}_p = I_s \mathcal{E}_s.$$

$$\therefore \quad \frac{\mathcal{E}_s}{\mathcal{E}_p} = \frac{I_p}{I_s}.$$

The ratio of the voltages in the coils is inversely proportional to the ratio of the corresponding currents.

Long-Distance Transmission of Electrical Power

Transformers are essential to long-distance transmission of electricity. An example will illustrate why it is more economical to deliver electrical power at high voltage than it is at low voltage.

Example: A generator at City A delivers power at the rate of 1.00 MW to City B. The total resistance of the very low resistance cables between A and B is only 10.0 Ω.

Situation I: Power is delivered at a low voltage of only 5 000 V.

The current in the cables would be $I = \dfrac{P}{V} = \dfrac{1.00 \times 10^6 \text{ W}}{5.00 \times 10^3 \text{ V}} = 2.00 \times 10^2 \text{ A}$.

The **power lost as heat** in the cables would be
$$P_L = I^2R = (2.00 \times 10^2 \text{ A})^2(10.0 \text{ } \Omega) = 4.0 \times 10^5 \text{ W}.$$
Of the 1 000 000 W supplied, 400 000 W would be wasted as thermal energy!
At this low voltage **40% of the power would be wasted.**

Situation II: Power is delivered at a higher voltage of 500 000 V.

The current in the cables would be $\dfrac{1.00 \times 10^6 \text{ W}}{5.00 \times 10^5 \text{ V}} = 2.0 \text{ A}$.

The power **lost as heat** in the cables would be
$$P_L = I^2R = (2.0 \text{ A})^2(10.0 \text{ } \Omega) = 4.0 \times 10^1 \text{ W}.$$
Of the 1 000 000 W supplied, only 40 W is lost as thermal energy, a waste of only 0.0004%!

In order to minimize power loss in transmission lines, the voltage produced at the generator is stepped up to higher voltages, typically 500 000 V, before transmitting the power. The step-up in voltage is accompanied by a step-down in current, since

$$\frac{I_s}{I_p} = \frac{\mathcal{E}_p}{\mathcal{E}_s}.$$

Exercises (Assume all transformers are 100% efficient)

1. Why will a transformer not work with DC current?

2. A transformer has 120 turns in the primary coil and 600 turns in the secondary coil. If 120 V is applied to the primary coil, what will the secondary coil voltage be?

3. The primary coil of a transformer has 5 000 turns and the voltage across it is 120 V. The secondary coil has 50 turns.

   (a) What is the voltage across the secondary coil?

   (b) What is the primary coil current if the current in the secondary coil is 10.0 A?

4. A transformer has 50 primary turns and 2 000 secondary turns. The primary coil is connected to a 240 V source. If the secondary current is 2.5 mA, what is the

   (a) secondary voltage?

   (b) primary current?

   (c) power output of the secondary coil?

   (d) power input at the primary coil?

5. Why is a step-down transformer inserted between your circuit box and your doorbell circuit?

6. Find out why the iron core of a transformer is made in insulated layers (laminated) instead of one solid block of steel. What are 'Eddy currents'?

Chapter Review Questions

1. A straight piece of wire 10.0 cm long is moved through the poles of a magnet of strength 0.25 T at a speed of 4.0 m/s. What emf is induced between the ends of the wire? What is the **electric field strength** in the wire while it is moving?

2. What is the difference between **magnetic field strength** and **magnetic flux**?

3. What is **Faraday's Law of Induction** (a) in symbols and (b) in words?

4. What is **Lenz's Law**?

5. A loop of area 225 cm² has 24 turns of wire. It is in a magnetic field of strength 3.6 x 10⁻² T. To begin with, its plane (face) is parallel to the lines of force of the field. In a time of 0.15 s it is rotated so that its plane is perpendicular to the lines of force. What is the average emf induced in the loop during the one-quarter rotation?

6. Draw a solenoid with a few representative turns. A permanent magnet is moving toward it from the right, with the south pole about to enter the solenoid. What will be the polarity of the right end of the solenoid at this instant? Sketch which way current will move in the solenoid if it is connected to a conducting path.

7. By how much must the **magnetic flux** inside a coil of 100 turns change in a time of 1.0 ms to produce an emf of 2.0 V?

8. What is the peak emf of a generator which has a frequency of 60 Hz, a magnetic field strength of 0.64 T, a coil of area 0.120 m², and 250 turns in its coil?

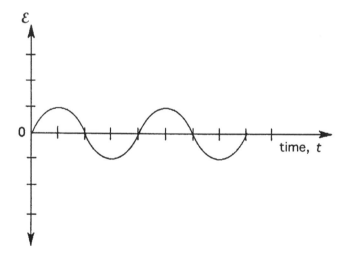

Figure 8.18

9. **Figure 8.18** shows how the emf produced by an AC generator varies with time. Sketch this graph, then show on the same diagram how this graph would change if **both** the number of turns on the generator's rotating armature **and** the frequency of rotation of the armature were doubled.

10. The armature resistance of a motor is 1.8 Ω. If the source voltage is 12.0 V, what is the back emf of a motor which draws 2.0 A when running at full speed?

11. What is the efficiency of a motor if its back emf is 8.0 V when the source voltage is 12.0 V?

12. The back emf of a motor is 6.3 V when the current is 3.0 A. What is the armature resistance if the source voltage is 9.0 V?

13. The armature of a DC motor has a resistance of 5.0 Ω. The motor is connected to a 120 V line, and when the motor reaches full speed the back emf is 108 V.

(a) What is the current at 'start-up' (before the motor turns over)?

(b) What is the current when the motor is being used?

14. The primary voltage of a step-up transformer is 120 V. There are 50 turns in the primary coil and 800 turns in the secondary coil.

(a) What is the output voltage in the secondary?

(b) What is the current in the secondary if the primary coil current is 16 mA?

(c) What is the power input to the primary coil?

15. A transformer has 400 primary turns and the input voltage to the primary coil is 120 V. The secondary coil voltage is 6 000 V. How many turns are there in the secondary coil?

16. A transformer has an efficiency of 98%. A primary voltage of 240 V is stepped down to 12.0 V. If the secondary current is 20.0 A, what is the primary current?

17. A coil of radius 0.072 m and with 36 turns is in a magnetic field of 0.80 T. If the coil is completely removed from the field in a time of 20.0 ms, what is the induced emf in the coil?

18. If the magnetic flux through a coil of wire with 300 turns changes from + 5.0 Wb to − 10.0 Wb in a time of 0.050 s, what emf is induced in the coil?

19. The magnetic field perpendicular to a coil of wire with radius 4.2 cm and with 24 turns changes from + 0.25 T to − 0.25 T in a time of 0.15 s. What is the magnitude of the induced emf?

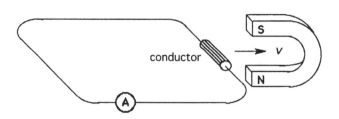

Figure 8.19

20. Will the induced current in the conductor in **Figure 8.19** be 'into the page' or 'out of the page'? Explain why.

Brain Busters

21. A voltage of 12 V is applied to an electric motor with an armature resistance of 5.0 Ω. When the armature is rotating at its peak speed, the current in it is 0.48 A. When a load is placed on the motor, its speed (frequency) is reduced to 1/3 of its peak speed. What is the 'back emf' of the motor under this load?

22. A town receives 10 MW of power delivered at 50 kV from a generator over lines which have a resistance of 5.0 Ω. What percentage of the power generated is lost as heat in the lines?

Test Yourself!

Multiple Choice

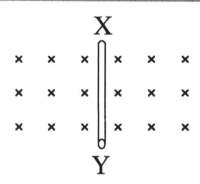

1. One can induce an emf in the wire XY if one moves the wire
   A. into the page.
   B. out of the page.
   C. toward X.
   D. toward Y.
   E. left or right.

2. A DC motor is connected to a battery. The load on the motor increases, so the armature slows down. How will this affect the **back emf** and the **current** through the motor?

	Back emf	Current
A	increases	decreases
B	increases	increases
C	decreases	decreases
D	decreases	increases

3. In a step-down transformer,

A. $V_s < V_p$ and $I_s < I_p$.
B. $V_s < V_p$ and $I_s > I_p$.
C. $V_s > V_p$ and $I_s < I_p$.
D. $V_s > V_p$ and $I_s > I_p$.

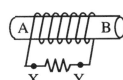

4. When the north end of the bar magnet is moved out of the solenoid as shown above, what is the direction of the induced current in the solenoid, and what is the polarity of end **B** of the solenoid?

	Current Direction	Polarity of end B
A	X to Y	N
B	Y to X	N
C	X to Y	S
D	Y to X	S

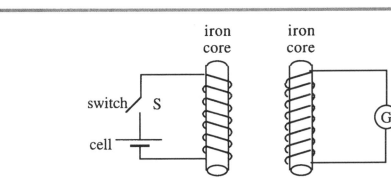

5. The galvanometer G will indicate a small current
A. only while switch S remains closed.
B. only while switch S remains opened.
C. only while switch S is being opened.
D. while switch S is being opened or being closed.

Open-Ended Questions

6. What is the magnetic flux, ϕ, through a coil of wire having an area of 5.0×10^{-2} m², whose plane is perpendicular to a magnetic field of magnitude 2.0×10^{-3} T?

7. A generator coil has 170 turns. It has a cross-sectional area of 4.00×10^{-2} m². In a time of 0.20 s, the magnetic field changes from 1.20 T to 1.50 T. What is the average emf induced in the coil?

8. A square coil with 85 turns, measuring 0.15 m on each side, is in a magnetic field of strength 5.0×10^{-2} T. If the coil is removed from the field in 0.20 s, what is the average emf induced in the coil?

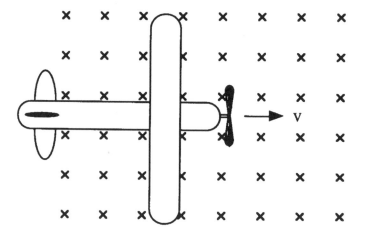

9. An airplane with a wingspan of 12.0 m travels at right angles through a magnetic field of strength 5.0×10^{-3} T. An emf of 1.5 V is induced between the ends of the wingtips. How fast was the airplane moving?

10. A DC motor is connected to a 12.0 V power supply. When the armature is rotating, the current is 3.80 A and the back emf is 10.40 V.
(a) What is the resistance of the armature?
(b) If the armature 'jams' and cannot turn, what will the current in the armature be?

11. When a 3.0 V battery is connected to a motor with armature resistance 0.20 Ω, a current of 1.5 A exists in its windings. What is the back emf of the motor?

12. A transformer is plugged into a 120 V AC source. It has an output of 16 V AC. If the primary coil has 300 turns, how many turns are there in the secondary coil?

13. A transformer has 600 turns in the primary coil and 120 turns in the secondary coil. If the potential difference across the primary coil is 115 V AC, what emf is induced in the secondary coil?

14. A power station delivers 500 kW of power to a village through lines with a total resistance of 5.00 Ω. The input voltage is 400,000 V. If the input voltage was reduced to 10,000 V, by what factor would the power wasted as heat in the lines be multiplied?

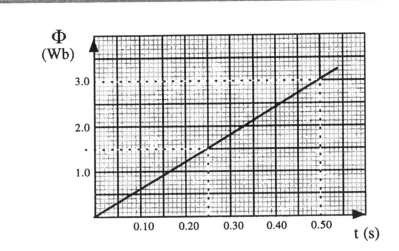

15. The above graph shows how magnetic flux through a single loop of wire changes with time. What is the average emf induced in the loops, between $t = 0.25$ s and $t = 0.50$ s?

Answer Key

Exercises

Page 7

1. The same
2. zero

Page 8

1. six ways
2. No difference
3. 260 m, 23° E of N
4. (a) 5 steps, 37° E of S (b) 17 steps

Page 11

1. (a) 720 N
   (b) 624 N
   (c) 360 N
   (d) 0 N
2. 130 N, 22.6° E of N
3. 130 N, 67.4° S of E

Page 17

1. $F_1 = 41.6$ N, $F_2 = 20.8$ N
2. (a) 0 (b) 0 (c) 0
3. F_4 is 2 grid squares in length, pointing right.
4. $F_x = 55$ N. This component acts along the road.
5. 386 N

Page 20 (top)

1. (a) v_y (b) 12.3 m/s (c) 20.8 s
2. (a) v_x (b) 8.60 m/s (c) 179 m
3. 29.8° upstream

Page 20 (bottom)

1. 60 N
2. 257 m, 29° E of N
3. 0.49 m/s, 12° to the right.

4. (a) 22 km/h, 56° to the west
   (b) 1.5 km
5. 6.9 m/s²
6. (a) 240 N
   (b) 351 N
7. 102 N
8. 19 km/h, 51.3° S of W

Page 24

1. 75 N·m

Page 29

1. 5.3 N
2. 37 cm
3. 6.1×10^2 N
4. 5.1×10^5 N
5. 69 N

Chapter Review

Page 31

1. Vectors have direction.
2. 2.60×10^2 m, 67.4° E of S
3. 5.8 N, 31° W of N
4. (a) 56.0 N (b) 10.0 N (c) accelerate
5. 545 km/h (W), 779 km/h (N)
6. 852 km/h, 2.42° E of S
7. 5.0 km, 37° E of S
8. (a) 5.9×10^4 N
   (b) 6.9×10^3 N
   (c) 6.9×10^3 N
9. (a) 3.2×10^2 N   (b) 6.9×10^2 N
10. (a) 250 N
    (b) 354 N
    (c) 500. N
    (d) 2.86×10^3 N
    (e) undefined (infinite)
11. (a) 500.0 N straight up
    (b) $F_A = 250$ N (c) $F_B = 433$ N
12. 8.0 m/s at 37° E of the vertical; 2.5×10^3 s (42 min)
13. 1.9 m
14. 2.0×10^1 N
15. 9.9×10^2 N
16. $F_A = 1.1 \times 10^3$ N, down;
    $F_B = 2.3 \times 10^3$ N, up.

17. 385 m
18. 1.5 s
19. 4.7 x 10^3 km from the centre of the earth, or 1.7 x 10^3 km below the crust of the earth!
20. 34 N
21. $F_f L \cos\theta = \frac{1}{2}mgL\sin\theta$, so

$$F_f = \frac{1}{2}mg \cdot \frac{\sin\theta}{\cos\theta} = \frac{1}{2}mg \cdot \tan\theta$$

Chapter 2

Motion in Two Dimensions

Exercises

Page 44

1. 5.3 x 10^2 km
2. (a) 0.28 m/s
   (b) 14 m/s
   (c) 22 m/s
   (d) 28 m/s
3. (a) 38 m/s
   (b) 47 m
   (c) 1.2 x 10^2 m
4. (a) Yes. Car stops in 47 m
   (b) No. Car stops in 59 m
5. (a) (i) 49 m/s^2
       (ii) -9.8 m/s^2
       (iii) 49 m/s^2
   (b) B (time 1.2 s)
   (c) 5.9 m
6. (a) $v_f^2 = v_o^2 + 2ad$, but $d = 0$,
       $\therefore v_f^2 = v_o^2$,
       $\therefore |v_f| = |v_o|$
   (b) No. Same speed but in the opposite direction.
7. 3.0 m/s^2
8. (a) 0.43 m/s^2
   (b) 2.6 s

Page 54

1. (a) 4.5 s
   (b) 1.2 x 10^2 m
2. (a) 34 m/s (b) 6.9 s (c) 2.4 x 10^2 m

3. 4.1 x 10^2 m
4. (a) 1.0 x 10^1 m
   (b) 2.8 x 10^2 m
   (c) Ouch! Yes!
5. 1.9 x 10^2 m
6. (a) 21 m/s
   (b) 12 m/s
   (c) 2.4 s
   (d) 51 m
   (e) 7.3 m
7. For 45°: (a) 17 m/s (b) 17 m/s
   (c) 3.5 s (d) 6.0 x 10^1 m (e) 15 m
   For 60°: (a) 12 m/s (b) 21 m/s
   (c) 4.3 s (d) 51 m (e) 23 m
8. (c) $v = (10.0 \text{ m/s}^2)t + 2.50$ m/s
   (e) $v_x = 2.12$ m/s

Chapter Review

Page 56

2. 39.4 m
3. 34.3 m
4. 41 m (too short for a home run)
5. Misses by 3.0 cm
6. 34.5 m. It hits the wall 17.7 m above the firing point.
7. 12.1 m
8. 27.7°
9. 28.5 m ($\cong$ 29 m)
10. $v_f = \pm 8.3$ m/s, $t = 0.68$ s and 2.4 s
11. Pebble dropped from 1.8 m above the top of the window. Detailed solution follows:
    $h_2 - h_1 = \frac{1}{2}a (t_2^2 - t_1^2)$
    -1.8 m $= -4.9$m/s^2 $(t_2 + t_1)(t_2 - t_1)$
    Since $t_2 - t_1 = 0.25$ s, (I)
    -1.8 m $= -4.9$m/s^2 $(t_2 + t_1)(0.25$ s$)$
    $\therefore t_2 + t_1 = 1.47$ s (II)
    Add (I) and (II): $2t_2 = 1.72$ s,
    $\therefore t_2 = 0.86$ s and
    $\therefore t_1 = 0.61$ s
    Solve for $d_1 = \frac{1}{2}at_1^2 = 1.8$ m above the top of the window.

Chapter 3
Momentum and Energy

Exercises

Page 66

1. 0.17 m/s² upward
2. $a = 0$
3. (a) 3.3 m/s²
   (b) 6.5 N No.
4. If he allows himself to be accelerated down the rope at 1.3 m/s², the tension force in the rope will be lessened from 735 N to 637 N, which the rope can handle.
5. (a) 4.66 m/s²
   (b) 37 m/s
6. 4.5 m/s². Constant velocity when $F = 0$. (Terminal velocity)

Page 70

1. 3.0×10^{-3} kgm/s
2. (a) 5.4×10^2 kgm/s
   (b) -5.4×10^2 Ns
   (c) -4.5×10^2 N
3. Throw the camera in a direction away from the shuttle.
4. Thrust is 6.0×10^7 N, which is greater than the force of gravity on the rocket.
5. 0.77 m/s
6. 5.3 m/s
7. zero
8. - 0.57 m/s
9. The bullet which rebounds has $\Delta p = -\frac{3}{2}mv$. The bullet hitting Plasticine has $\Delta p = -mv$. Since $F \propto \Delta p$, the rebounding bullet must exert a greater force.
10. (a) - 13.0 Ns   (b) - 1.3×10^4 N
11. 3.6×10^2 m/s
12. 12 m/s
13. - 8.0×10^1 Ns, $F = - 16$ N

Page 80

1. 2.7 m/s, 37.5° E of N
2. 3.3 m/s, 58° S of W
3. 47 kJ
4. (a) 5.0 kgm/s
   (b) 33 m/s, 37° to direction of first mass
5. Struck proton: 3.0×10^6 m/s, 60° from the incident proton's original direction.
   Incident proton: 5.2×10^6 m/s.
6. 22 km/h, 12° E of S
7. 259 kgm/s, force exerted 17° E of S

Page 83

1. (a) 1.2×10^3 J (b) 1.4×10^3 J.
   No. Effort **force** is less.
2. 6.8×10^2 J

Page 86

1. 0.72 J
2. 0.41 m

Page 87

1. Doubling speed increases E_k by 4 times, while doubling mass only doubles E_k.
2. 42 kJ
3. 180 kJ
4. 7.2×10^{-2} J
5. 9 times

Page 88

1. 2.6×10^3 J
2. (a) 0.036 J   (b) 2.7 m/s
3. $E_{p(grav)}$ to E_k to $E_{p(elastic)}$ to E_k to $E_{p(grav)}$ etc...

Page 92

1. (a) 1.3×10^2 J   (b) 2.9×10^2 m
2. 0.24 J
3. 5.4 m/s, No.
4. 15 m/s. No
5. 2.2×10^2 J

Page 93

1. 5.0×10^2 m/s
2. 4.7 kg
3. 5.5×10^2 J, 4.4 m/s

Page 94

1. 2.3 MJ
2. (a) 750 W (b) 1 hp
3. 39.2 s
4. (a) 2.7×10^2 W   (b) 0.36 hp
5. (a) 2.63×10^5 W (b) 263 kW

Chapter Review

Page 95

1. 0.467 m/s², 205 N
2. 5.88 m/s², 4.70 N
3. 12.5 kgm/s
4. 4.00 Ns
5. 0.37 m/s
6. 2.2 m/s
7. 0.97 m/s
8. (a) - 15 m/s   (b) - 0.30 m/s
9. 0.59 m/s, 23° W of S
10. (b) 1.04 m/s
    (c) 0.60 m/s
    (d) 9.0×10^{-4} J
11. 12.3 kJ
12. 6.9 kJ
13. 760 J
14. 3.3 m/s
15. 3.1×10^5 J
16. 1.47 MJ
17. Energy is used to change the shape of the Plasticine. Internal friction results in heating.
18. 1.71 m/s
19. The girl. The weightlifter does no work.
20. 5.6 kW
21. 130 MJ
22. 21 m/s, 2.1° W of N. (Solution may require use of sine or cosine law.)
23. 2.9 m/s²

24. 1.7 m/s²
25. If the block has a steady speed down the ramp, then $F_f = F_p$ (magnitude only).

$$\mu = \frac{F_f}{F_N} = \frac{F_p}{F_N} = \frac{mg\sin\theta}{mg\cos\theta} = \tan\theta.$$

26. 7.9×10^2 m/s
27. The small ball lands above the large ball. It 'meets' the large ball on its rebound, and so is given energy and momentum by the large ball before it (the small ball) rebounds off the large ball and reverses its own direction. (This is only a partial answer.)

Chapter 4

Circular Motion and Gravity

Exercises

Page 108

1. (a) 12 m/s
    (b) 93 m/s²
    (c) 93 N
    (d) the rope
    (e) No. The force of gravity on the mass will make the rope dip below the horizontal.
2. (a) 1.2 m/s
    (b) 1.0×10^1 m/s²
    (c) 1.0×10^{-2} N
3. 8.91 m/s²
4. (a) 9.68 m/s²
    (b) 1.2×10^4 N
    (c) Car skids. (F_f is only 2.9×10^3 N)
5. 19.3 N
6. 2.4×10^2 N
7. 7.1×10^4 N
8. 27 m/s
9. (a) 3.4×10^{-2} m/s² (b) 2.0×10^{-4} Hz
        17 x faster than normal)
    (c) You would feel 'weightless'.

10. 2.0×10^2 N, 4.5×10^2 N
11. 6.5×10^3 N
12. 7.1 m/s
13. 3.6×10^{22} N (gravity)
14. 11 m/s
15. 33 m, banked facing centre. A component of F_g provides some centripetal force.

Page 119

1. 1.9×10^8 s
2. 2.8×10^4 s (7.9 h)
3. $4R$

Page 121

1. 686 N
2. (a) 7.5×10^{-8} N
   (b) 4 times as much.
3. 113 N
4. 253 N
5. 1.72×10^3 N
6. 2.7×10^{-3} m/s^2
7. 1.0×10^3 m/s
8. G appears to be constant anywhere in the universe, but g varies as $1/R^2$, therefore g is constant only at a given distance from the attracting planet.
9. (a) 1.62 m/s^2, or 0.17 g
   (b) 3.31 m/s^2, or 0.34 g
   (c) 1.47 m/s^2, or 0.15 g
   (d) 273 m/s^2, or 28 g.
   Mercury
10.
$$\frac{GMm}{R^2} = \frac{m4\pi^2 R}{T^2};$$
$$\therefore M = \frac{4\pi^2 R^3}{GT^2} = 6.02 \times 10^{24} \text{ kg.}$$
11. 2×10^{18} N

Page 124 (top)

1. $a = g$
2. 616 N
3. 7.9×10^3 m/s

4. Your 'weight' is primarily due to the gravitational attraction of the massive earth.
5. 5.4 m/s
6. 41 m

Page 124 (bottom)

7. 35×10^3 m/s.   No. $mv^2/R = GMm/R^2$; then 'm' cancels!

Page 127

1. 1.1×10^4 m/s
2. Sun: 6.2×10^5 m/s
   Moon: 2.4×10^3 m/s
   Mars: 5.0×10^3 m/s
3. Venus is easier. To go to Mars you have to move *away* from the Sun. Toward Venus, the sun's gravitational pull helps you.

Chapter Review

Page 127

1. 3.3×10^2 N
2. 6.0×10^2 N
3. (a) 14 m/s   (b) 56 m/s^2 (c) 69 N
4. 5.2×10^3 s (1.4 h)
5. (a) 1.0×10^4 N   (b) 0.85
6. 1.8×10^3 N
7. 542 N
9. 90.0 N
10. At D (Kepler's Second Law)
11. (a) January (Kepler's Second Law)
    (b) January ($F \propto 1/R^2$)
12. 27 a
13. (a) 686 N   (b) 2.3×10^{-9} N
14. 2.0×10^1 N
16. 7.4×10^3 m/s
17. 7.48 m/s^2
18. 3.1×10^6 m
19. 12 a
20. 2.64×10^6 m
21. (a) 7.9×10^3 m/s
    (b) $V_{escape} = \sqrt{2} \ V_{surface\ orbit}$.
22. 0.62 a

23. 3.0×10^4 m/s
24. 22 m/s
25. 3.4×10^8 m
26. (a) 76 a
    (b) $R_{mean} = 2.7 \times 10^{12}$ m
    (c) $R_{max} = 5.3 \times 10^{12}$ m
    (d) Between Neptune and Pluto.
27. 5.9×10^{23} kg
28. 0.472 km
29.

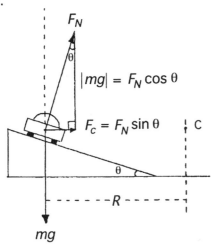

$$|mg| = F_N \cos \theta$$

$$F_c = F_N \sin \theta$$

mg

The road is banked so that the force F_N exerted by the road on the car is perpendicular, or **normal** to the road surface. Since the surface is frictionless, the only forces acting on the car are the normal force F_N and the force of gravity, *mg*. A horizontal component of the normal force provides the centripetal force F_c. Note that on a truly frictionless surface, the required angle will only work for *one particular speed v!* On the diagram, $\sin \theta = F_c/F_N$ and $\cos \theta = mg/F_N$.

$$\tan \theta = \frac{\sin \theta}{\cos \theta} = \frac{\dfrac{F_c}{F_N}}{\dfrac{mg}{F_N}} = \frac{\dfrac{mv^2}{R}}{mg} = \frac{v^2}{gR}.$$

30. 1.3×10^{20} kg
31. 1.98×10^{30} kg

32. $g =$
$$\frac{GM}{R^2} = G\frac{\rho V}{R^2} = G\frac{\rho}{R^2} \cdot \frac{4\pi R^3}{3} = \frac{4}{3}\pi G \rho R$$

Chapter 5
Electrostatics

Exercises

Page 137

1. If an excess charge developed on the metal rod, it would be conducted away through his hand to the ground.
2. The acetate strip will attract electrons, which will flow through the metal conductor to the acetate. The metal becomes positive and attracts electrons off the metal sphere of the electroscope. Both the sphere and the rod are positive, so they repel each other.
3. Charge an electroscope positive, see if the comb repels it. If not, charge an electroscope negative and see if the comb repels it. Repulsion of like charges is the only sure test.

Page 145

1. (a) $2F$ (b) $4F$ (c) $F/4$
   (d) $F/9$ (e) F (f) $16F$
2. 9.0×10^{-3} N
3. 3.2×10^{11} N
4. 9.2×10^{-8} N
5. 1.8×10^{11} C, 2.8×10^{26} N
6. 12 μC
7. 0.39 N directed along a line bisecting adjacent sides.
8. (a) 2.9×10^{26} N
   (b) 6.7×10^{-17} N
   (c) 4.3×10^{42}!!!
9. Electrical force is 10^{39} times greater than the gravitational force between a proton and an electron in a hydrogen atom.
10. 1.5×10^{-8} m

Page 152

1. 2.0×10^2 N/C, down.
2. 1.4×10^{-16} N
3. 1.0×10^{10} N/C in a direction away from the charge.
4. 4.0×10^6 N/C toward the 36 μC charge.
5. 9.6×10^{10} m/s^2
6. 5.0 N/C from + to - terminal.
7. (a) 5.0×10^4 N/C
   (b) 8.8×10^{15} m/s^2
8. (a) 9.8×10^{-15} N upward
   (b) 4.8×10^{-19} C
   (c) Sphere is negatively charged
   (d) 3 excess electrons
9. $E_A = 2.6 \times 10^5$ N/C, 11° left of the vertical and upward.

Page 162

1. 1.9×10^7 m/s (0.063 c)
2. 4.4×10^5 m/s
3. (a) 1.6×10^7 m/s
   (b) 2.5×10^3 N/C
   (c) 4.0×10^{-16} N
   (d) 4.4×10^{14} m/s^2
   (e) 3.1×10^{-9} s
   (f) 2.1 mm
   (g) 19 mm
4. 0.60 cm

Page 166

1. 0.56 J
2. $- 3.1 \times 10^{-18}$ J (- 19 eV)
3. $- 1.6 \times 10^{-18}$ J (- 10 ev)
4. 2.3×10^{-17} J   (144 eV)
5. (a) 5.0×10^5 V   (b) - 5.0×10^5 V

Chapter Review

Page 166

1. (a) $4F$ (b) $4F$ (c) 256 F
2. Positive. Electrons are repelled to ground, leaving the sphere positive.
3. (a) 6.0×10^5 J (b) 3.0×10^2 V
4. 9.2×10^{-16} N

5. 1.5×10^{-11} m
6. 1.0×10^3 N/C
7. 4.8×10^{11} m/s^2
8. 9.0×10^5 N/C toward the -25 μC charge
9. 9.0×10^1 V
10. (a) 4.2×10^3 V/m
    (b) 6.7×10^{-16} N
    (c) 7.4×10^{14} m/s^2 toward the + plate.
11. 3.2 cm
12. 2.4 cm
13. 45 J
14. 144 V
15. 0.75F
16. 1.8×10^6 V
17. 2.0×10^{-14} m
18. 6.9×10^{-17} J

Chapter 6

Resistor Circuits

Exercises

Page 180

1. 3.0×10^2 C
2. 1.0×10^1 A
3. 2.7×10^{23} electrons
4. 23 days
5. 1.8 g
6. 4.02 g

Page 181

1. 1.5 kΩ
2. 12 A
3. 25 V

Page 182

1. $2200 \pm 220\Omega$
2. $10\,000\ \Omega \pm 500\Omega$
3. $1\,500\,000\ \Omega \pm 150\,000\ \Omega$
4. $470\,000\ \Omega \pm 94\,000\ \Omega$

Page 184

1. 240 Ω

2. (a) 24 Ω (b) 2.2 x 10^5 J

3. (a) 3.6 x 10^6 J (b) 72 kWh (c) $4.32

4. 0.045 kWh

5. 22 V

Page 186

1. 1.20 V

2. 0.030 Ω

3. 5.0 A

Page 191

1. (b) 1.1 A

2. (a) 9.0 Ω (b) 2.0 kΩ (c) 314 Ω

3. 6.0 A

4. $R/16$

5. 1.5 A

6. (a) 6.0 Ω (b) 1.0 A

Page 196 Challenges

2. (a) 50 Ω   (b) 1.0 A

   (c) 0.13 A   (d) 7.3 V

Chapter Review

Page 197

2. 4.0 x 10^1 A

3. 2.7 x 10^{24} electrons

4. 24.7 g

5. 1.29 V

6. (a) 15 V   (b) 120 V

7. 30 kΩ

8. 80. V

9. 100 000 Ω ± 5 000 Ω

10. yellow, violet, green

11. 33 V

12. 12.5 A

13. 960 W

14. 144 Ω

15. I = 21.3 A; breaker is activated.

16. 60 kWh, $3.60

17. 0.25 V

18. 7.5 V

19. (a) 44 Ω (b) 4.0 Ω

20. 51.28 kΩ

21. 3.0 V

22. 0.75 Ω

23. 18 kΩ, 9.0 kΩ, 2.0 kΩ, 4.0 kΩ

24. (a) 167 kΩ, 0.48 mA

    (b) 77 Ω, 0.13 A

    (c) 314 Ω, 5.2 mA

25. 3.0 V

26. 0.83 Ω

Chapter 7

Magnetic Forces

Exercises

Page 212

1. (a) Lines are circular and clockwise around the conductor with current going into the page, and counterclockwise around the conductor with current coming out of the page.

   (b) Repel. Lines of force in the space between the conductors run in the same direction (*down* on the diagram), just as they would with two bar magnets lined up with like poles adjacent to each other.

2. End **B** is north.

Page 218

1. 2.0 cm

2. (a) 0.70 cm   (b) 0.35 cm

3. 2.0 x 10^3 V

Page 220

1. (a) 8.0 x 10^{-15} N (b) 8.8 x 10^{15} m/s², perpendicular to the velocity.

2. 1.0 x 10^{-15} N

3. (a) Up, perpendicular to magnetic field lines.

    (b) 1.2 x 10^{-10} N

Page 221

1. 8.0×10^{-3} T
2. 300 turns
3. 159 turns
4. 3.1×10^{-4} T

Page 227

1. (a) 2.5×10^{-2} T   (b) 1.5×10^{-3} N
2. 9.1×10^{-3} T
3. 0.74 A
4. (a) 0   (b) 4.3×10^{2} N   (c) 6.1×10^{2} N
5. (a) 3.1 N   (b) 125 T

Page 233

1. 9.1×10^{-31} kg
2. 1.7×10^{-27} kg
3. 1.6 m
4. 1.1×10^{5} m/s

Page 235

1. $2R$
2. (a) 3.0×10^{5} m/s   (b) 8.4 cm

Chapter Review

Page 237

1. iron, cobalt, nickel.
2. Electric field. A constant magnetic field will not affect a stationary charged particle.
3. Lines of force are clockwise and circular.
4. Lines are parallel for the length of the solenoid, going from **S** to **N** *inside* the solenoid.
6. 'Out'.
7. 2.9×10^{-12} N
8. 6.3×10^{-2} T
9. 1.60 cm
10. 0.32 cm
11. 26 N
12. 1.7×10^{-3} T
13. 3.2×10^{-4} N
14. 1.5×10^{-2} T
15. 6.7×10^{-27} kg

17. Attract
18. 6.5×10^{5} V/m, 3.3×10^{3} V
19. 2.0×10^{6} m/s, 3.8 mm

Chapter 8
Electromagnetic Induction

Exercises

Page 248

1. 0.38 V
2. 0.30 V
3. 60 km/s!
4. Into the page.

Page 251

1. Use a split-ring commutator.

2. $\mathcal{E} = 4\pi NB\ell fR\sin\theta$
3. $\mathcal{E} = 2\pi NABf\sin\theta$
4. 5.2×10^{2} V
5. Increase *any* of *N, B, A* or *f*.

Page 256

1. - 0.10 V
2. - 5.0×10^{3} V
3. A to B. Left end becomes north (Lenz's Law)   Ampère's Right Hand Rule indicates current is from A to B.
4. (a) 0.090 V
   (b) Top end (Lenz's Law, Ampère's Rule)
   (c) 1.2 V/m

Page 260

1. (a) $1.5 \ \Omega$ (b) 2.4 V   (c) 1.8 V
2. 11.1 V
3. 5.6 V
4. (a) $1.2 \ \Omega$ (b) 1.5 A

5. Overloading decreases *f*, which decreases back emf and increases current *I*, which may burn out the armature.

6. Efficiency =
$$\frac{IV - I^2R}{IV} = \frac{I(V - IR)}{IV} = \frac{\mathcal{E}_B}{V}.$$

7. Since Efficiency $= \mathcal{E}_B / V$, and $\mathcal{E}_B \propto f$, therefore efficiency increases at higher frequency.

Page 263

1. With DC, the rate of change of magnetic flux is zero, therefore the induced emf is zero also.
2. 600 V
3. (a) 1.20 V (b) 0.10 A
4. (a) 9.6×10^3 V (b) 100 mA
   (c) 24 W (d) 24 W
5. Lower voltage is safer.
6. Reduces 'eddy currents' in the iron, that may cause energy loss as heat, I^2Rt.

Chapter Review

Page 264

1. 0.10 V, 1.0 V/m
2. $\phi = BA$
3. $\mathcal{E} = -N\frac{\Delta\phi}{\Delta t}$. See text.

5. - 0.13 V
6. Right end is south.
7. - 2.0×10^{-5} Wb
8. 7.2×10^3 V

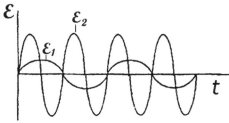

9. $\mathcal{E}_2 = 4\mathcal{E}_1$ and $t_2 = \frac{1}{2}t_1$
10. 8.4 V
11. 0.67
12. 0.90 Ω
13. (a) 24 A (b) 2.4 A
14. (a) 1.92×10^3 V
    (b) 1.0 mA
    (c) 1.9 W
15. 2.0×10^4 turns
16. 1.02 A
17. 23 V
18. 9.0×10^4 V
19. 0.44 V
20. Out of page (Lenz's Law, Ampere's Right Hand Rule)
21. 3.2 V
22. 2.0 %

Test Yourself! Answer Key

Chapter 1

1. D   2. A   3. C   4. B   5. C
6. 50 m/s (toward north)
7. One putt would travel 8.0° W of S, a displacement of 8.6 m.
8. 2.9 kg
9. 1.0 m
10. (a) 2.1×10^3 N
    (b) As $\theta \to 90°$, $T \to \infty$. The cord will break if you try to make it perfectly straight.
11. 6.7 kg
12. 20.6 N
13. 2.24×10^3 N

Chapter 2

1. A   2. A   3. C   4. B   5. D   6. A
7. (a) 2.7 s (b) 35 m
8. 0.34 m
9. 3.9 *kilometres!*
10. (a) 91 m/s (b) 112 m/s

Chapter 3

1. B   2. C   3. A   4. A   5. D
6. (a) 20.0 N (b) 10.0 N (c) 0.204
7. 8.4 m/s^2
8. 15 m/s
9. Pulling up is easier because the vertical component of your pulling force is 'up', and helps you lift the mower.
10. (a) 25.5 N (b) 23.0 N (c) 0.900
11. 8.0×10^1 N
12. (a) 3.9 m/s^2 (b) 47 N
13. The third piece flies off at 2.2 m/s, in a direction 53° S of W, or 37° W of S.

Chapter 4

1. D   2. C   3. E   4. D   5. B   6. C
7. (a) 0.50 s (b) 1.0×10^2 N
8. 9.9×10^{21} kg
9. (a) 1.47 N/kg, or 1.47 m/s^2
   (b) 2.79×10^3 m/s
10. (a) 3.7×10^2 N (b) 5.2×10^2 N
11. (a) 5.2×10^3 m/s
    (b) 1.8 m/s^2 or 1.8 N/kg
    (c) No effect (because *m* cancels).
12. 25 s

Chapter 5

1. D 2. E 3. B 4. E 5. A 6. B 7. B 8. A
9. 4.0 N
10. 8.0×10^{-8} C
11. 8.4×10^6 m/s
12. 5.0×10^4 V/m, or 5.0×10^4 N/C
13. 3.2×10^{-15} N (down)
14. 2.0×10^6 N (to the right)
15. 8.2×10^{-3} J
16. $- 4.3 \times 10^{-18}$ J
17. 5.4×10^4 J (total)

Chapter 6

1. D   2. D   3. A   4. B   5. D
6. 2.0 A
7. 8.1 Ω
8. 1.50 V
9. 10.0 V
10. 72 V
11. 0.50 Ω
12. (a) 91 Ω
    (b) 0.13 A
    (c) 0.93 W
13. 1.71 V
14. (a) 16 V
    (b) 1.8×10^2 W

Chapter 7

1. C   2. A   3. B   4. C   5. D
6. A   7. B   8. A   9. C
10. 7.9×10^{-6} N
11. 3.0 N
12. 5.3 A
13. (a) $R = mv/Bq$
    (b) 0.13 m
    (c) 2.9×10^{-21} kg·m/s
14. 0.13 T

Chapter 8

1. E   2. D   3. B   4. D   5. D
6. 1.0×10^{-4} Wb
7. $- 1.0 \times 10^1$ V
8. 0.48 V
9. 25 m/s
10. (a) 0.42 Ω
    (b) 28.6 A
11. 2.7 V
12. 40 turns
13. 23 V
14. 1600 times as much wasted power.
15. 6.0 V

Useful Mathematical Information

Right-Angled Triangles

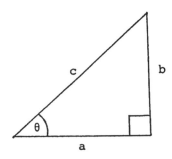

Pythagoras

$$a^2 + b^2 = c^2$$

Trigonometric Functions

$$\sin\theta = \frac{b}{c}$$

$$\cos\theta = \frac{a}{c}$$

$$\tan\theta = \frac{b}{a}$$

$$\sin2\theta = 2\sin\theta\cos\theta$$

$$\frac{\sin\theta}{\cos\theta} = \tan\theta$$

Area of Triangle = ½ab

Quadratic Equation

If $ax^2 + bx + c = 0$, then

$$x = \frac{-b \pm \sqrt{b^2 - 4ac}}{2a}$$

All Triangles

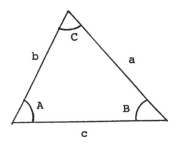

Sine Law

$$\frac{a}{\sin A} = \frac{b}{\sin B} = \frac{c}{\sin C}$$

Cosine Law

$$c^2 = a^2 + b^2 - 2ab\cos C$$
$$b^2 = a^2 + c^2 - 2ac\cos B$$
$$a^2 = b^2 + c^2 - 2bc\cos A$$

Prefixes

centi (c) = 10^{-2}

milli (m) = 10^{-3}

micro (μ) = 10^{-6}

nano (n) = 10^{-9}

pico (p) = 10^{-12}

giga (G) = 10^{9}

mega (M) = 10^{6}

kilo (k) = 10^{3}

Summary of Key Formulas Used in Physics 12

Vector Kinematics

$$v_f = v_0 + at$$

$$\bar{v} = \frac{v_0 + v_f}{2}$$

$$d = v_0 t + \tfrac{1}{2}at^2$$

$$v_f^2 = v_0^2 + 2ad$$

Vector Dynamics

$$F_{net} = ma$$

$$F_f = \mu F_N \quad \mu = \frac{F_F}{F_N}$$

$$F_g = mg$$

Momentum

$$p = mv$$

$$F\Delta t = \Delta p$$

Equilibrium

$$\tau = F\ell$$

Work, Energy, Power

$$W = Fd$$

$$E_{p(grav)} = mgh$$

$$E_k = \tfrac{1}{2}mv^2$$

Circular Motion and Gravity

$$a_c = \frac{v^2}{R} = \frac{4\pi^2 R}{T^2}$$

$$F_c = m\frac{v^2}{R} = m\frac{4\pi^2 R}{T^2}$$

$$F_g = G\frac{m_1 m_2}{R^2}$$

$$g = \frac{GM}{R^2}$$

$$E_{p(grav)} = -G\frac{m_1 m_2}{R}$$

$$\frac{R^3}{T^2} = K$$

Electrostatics $R = nc$

$$F = k\frac{Q_1 Q_2}{R^2}$$

$$E_{p(electric)} = k\frac{Q_1 Q_2}{R}$$

$$V = k\frac{Q}{R} = \frac{W}{Q}$$

$$\Delta V = \frac{\Delta E_p}{Q}$$

$$\text{Electric Field } E = \frac{F}{Q} = \frac{V}{d}$$

Electric Circuits

$$I = \frac{Q}{t}$$

$$R = \frac{V}{I}$$

$$P = IV$$

$$V_{terminal} = \mathcal{E} - Ir$$

$$R_s = R_1 + R_2 + R_3 + ...$$

$$\frac{1}{R_p} = \frac{1}{R_1} + \frac{1}{R_2} + \frac{1}{R_3} + ...$$

Electromagnetism

$$F = BI\ell$$

$$F = BQv$$

$$B = \mu_o n I = \mu_o \frac{N}{\ell} I$$

$$\mathcal{E} = B\ell v$$

$$\phi = BA$$

$$\mathcal{E} = -N \frac{\Delta\phi}{\Delta t}$$

$$\mathcal{E}_{back} = V_{terminal} - IR$$

$$\mathcal{E} = 2\pi f NAB$$

Transformer

$$\frac{V_S}{V_p} = \frac{N_S}{N_p} = \frac{I_p}{I_s}$$

Index

Table of Constants and Other Useful Data

Universal Gravitation Constant $\qquad$ $G = 6.67 \times 10^{-11}$ Nm^2/kg^2
Gravitational acceleration, earth's surface $\qquad$ $g = 9.80$ m/s^2

Earth

Radius of planet $\qquad$ $R_E = 6.38 \times 10^6$ m
Mean Orbital Radius about the Sun $\qquad$ $R = 1.50 \times 10^{11}$ m
Rotational Period $\qquad$ $T_E = 8.61 \times 10^4$ s
Period of Revolution around the Sun $\qquad$ $T = 3.16 \times 10^7$ s
Mass of Earth $\qquad$ $M_E = 5.98 \times 10^{24}$ kg

Moon

Radius of Moon $\qquad$ $R_M = 1.74 \times 10^6$ m
Mean Orbital Radius about the Earth $\qquad$ $R = 3.84 \times 10^8$ m
Rotational Period $\qquad$ $T_M = 2.36 \times 10^6$ s
Period of Revolution around the Earth $\qquad$ $T = 2.36 \times 10^6$ s
Mass of Moon $\qquad$ $M_M = 7.35 \times 10^{22}$ kg

Sun

Mass of Sun $\qquad$ $M_S = 1.98 \times 10^{30}$ kg

General

Speed of Light $\qquad$ $c = 3.00 \times 10^8$ m/s
Coulomb's Constant $\qquad$ $k = 9.00 \times 10^9$ Nm^2/C^2
Mass of Electron $\qquad$ $m_e = 9.11 \times 10^{-31}$ kg
Elementary Charge $\qquad$ $e = 1.60 \times 10^{-19}$ C
Mass of Proton $\qquad$ $m_p = 1.67 \times 10^{-27}$ kg
Mass of Neutron $\qquad$ $\tilde{m}_n = 1.68 \times 10^{-27}$ kg
Permeability of Free Space $\qquad$ $\mu_o = 4\pi \times 10^{-7}$ Tm/A
Electron Volt $\qquad$ $1 \text{ eV} = 1.60 \times 10^{-19}$ J

Mathematical

Pi $\qquad$ $\pi = 3.14$
Circumference of a Circle $\qquad$ $2\pi r$
Area of a Circle $\qquad$ πr^2
Volume of a Sphere $\qquad$ $4/3 \ \pi r^3$

$\sin \theta = o/h \qquad\qquad \cos \theta = a/h \qquad\qquad \tan \theta = o/a$

Troy Pettrisch illustrates the shape of the electric field around his head, using his hair, as he holds on to the charged dome of a model **Van de Graaff** static electricity generator.

This book was printed in Canada by
Hignell Book Printing
in Winnipeg, Manitoba.